The Constables
First Family of the Adirondacks

CONSTABLE FAMILY TREE

Emphasizing inheritance line of Constable Hall, omitting children who died in infancy.

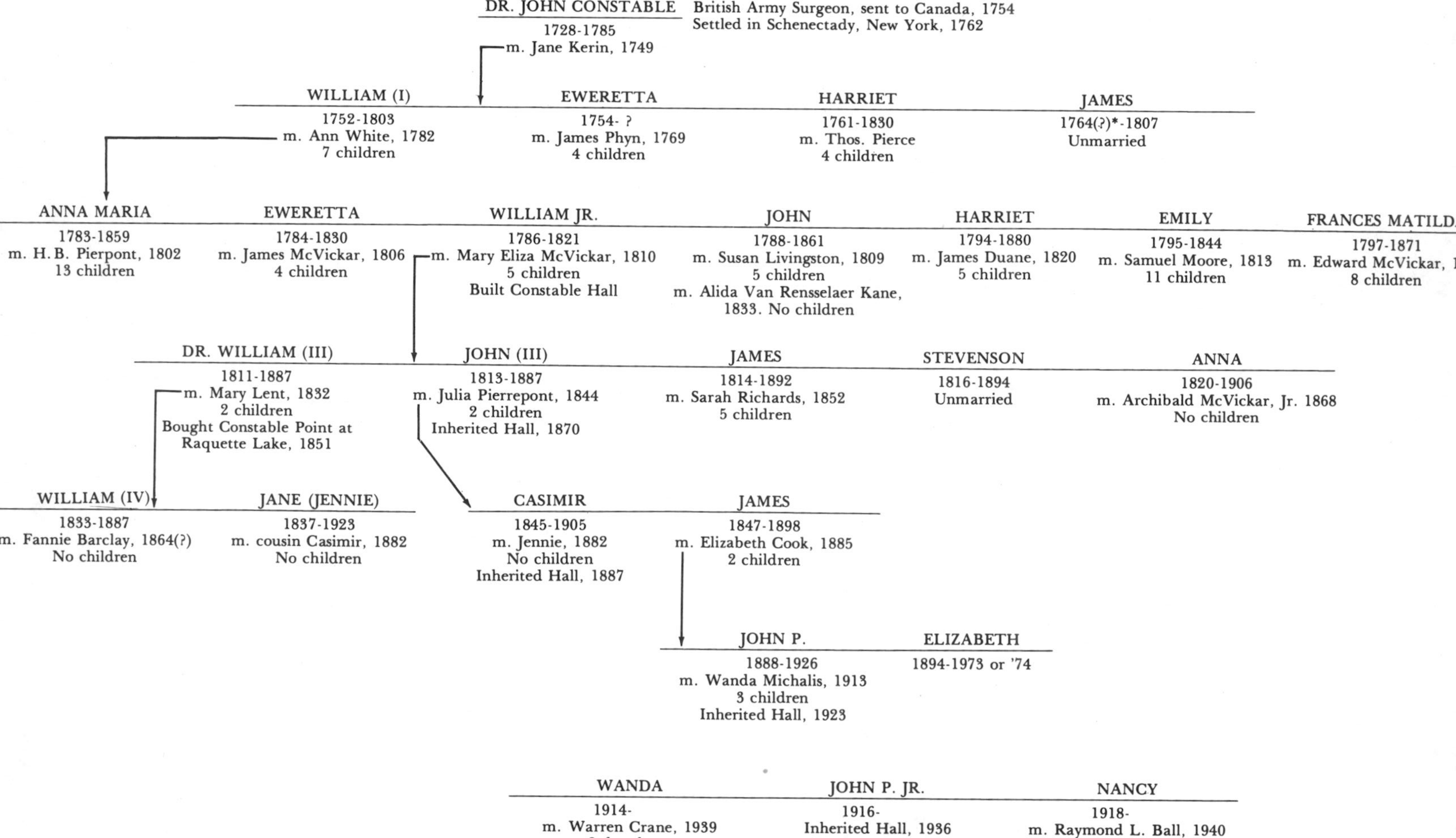

*See *Notes*, Ch. I, #2, page 144.

The Constables
First Family of the Adirondacks

by
Edith Pilcher

North Country Books, Inc.
Utica, New York

The Constables
First Family of the Adirondacks

ISBN 0-925168-04-1

ISBN 0-925168-05-X

Library of Congress Cataloging-in-Publication Data

Pilcher, Edith, 1928-
The Constables : first family of the Adirondacks / by Edith Pilcher.
p. cm.
Includes bibliographical references.
ISBN 0-932052-63-0 :
1. Constable family. 2. Pioneers—New York (State)—Adirondack Mountains Region—Biography. 3. Landowners—New York (State)—Adirondack Mountains Region—Biography. 4. Businessmen—New York (State)—Adirondack Mountains Region—Biography. 5. Adirondack Mountains Region (N.Y.)—History. 6. Adirondack Mountains Region (N.Y.)—Genealogy. I. Title.
CT274.C648P55 1992
929'.2'0973—dc20 92-8393
CIP

Book design by
John D. Mahaffy

Published by
North Country Books, Inc.
18 Irving Place
Utica, New York 13501-5618

DEDICATION

To Ennis—who shares so much with me

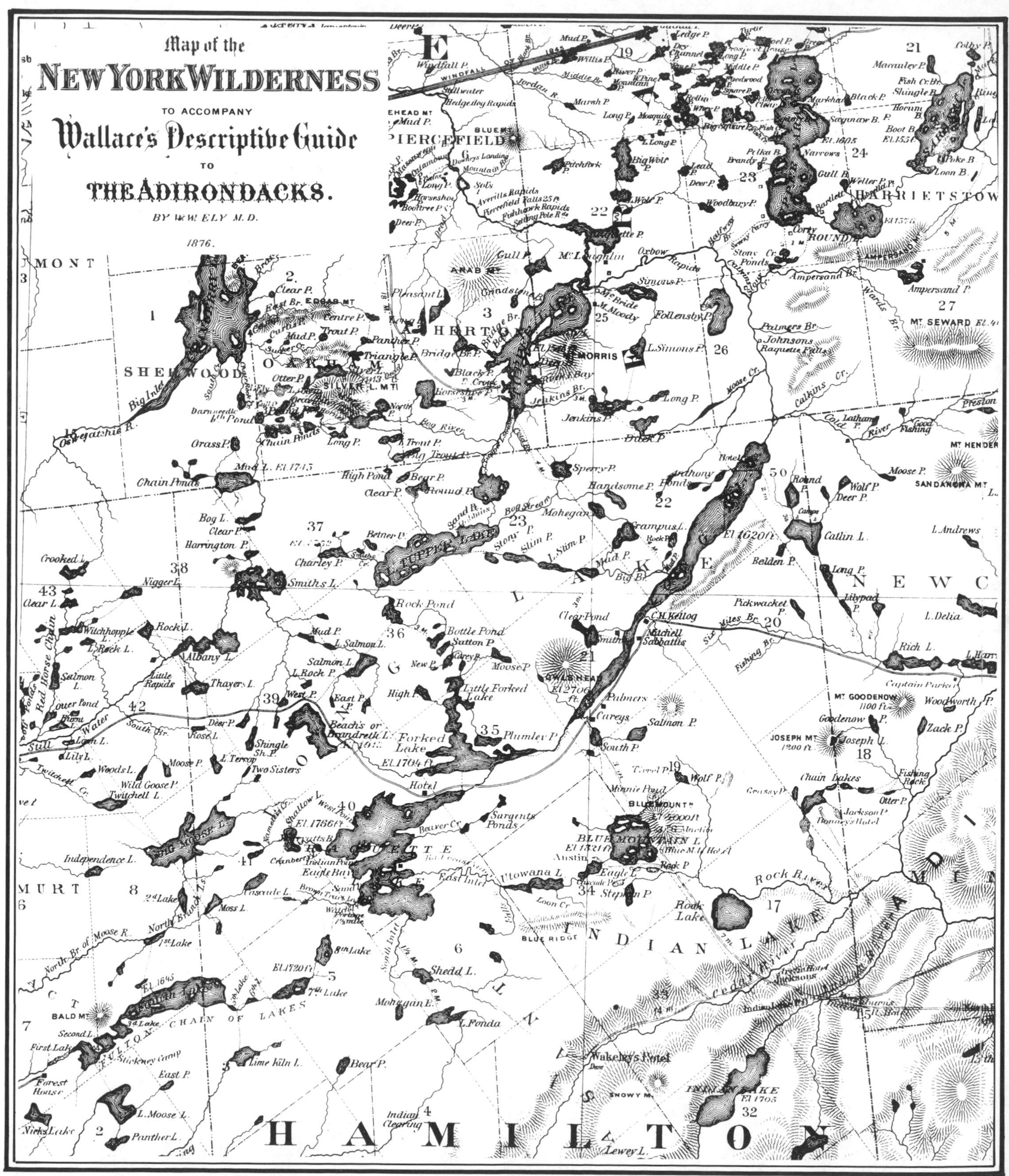

Map of the
NEW YORK WILDERNESS
TO ACCOMPANY
Wallace's Descriptive Guide
TO
THE ADIRONDACKS.
BY W. W. ELY M.D.
1876.
HAMILTON
INDIAN LAKE
TUPPER LAKE
PIERCEFIELD
HARRIETSTOWN
SHERWOOD
RAQUETTE
FULTON CHAIN OF LAKES
Big Inlet
Oswegatchie R.
Bog River
Chain Ponds
Mud L. El. 1745
High Pond
Clear P.
Bear P.
Round P.
Bog L.
Harrington P.
Crooked L.
Nigger L.
Smiths L.
Rock Pond
Charley P.
Betner P.
Witchhopple L.
Rock L.
Albany L.
Little Rapids
Thayers L.
Salmon L.
Otter Pond
Still Water
Lily L.
Woods L.
Wild Goose P.
Twitchell L.
Moose P.
Shingle Sh. P.
Two Sisters
Deer P.
Rose L.
West P.
East P.
Beach's or Brandreth L.
Forked Lake
El. 1704 ft.
Little Forked Lake
Plumley P.
Hotel
Big Moose L.
Independence L.
Shallow L.
El. 1766 ft.
Eagle Bay
Utowana L.
Eagle L.
Blue Mountain L.
BLUE MOUNTN
Minnie Pond
Wolf P.
Austin
Stephen P.
Rock Lake
Rock River
Cedar River
Indian Lake
Jacksons
Wakeleys Hotel
SNOWY M.
BLUE RIDGE
Loon Cr.
Cascade L.
Moss L.
2d Lake
1st Lake
North Branch
North Br. of Moose R.
8th Lake
7th Lake
El. 1720 ft.
Shedd L.
Mohegan L.
L. Fonda
Fourth Lake
El. 1645
3d Lake
Second L.
First Lake
BALD MT
Stickney Camp
Forest House
East P.
L. Moose L.
Panther L.
Nicks Lake
Lime Kiln L.
Bear P.
Indian Clearing
Lewey L.
El. 1705
Sargents Ponds
Beaver Cr.
Salmon P.
South P.
Careys
Palmers
OWLS HEAD
El. 2706 ft.
Clear Pond
Smiths
Mitchell Sabbattis
C. H. Kellog
Six Miles Br.
Fishing Br.
Pickwacket P.
Rich L.
Captain Parker
MT GOODENOW
Goodenow P.
Woodworth P.
Zack P.
JOSEPH MT
Joseph L.
Chain Lakes
Fishing Rock
Otter P.
Jackson P.
Lilypad P.
L. Delia
Long P.
Belden P.
Catlin L.
L. Andrews
Round P.
Wolf P.
Deer P.
Moose P.
SANDANONA MT
Anthony Ponds
Handsome P.
Sperry P.
Mohegan
Grampus L.
Slim P.
L. Slim P.
Mud P.
Big Br.
Bottle Pond
Sutton P.
Moose P.
Mud P.
L. Salmon L.
Salmon L.
Long P.
Jenkins P.
Jenkins Br.
MT MORRIS
L. Simons P.
Follensby P.
Simons P.
Oxbow Rapids
Moose Cr.
Johnsons Raquette Falls
Palmers Br.
Calkins Cr.
Cold River
Latham P.
Good Fishing
Preston
MT HENDER
MT SEWARD
Ampersand P.
Ampersand Br.
Wards Br.
Stony Ponds
ROUND L.
Corey
Bartlett
Gull B.
Narrows
Weller P.
Loon B.
Poke B.
Boot B.
Hoosier B.
Shingle B.
Fish Cr. B.
Macauley P.
Colby P.
Saginaw B.
Black P.
Markham
Middle P.
Long P.
Dry Channel
Ledge P.
Willis P.
Mud P.
River P.
Windfall P.
WINDFALL
Jordan R.
Stillwater
Hedgehog Rapids
Mud P.
Marsh P.
Long P.
Mosquito P.
L. Long P.
Big Wolf P.
Pitchfork P.
Lead P.
Deer P.
Woodbury P.
Brandy P.
Wolf P.
McLaughlin
Gull P.
Grindstone
ARAB MT
Pleasant L.
Bridge Br.
Black P.
Horseshoe P.
Mountain Br.
Averills Rapids
Piercefield Falls 25 ft.
Fishhawk Rapids
Setting Pole Rd.
Downeys Landing
Long P.
Horseshoe
Bootree P.
Deer P.
Clear P.
East Br.
EDGAR MT
Centre P.
Trout P.
Mud P.
Panther P.
Triangle P.
Otter P.
SILVER L. MT
Darning-needle Pond
Grass P.
Long P.
Trout P.
Chain Ponds
MONT
MURT

Contents

Dedication v

List of Illustrations ix

Acknowledgements xiii

I. The Early Constables: Founders and Fortunes 3
- Dr. John Constable, Immigrant 3
- William Constable I 7
- The Macomb Purchase, 1792 12
- James Constable, Guardian and Executor 16
- William's Widow and Children 18
- William Constable Jr., Builder of Constable Hall 20

II. Earliest Adirondack Explorations: 1830s and 1840s 29
- Annotated Maps 30
- Earliest Excursions 35
- First Visit to Raquette Lake, 1835 35
- First Exploratory Trip Through Adirondacks, 1836 37
- 1839 and 1840 Circuits 37
- 1843 Trip to Raquette Lake 39
- Who was Bob Racket? 39
- Reprint from *Spirit of the Times*, 1843 Trip 40
- Salmon Trout 49
- Higby the Hunter 49
- Hermits Wood and Beach at Raquette Lake 51

III. 1850: The First Ladies Expedition to the Woods 57
- William's Orders to Anna and John 58
- "The Intrepid Females" of Blue Mountain 64
- Fenton House at No. 4 64
- The Road East from No. 4 67

IV. Adventures in the 1850s 69
Summer, 1851 69
Naming of Big Moose, 1851 69
"A Month at the Racket," 1855 70
Reprint from *The Knickerbocker* 71
Guide Asa Puffer 88
Hermit James O'Kane at Stillwater 89
Constable Trips at Home and Abroad 90

V. The 1860s: Passing Campers and a New Generation 93
Albert Bigelow 93
Arthur F. Tait 93
Charles Themanen 95
"Adirondack" Murray 95
Constable Children Caught a Bear 96
Other Constable Trips 97
John & Stevenson's Winter Hunting Trip, 1864 98
Casimir's Courtship, 1867 101
The Impact of Murray's Book 105

VI. The 1870s: Time of Rapid Changes 107
Constable Camp at Big Moose Lake 110
Stevenson's Bachelor Trips 111
Notes from 1877 112
Summer Sojourn at Raquette Lake, 1878 116
Subsequent History of Constable Point 122
The Spring at Constable Point 125

VII. End of a Gracious Era: 1880s to Present 127
Game Conservation 127
Scholarly Studies of Adirondack Mammals 128
Young James' Adirondack Trip, 1883 129
Casimir's Legacy 130
John Pierrepont Constable Sr. 131
The Current John Constable (John P. Jr.) 131
The Restoration of Constable Hall 132
Contemporary History 139

Illustrations

Front Cover: *Autumn Morning, Racquette Lake*, 1872
by Arthur Fitzwilliam Tait
Oil on canvas, 36″ x 72″
(Courtesy of the Adirondack Museum)

Section of *1876 Map of the New York Wilderness and the Adirondacks* by W.W. Ely, M.D. vi

Frontis: Family Tree of the Constables, emphasizing the line of inheritance of Constable Hall

MAPS

I. Schenectady, Circa 1760 4
The Macomb Purchase and St. Lawrence Ten Towns ... 12
William Constable's Erroneous Version of Sauthier's Map (1792) 14

II. John Constable's note on 1840 map of Mohawk & St. Lawrence Railroad and Navigation Company 31
Annotated section of Stoddard's 1881 Map of the Adirondack Wilderness 34
1853 Map of Raquette Lake 36
1843 Map of Blue Mountain Lake 38
Constables' Route in 1843 from Constableville to Raquctte Lake 43

III. Constables' Route in 1850 from Constableville to Raquette Lake 61
Settlement at Raquette Lake in early 1850s 62

IV. John Constable's Notes on section of Stoddard's Map around Big Moose Lake 68

V. Merritt's 1860 Map of Raquette Lake Area 103

VI. Lakes & Ponds visited by Stevenson Constable in 1877 and 1878 115
Settlement at Raquette Lake in the 1870s 120

VII. Section of Butler's 1879 Map of the New York Wilderness 138

OTHER ILLUSTRATIONS

I. Reappointment of Dr. John Constable to First New York Regiment, 1763 2
Sir William Johnson 5
Indian Confab at Johnson Hall 6
William Constable 7
Marquis de Lafayette & Note 10
Constable's Coat of Arms 11
Constable Graveyard Monument 16
Anna Maria Constable Pierrepont 19
Hezekiah Beers Pierpont 19
Pierrepont Home on Brooklyn Heights 20
William Constable Jr. 21
William Constable's Portrait of Washington 23
Constable Hall (front & rear views) 24
Buckskin Coat 25
Kitchen & Old Flintlock Gun 25
Mary Eliza McVickar Constable 26

II. William Constable III and Guide 28
John Constable III 28
James Constable (with daughter) 28
Stevenson Constable 28
Note re Raquette River in Merritt's Book 33
Farrand N. Benedict 37
Compass presented to John by Casimir de Rham 38
Arnold's Inn in Herreshoff House 41
Fulton Chain of Lakes from Bald Mountain 42
McEntee Sketch of Deer Feeding at Raquette Lake 47
View on Raquette Lake by John W. Hill 52
McEntee Sketch of Wood's Cabin on Raquette Lake 54

III. William III's handwritten title for First Ladies Expedition to the Woods 56
Portrait of William III 56
Sketch of Constable Hall by William III 59
Tait Painting of Constable Point Lakeshore 60
Tait Painting of Leanto at Constable Point 63
The Road to Fenton's 65
Fenton House 65
Gignoux Painting of Log Road in Hamilton County 66

IV. "Floating for Deer" Sketch by Theodore R. Davis 75
South Inlet, Raquette Lake, Stoddard Photo 77
"A Swim for Life" by Thomas Moran 79

McEntee Sketch of Blue Mountain from Constable Point 81
Tyler Painting of West Mountain from Raquette Lake 82
"Evening on Raquette Lake" by James D. Smillie 86
McEntee Sketch of Asa Puffer 89
Schoolboys: Casimir and James Constable 90

V. Constable Point Camp by Charles Themanen 92
Tait Painting: "An Early Start" 94
Tait Painting: "A Good Time Coming" 94
Raquette Lake & Murray's Island 96
Prentice's Painting of Smith's Lake 97
Winslow Homer's "Deerstalking" 99
John Constable III 100
John Constable's Snowshoes 100
William Constable IV 102
Casimir Constable 102
"Murray's Fools" 105
"Adirondack" Murray 106

VI. Adirondack Railway Station, North Creek 107
First *Utowana* Steamer on Eagle Lake 108
Moose River Inn 109
The Forge House 109
Aerial View of Big Moose Lake 110
Stevenson Constable in hunting outfit 112
Stevenson's List of Supplies 113
Guideboat Beached on Constable Point 117
Guide Rueben Cary 118
Antlers' Boathouse 123
Current view of Constable Point 123
Current view of Constables' Spring (two views) 124

VII. Deer Harvest at Sportsmen's Hotel 126
Charles Fenton 126
John Pierrepont Constable Sr. 131
The Drawing Room & the Library at Constable Hall 133
Master Bedroom & Dining Room at Constable Hall 134
Pistol Collection at Constable Hall 135
Gun Collection 136
Some of John Constable's Hunting Trophies 137
The Registered Flyer 137
John P. Constable Jr. 139
Constable Pond 140
Constable Creek 141

Acknowledgements

I am most grateful to John Pierrepont Constable Jr., one of the seventh generation of the Constables in America and the last private owner of Constable Hall. He has generously provided me with maps, letters, notes, photos and other family records and mementos which contain information hitherto unknown about activities of many of his forbears in the Adirondacks.

This book would never have been written without the advice and encouragement of Warder H. Cadbury and the late William K. Verner. They helped me evaluate which items were newsworthy and of interest in the world of Adirondack scholarship. Then they suggested other contemporary writings, many unpublished, which relate to the Constable materials, as well as appropriate illustrations. Professor Cadbury has kindly read through preliminary drafts of the manuscript, enhancing its final form.

Edward Comstock Jr., formerly of Wildwood Books in Old Forge, also suggested sources of information and allowed me to copy historic photos and documents.

Robert H. McNeilly, Director at Constable Hall, loaned materials for copying and assisted arrangements for photos.

The staff of the Schenectady Historical Society suggested and made available a variety of records which shed light upon the early Constables in Schenectady. Particular thanks to Elsa Church for her detailed knowledge of these archives.

Union College librarians facilitated procurement of many research materials, particularly Ruth Anne Evans (now retired) and David Gerhan. Ellen Fladger, Archivist, offered expert advice about care and handling of valuable 19th century photographs.

The Adirondack Museum is an invaluable resource. Jerold Pepper, Librarian, provided expertise and access to books, maps, microfilm records and several unpublished manuscripts. Tracey and Jim Meehan helped find suitable illustrations, and Caroline Welsh, Curator of Exhibits and Paintings, arranged for their duplication.

The Geography and Map Division of the Library of Congress provided fine copies of old maps.

The late William Judson of Big Moose Lake lent his copy of the Higby Family genealogy, enabling identification of Higby the Hunter.

Rosemary L. Van Derhoof at St. George's Episcopal Church in Schenectady provided access to the earliest church records to verify details of births, baptisms and deaths.

John Keating and Robert McCracken of the Bureau of Real Property at the New York Department of Environmental Conservation helped me search—unfortunately, in vain—through Colvin Reports and other state records, seeking information on the naming of Constable Pond and Constable Creek.

Ruth Timm, Raquette Lake historian, contacted Joe Pierson of the Cortland College Environmental Center at Antlers Point (formerly Constable Point). He made inquiries and finally aimed me in the right direction to rediscover the "spring at Sand Point" which was used by the Constables when camping there.

J.H. Swinney, former Director of The Adirondack Museum and of the Strong Museum, painstakingly assisted me in formulating descriptions of the various models in the gun collection at Constable Hall.

Faye K. Brown of No. 4 and Syracuse guided me and my husband around the settlement at No. 4, showing us remains of Fenton's Hotel as well as his own photo album and scrapbook.

Charles Bunke, Town Historian of Watson, showed me a diary kept by Almeron Higby (son of Higby the Hunter), and also identified the houses and workshop formerly owned by that family.

George N. Davis of Lowville tapped his personal scrapbooks, as well as records at the Lewis County Historical Society, to provide photos of Charles Fenton and the Fenton House at No. 4.

Casimir de Rham, of Cambridge, Massachusetts, responded to inquiries about early family members and relationships, and corresponded regarding the location and circumstances of Clement Clarke Moore's composition of the poem "The Night Before Christmas." He convinced me it was not written at Constable Hall, and saved me from error in asserting that it was composed there.

The late Mary Rustad, my very good friend, copy-edited this manuscript during her last visit with us in the summer of 1991.

My husband, Ennis, chauffeured me and my copier around the North Country, took photographs on many occasions, critiqued and proofread successive drafts of this manuscript, and in many other ways facilitated its production.

I greatly appreciate the kind assistance from all these very helpful folks.

THE CONSTABLES

First Family of the Adirondacks

Dec 7th 1763

By the Honourable

CADWALLADER COLDEN, Esq;

His Majesty's Lieutenant Governor and Commander in Chief of the Province of New-York, and the Territories depending thereon in America.

To John Constable Gentleman Greeting

Reposing special Trust and Confidence, as well in the Care, Diligence, and Circumspection, as in the Loyalty, Courage, and Readiness of You, to do His Majesty good and faithful Service; Have nominated, constituted, and appointed, and I Do, by Virtue of the Powers and Authorities to Me given by His Majesty, Hereby Nominate, Constitute, and appoint You the said John Constable to be Lieutenant of the Company in the pay of the Province of New-York [illegible] whereof John Th. Muller Esq. is Captain

You are therefore to take the said Company into your Charge and Care, as Lieutenant thereof, and duly to exercise both the Officers and Soldiers of that Company in Arms. And as they are hereby commanded to obey You as their Lieutenant so are you likewise to observe and follow such Orders and Directions from Time to Time, as you shall receive from Me, or any other your superior Officer, according to the Rules and Discipline of War, in Pursuance of the Trust reposed in you; and for so doing this shall be your Commission.

Given under m Hand and Seal at Arms, in New-York, the Seventh Day of December in the fourth Year of His Majesty's Reign, Annoque Domini One Thousand Seven Hundred and Sixty three

By his Honour's Command,

Cadwallader Colden

[illegible] Secry

This engraved parchment reappointed Dr. John Constable, Gentleman, a lieutenant in the First New York Regiment, whereof John Th. Muller, Esquire, was captain. It was signed by Cadwallader Colden, Governor of New York, on December 7, 1763. An embossed seal on the top left side indicates this was an official document. Now it is difficult to read because of the spots and stains from aging, and the fading of the inked sections. It presently hangs in the office at Constable Hall.

fort from her church and personal devotions. As she aged, she suffered increasingly from the severity of upstate winters. She lived until 1826 —time to see all seven of her children happily married and with children of their own, on whom she doted. She visited them often and wrote frequent, affectionate letters filled with family news and pious platitudes about love and duty, hand in hand with complaints about the weather and her rheumatism.

One of the most exciting events of her last years was a visit from General Lafayette on July 12, 1825. During his triumphal visit to New York City, he heard that "the widow of his dear friend and companion-in-arms" was living with her daughter, Anna, in Brooklyn at that time. He crossed the river from Manhattan to pay his repsects; although the visit lasted only one-quarter of an hour, it was an emotional reunion which she and Anna considered a great honor.[11]

Anna had married Hezekiah B. Pierpont in 1802; over the ensuing years they had 13 children. He became extremely wealthy and purchased considerable city real estate, including Brooklyn Heights on which he and Anna established their home and founded a prestigious residential district. It was he who changed the spelling of the family name to *Pierrepont* for his wife and children, but he retained the former spelling for himself, as his signature was so well known in business circles.

Anna's siblings also married into prominent and wealthy families. Three of them wed chil-

Mrs. Hezekiah Beers Pierrepont
née Anna Maria Constable

Hezekiah Beers Pierpont

Pierpont, like William Constable, made a family fortune from enterprising trade and investments, as well as from manufacturing. He acquired large portions of the Macomb Purchase directly from William Constable and later from his heirs, after serving as one of the estate executors. Thereafter he contributed to upstate development by promotion of roads, canals and railroads.

The old Pierrepont home on Brooklyn Heights, 1838.

dren of John McVickar, their father's good friend and business associate; Eweretta, the second daughter, married James McVickar in 1806, and in 1810 William Jr. married Mary Eliza. Their youngest sister, Frances Matilda Constable, married Edward in 1819.

John Constable married Susan Livingston in 1809; they resided in Schenectady, where all five of their children were born.[12] She died in 1830, and three years later John wed Alida Van Rensselaer Kane; they later moved to Philadelphia.

Harriet Constable was wed in 1820 to James Duane, scion of a very notable and wealthy family in Schenectady, and her sister Emily married Dr. Samuel Moore of Troy, a nephew of the Episcopal bishop of New York City.

All the Constable children were themselves prolific, and they named many of their children after family members. The practice was repeated over ensuing generations so that parents, children, aunts, uncles and cousins often bore the same names. The problem is more confusing than appears on the family tree printed in this book because those whose children are not shown also repeatedly named their offspring William, John, James, Eweretta, Ann and Anna.

All of William Constable's children inherited some Macomb Purchase lands, but only William Jr., the elder son, devoted himself entirely to their development.

WILLIAM CONSTABLE JR.
BUILDER OF CONSTABLE HALL

William Jr., third child and oldest son, was born in New York City where he spent most of his early childhood. He was left home in the care of his grandmother while his parents were in Europe from 1792 until 1795. However, he was old enough to accompany them on their next European trip, 1798-1801. Following their departure, he stayed on in England to complete his education, but his schooling was interrupted by his father's death and when he was seventeen years old, he returned home.

His personality and character are something of an enigma; no activities or experiences in his early life seem to have provided the impetus for his later becoming a wilderness settler. He does not appear to have inherited his father's broad interests and abilities or his personable charm; his Uncle James, as guardian, found William Jr. rather difficult to handle.

After resettling in Schenectady, he attended Union College for three years, from which he graduated in 1808 with an A.B. degree. Although a satisfactory student, he was not an outstanding scholar.

Students lived under numerous regulations and restrictions in those days, as many were only in their middle-teens. William Jr. was required to room at the College, despite the fact that it was only three blocks from his home, but he was allowed to eat his meals with his family. Small fees were levied for use of the library, candles and wood, and unspecified "damages"—both "public" and "private." These included fines for being tardy or missing study hours in his room, or classes or chapel.

Other financial records indicate some of his recreational interests during his college years: he kept a horse, took dancing lessons and ran up a "substantial bill" at a local tavern. He joined a student literary and social organization, the Philomethian Society and left among his papers a rather flowery essay entitled "Belles Lettres" which may have been written for delivery to this group. It is also possible that the paper was his graduation oration, which was a common feature of such ceremonies at Union College at that time.

William Jr. was twenty years old when he first visited his Adirondack lands with his Uncle James during the summer of 1806; it is regrettable that he left no record of his own impressions of that trip. His inheritance included large tracts in Townships III and IV in Lewis County containing Turin, West Turin, Martinsburgh and High Market. However, these were subject to contract with Nathaniel Shaler, land agent, and under bond to Daniel McCormick. These encumbrances put the young man heavily in debt. He was also heir to an estate in Ireland, which yielded some income from tenants.

William Constable Jr.
(1786-1821)

The builder of Constable Hall is commemorated by this portrait which hangs near its entrance.

Chafing under his uncle's guardianship as he approached his 21st birthday and his college graduation, William sought to make his Irish business interests an excuse for a European trip. Instead, James endeavored to persuade the young man to study law, in compliance with his father's last wishes.

This disagreement is revealed in a letter which James wrote in April 1807, just a few months before his death, to James Forsyth, who looked after their British business affairs. He described William as "not very tractable," implored Forsyth to intercede by writing to the youth "and state to him that his presence is not at all necessary in Europe on account of his Irish estate . . . for I have an idea he looks forward to such a voyage after College. . . ." James, in requesting Forsyth to counsel William to comply with his father's last wishes, carefully quoted:

> "I wish my son William after leaving College to engage in reading Law in some reputable Attorney's Office, not with a view to it as a Profession, but as himself and the rest of the family will have a considerable landed Property, it will be well for him to know how to defend it."[13]

It is not known whether the young man followed his father's advice about studying law. However, if he did, it was not for long. He was married only two years after graduation, and the young couple chose to live on their remote northern estates and devote themselves to development of their lands. This decision may have been purely a business necessity, as his wealth lay mainly in the land's potential.

Nevertheless, he must have inherited his father's adventurous spirit, if not his business acumen. He probably relished the challenge of living in the upstate wilds, but it is difficult to know his character from the disparate pieces of information which are available about him.

He and Mary Eliza immediately began plans for building a suitable home of their own in Shalerville (now Constableville). They planned a grandiose mansion to be named Constable Hall; its construction period lasted nine full years, through 1819. During warmer months of the year, they lived in the frame home built by Nathaniel Shaler; winters were divided between New York City and Schenectady.

William Jr. was often short of ready funds. In 1812, his distress was alleviated by his sister Anna, who prevailed upon her husband to purchase from him, for $600, a valuable portrait of General George Washington which he had inherited from their father. It then adorned the Pierrepont home for many years and now hangs in the New York Public Library.

During 1812, William Jr. and his wife traveled to England and Ireland to confer on business affairs and visit his father's elderly aunts. On another visit to Ireland in 1816, he purchased and brought home "two beautiful bloodhounds."[14]

Daniel McCormick visited them at Shaler's in 1812, probably on business, but the tone of a letter which he wrote afterwards indicates a warm affectionate relationship as well:

> ". . . The kindness and attention I received from you and your good lady has made a lasting impression, and particularly your care of me upon the journey in providing me with some good wine. . . . I have sent you two days ago a Quarter Cask of Good old Madeira . . . and I hope to have a glass of it with you next year . . ."[15]

William Jr. sacrificed the increasing long-term value of his land holdings for immediate cash needs. He sold off much of his land in order to finish buying out Daniel McCormick's interests and to finance construction of Constable Hall. Years later, his punctilious grandson, Casimir, noted:

> "Grandfather was not a good businessman . . . although honorable, he was unmethodical and reckless."

He retained so little of his original holdings that Eliza later told her sons she felt mortified by his giving up the lands around them and

This Gilbert Stuart portrait of George Washington was commissioned by William Constable, along with a smaller bust-sized portrait. The two were painted simultaneously with the more famous "Lansdowne" portrait by Stuart in Philadelphia in 1796; the full-length view cost $500, and the smaller was $250. Constable presented the bust-sized portrait to his good friend, General Alexander Hamilton, and retained the larger work for himself. The portrait was bequeathed to his son William Jr., was later sold to Hezekiah B. Pierpont, and remained in the Pierrepont family for many years. It was presented to the Brooklyn Museum on February 22, 1947 and now hangs in the New York Public Library on the third floor.

"would rather have cut off either hand" than "surrender the inheritance."[16]

During most of the decade, William Jr. immersed himself in the infinite planning and close supervision of his mansion's construction. The work force for this enormous undertaking included artisans imported from the cities, local laborers and some Oneida Indians who lived in the region.

As the area around them was slowly settled, roads were improved and extended. It was no longer a wilderness, but rather a frontier. William joined with other early settlers in supporting civic improvements. In 1815, he helped establish the first school in Constableville and in the following year he and his brother-in-law, James McVickar, both subscribed liberally to the construction of an Episcopal church in the nearby village of Turin.

William Jr. chanced to meet another struggling land owner, John Brown Francis, in Boonville in 1817. Francis was descended from a prominent merchant from Rhode Island, and was owner of a sizeable part of the John Brown Tract in the Adirondacks, the most easterly part of the Macomb Purchase. At that time Francis was engaged in arranging construction of the Moose River Road, leading to the area which later became Old Forge. He recorded in his diary:

> ". . . Introduced to Mr. Constable, one of the landed proprietors in this neighborhood. Has the manners of a man who has seen good company."[17]

When finally completed in 1819, Constable Hall was a monumental achievement, an imposing and stately 16 room mansion built in the style of a Georgian country manor. From the front it appeared to be two stories high; however, three floors faced the rear, with kitchen and utility rooms on the ground level. The walls were of limestone slabs set off by four

Constable Hall was built by William Constable Jr. during the period from 1811 to 1819. It is a gracious, Georgian-style mansion, which crowns a gentle hillside.

A rear view of the mansion shows that three floors face the rear. Indian Room, kitchen, storage and utility areas are located on the ground floor.

tall round columns which adorned the front portico.

Grandiose amid the commonplace frame and log dwellings of that time and place, it was set upon the crest of a hill, overlooking the Black River Valley and the Adirondacks, rising to the east. It was the finest mansion west of the Hudson and north of the Mohawk.

An "Indian Room" was included on the ground floor, and it was used for many years by Iroquois in the region, who were welcome to stop there and receive hospitality and shelter. An old flintlock rifle hanging over the fireplace was available for their use and a place of honor was accorded to the old buckskin coat which had been presented to his father long ago. It hung in the room as a decoration and a symbol of enduring ties of friendship through generations.

Unfortunately William Jr. was never able to enjoy his grand new home; he was tragically injured in a construction accident shortly before the building was finished. The mishap occurred while he was supervising the installation of a ten-ton capstone designed for the front portico. As a wagon drawn by 18 oxen approached the house with this enormous load, he insisted that it deviate from a straight route to spare an oak tree in its path. The load shifted unexpectedly, and the stone split and

The kitchen at Constable Hall now displays the antique muzzle-loading flintlock gun which formerly hung in the Indian Room. The room and gun were reserved for use by neighboring or traveling Indians, who were always welcomed at Constable Hall. They customarily expressed their thanks for hospitality by giving a haunch of fresh meat to the Constables after a successful hunting trip.

The buckskin coat, now on display on the main floor of Constable Hall, used to hang in the Indian Room. It was presented to William Constable Sr. by Indians of the Six Nations as a token of their friendship.

Mary Eliza McVickar Constable
(1789-1870)
Daguerreotype circa 1860,
(Courtesy of John P. Constable Jr.)

fell. One piece knocked William to the ground, crushing his leg. Although he lived for two years after this calamity, those last years must have been a pain-wracked existence. He died in 1821 at the age of thirty-six, leaving five young children and a widow only thirty-three years old. Four sons had been born before the mansion was completed, and shortly after they moved in, a daughter was born.

Mary Eliza reigned as mistress of Constable Hall for the next 49 years, assisted by a large staff of domestic servants and agricultural workers. She furnished the manor with fine pieces, including many inherited from William Sr., and some antiques. Among them were a chair and table which had once belonged to Marie Antoinette; these had been purchased in Paris in 1794 and brought home by Hezekiah B. Pierpont, her brother-in-law.

Eliza, as she was called by the family, was accustomed to living amid elegant people of wealth and influence. She snobbishly refused to associate with the local residents in Constableville and nearby Turin; only the Episcopal minister was welcomed as her social equal.

Fortunately, her loneliness was alleviated by family members living nearby. Her two brothers, who had married William Jr.'s sisters, both developed estates in the vicinity. James McVickar, with his wife Eweretta Constable, had moved to Turin in 1813, where he served as a county judge until 1830. Her younger brother Edward, married to Matilda Constable, built a home nearby in West Turin.

Members of the Pierrepont family were also in the area. It will be recalled that Hezekiah B. Pierpont had married Anna Constable, and had also been an executor of William I's estate. Before and after William's death, Pierpont had bought some of the Macomb Purchase lands, and when William's estate was finally settled in 1819, he bought out the land interests of several heirs. In Lewis County alone, he amassed nearly half a million acres.

Pierpont viewed his lands as long term investments and he was active in developing roads and turnpikes, as well as encouraging the growth of canals and, later, railroads. He visited the region each summer, often accompanied by his two older sons who had been trained in surveying, and eventually they took over the management of these lands.

The elder son, William Constable Pierrepont, was in charge of tracts in Jefferson and Oswego Counties, and in 1822 built the elegant Pierrepont Manor across the Tug Hill Plateau from Constableville. Henry Pierrepont, his brother, managed family-owned lands in St. Lawrence, Lewis and Franklin Counties, and established a home near Constableville.

The presence of so many family members nearby was a comfort to Eliza as she took over personal management of the Constable household and estates. Income from land development supported her and her family; she managed the business alone until her sons were old enough to assist.

Eliza established a small private chapel off the pantry in her home, for worship when the winter weather prevented her attendance at church. She was a devoted member of the local Episcopal Church which her husband had helped found in the nearby village of Turin, and was instrumental in its relocation to Constableville in the early 1830s, when she donated a plot of land for a new building.

St. Paul's was then constructed on the same site that the former Shaler residence (her first home after marriage) had once stood; it had been destroyed by a fire. The little country church still stands in Constableville today, enhanced by such useful and decorative items as a marble altarpiece and baptismal font, candelabra, tapestries, vases and other gifts which were donated by generations of Constables, as well as other parishioners.

After William Jr. died, his magnificent mansion and remaining landholdings were passed on to his family, but perhaps his most valuable legacy was his five children, who were to rank among the Adirondack's first campers and hikers and finest sportsmen.

THE FOUR CONSTABLE BROTHERS

William III (1811-1887) and Guide
The guide is probably Higby the Hunter, William R. Higby, who guided for the Constables from the 1840s through the 1870s.

John
(1813-1887)

James (1814-1892) with daughter

Stevenson
(1816-1894)

(No photo is available of their sister Anna)

These daguerreotypes probably date from the 1840s and 1850s.
(Courtesy of John P. Constable Jr.)

CHAPTER TWO

Earliest Adirondack Explorations: 1830s and 1840s

The fatherless family which grew up at Constable Hall in the early 1800s was an unusually close group of siblings. William III was the oldest son, born in 1811; he was ten years old when his father died. His three brothers—John, James and Stevenson—followed closely in age, separated by only a year or two. Anna, their only sister, was four years younger than Stevenson.

Related to many prominent families in New York City, where they usually spent winters, they enjoyed close relationships with aunts, uncles and cousins among the Pierreponts, Jays, Livingstons, Duanes, McVickars, Moores, Bucknors, Bards and Lawrences. At Constable Hall the children had a lively group of first cousins of similar ages nearby. The James McVickar family included two sons (also named William and John) and two daughters (Anna and Mary). Edward McVickar's family was somewhat younger and included one boy and seven girls.[1]

Because of their mother's strong class-consciousness, the Constable youngsters were not allowed to mix with neighboring children or to attend local schools. Instead, they were tutored at Constable Hall by the local Episcopal minister.

As the Constable boys grew, they developed strength, agility and independence, often wandering in the nearby fields and forests. They honed their skills in hunting, fishing and camping, relishing all of these activities. Their little sister, Anna, probably tagged along as a small tomboy on some of their expeditions; her own later exploits indicate that she also loved camping and hiking.

The boys all attended European boarding schools in Paris and Geneva and acquired a solid academic foundation as well as the poise and polish of gentlemen. They must have been delighted, however, to return to the simpler pleasures of life at Constable Hall.

Nearby rivers and forests of the Tug Hill Plateau teemed with fish and game and each of the brothers was captivated by the quiet beauty of wilderness lakes and streams. As they grew to manhood, they undertook more adventurous fishing and hunting trips; the Adirondacks lured them eastward.

William III (known formally as William Sr., and informally as "Will") was the eldest and the only one to follow a profession. He became a doctor and lived in New York City, but stayed exceptionally close to all his family and visited often. Throughout his lifetime, he led them on periodic Adirondack expeditions and hosted jolly summer camping parties at Constable Point on Raquette Lake.

John remained at home at Constable Hall, becoming his mother's estate manager. He married his first cousin, Julia E. Pierrepont, and inherited the Hall from his mother in 1870. Enjoying life as an aristocratic gentleman-farmer, he was affectionate with family and intimate friends, indulgent toward tenants on his lands, and well-mannered but aloof to other neighbors. Through his frequent hunting trips to the Adirondacks, he achieved a reputation as an outstanding sportsman; some of his trophies still hang upon the walls of Constable Hall. His remaining guns are also on display and are of great interest to collectors. John contributed significant information to Clinton Hart Merriam's studies of Adirondack mammals. (Chapter Seven contains complete details.)

James, the third brother, resided in Philadelphia after his marriage, but he returned often to the Hall for visits and camping trips. A comment in family letters about James' health implies that he suffered from some chronic medical problem (possibly asthma) and had difficulty tolerating the cold winters of the north country.[2] Nevertheless, he was an avid outdoorsman.

Stevenson, youngest of the four, never married. He lived at Constable Hall throughout his life, assisting in running the estate. He too became a skilled sportsman, although his accomplishments paled alongside those of John. Members of the family affectionately called him "Stevie" or "Uncle Stevie."

Their sister Anna also lived at Constable Hall until she was married in 1868, at age forty-three, to her first cousin, Archibald McVickar. They then resided in Lyons Falls, only a few miles away.

The Constables were tantalized throughout their childhood by views from their home of the distant wilderness, which they simply called "the woods." The region was then popularly called "John Brown's Tract" and only later known as "the Adirondacks." All four brothers were among the earliest gentlemen sportsmen to range throughout the western and central mountains, under as rough and daunting conditions as those experienced by any guides, hunters and trappers. It is surprising that early histories of the region do not even mention their explorations.

The Adirondacks were still unmapped and largely unknown when the Constables first explored its waterways. Years later, after maps of the region were issued, John meticulously marked upon them routes of some of their trips and other useful notes. These valuable maps are still among the family possessions; from them it is possible to piece together a chronological sequence of some of the Constable's earliest Adirondack trips.

ANNOTATED MAPS

1840 Railroad Survey: This was John's earliest Adirondack map. A cloth-backed rectangle, 11½ by 28 inches, it was printed by Miller's Lithograph in New York City and was derived from a survey[3] for a route from Ogdensburgh to Lake Champlain for the Mohawk and St. Lawrence Railroad. It covers an area which includes parts of Montgomery, Oneida, Lewis, Herkimer, Hamilton, Franklin and St. Lawrence Counties. Despite its age and some brown stains, most of it is still legible.

On the back of the folded map, John wrote in pencil: "Very old and inaccurate. I used to take when moose hunting." On the face of the map, John made several more notes, some written in ink and others in pencil, which probably indicates they were made at different times.

"Tupper Lake" is marked upon Mort Lake. The location of "Plumley's" and "Seargeant's"

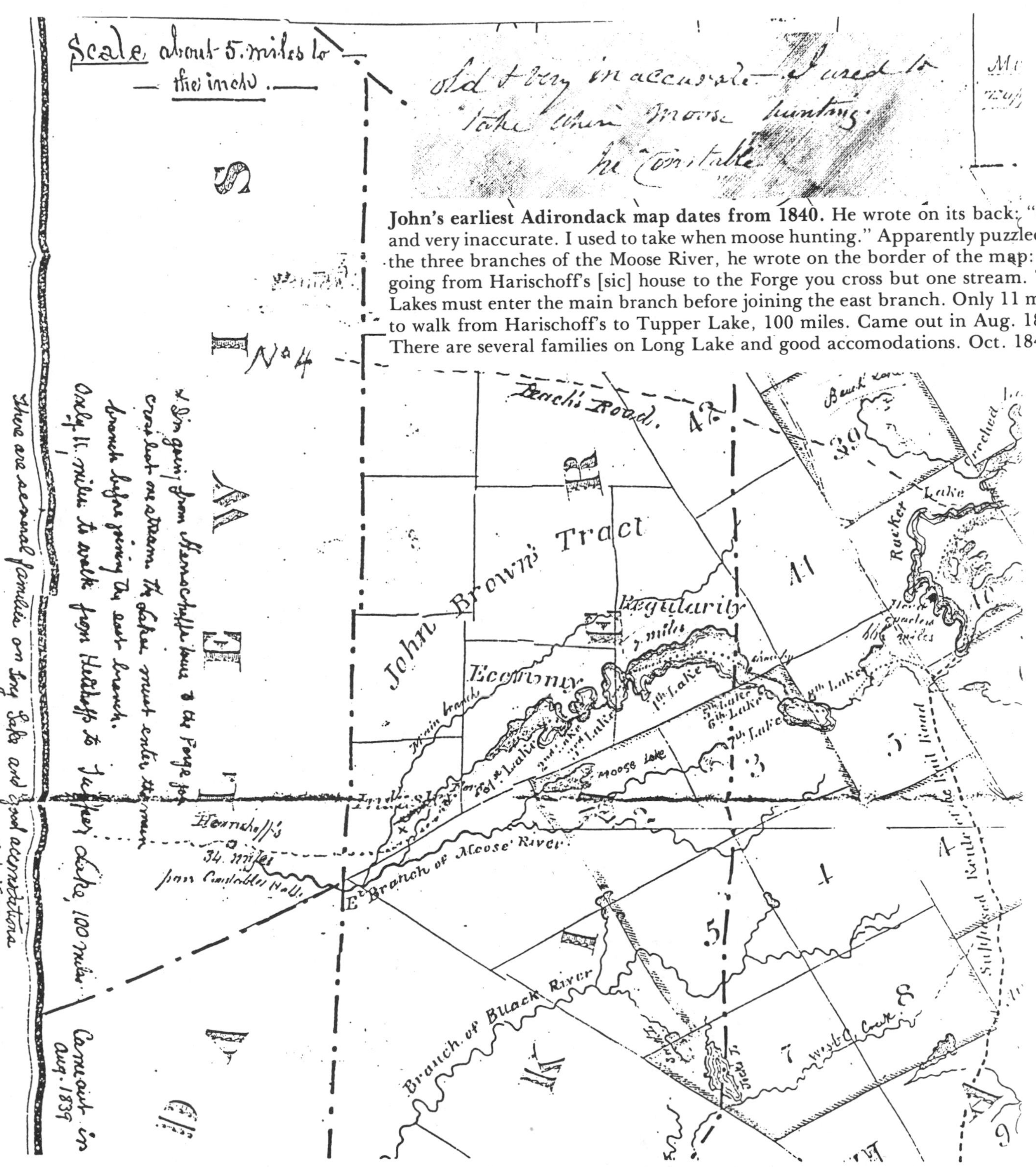

John's earliest Adirondack map dates from 1840. He wrote on its back: "Old and very inaccurate. I used to take when moose hunting." Apparently puzzled by the three branches of the Moose River, he wrote on the border of the map: "In going from Harischoff's [sic] house to the Forge you cross but one stream. The Lakes must enter the main branch before joining the east branch. Only 11 miles to walk from Harischoff's to Tupper Lake, 100 miles. Came out in Aug. 1839. There are several families on Long Lake and good accomodations. Oct. 1840."

is indicated on Long Lake and a note dated October 1, 1840 states: "There are five or six families on Long Lake and good accommodation."

The Beaver River is drawn in, as well as Albany Lake (now Nehasane), Smith's Lake (now Lake Lila), Beaches Lake (now Brandreth's) and a lake with an indecipherable name (now Little Tupper). Fenton's and No. 4 are also indicated, and the route from No. 4 to Racket [sic] Lake is drawn and then corrected.

Stoney Creek is marked, leading into the Raquette River, with the words "To Plattsburgh, 65 miles, 4 miles to Saranac Lake, only one mile portage."

Nearly obliterated is another notation on the western edge: "In going from Harischoff's [sic] house to the Forge, you cross but one stream. The lakes must enter the main branch before joining the east branch. Only 11 miles to walk from Harischoff's to Tupper Lake, 100 miles."

1843 Harris Survey of Blue Mountain Lake is a small map with a note indicating that John and Stevenson Constable with Casimir De Rham first visited the lake in 1836.

A. P. Edward's Survey of Raquette Lake was issued in 1853. Notes upon it indicated that William III and John Constable first visited the lake in 1835 on a hunting trip, guided by "Old Johnson and Chase." An X marks the point on which they had built a shanty; it later became known as Constable Point.

Merritt's Maps and Routes of Black River Waters is a pocket-sized booklet printed in 1860. It contains 12 pages of printed information relating to Adirondack water routes, including descriptions, mileages, guides and sources of supplies. The map itself is missing, probably indicating heavy usage, but copies available elsewhere emphasize the map-maker's optimistic view of a hunting and fishing paradise! The book contains two interesting notes:

> "1835: 1st Excursion to the Raquette Lake-
> W.C. Sr., Jn. C., Old Johnson, Chase.
> Headquarters at head of 4th lake since 1833.
>
> "The Raquette River derives its name from a large quantity of snowshoes found upon an island near Potsdam during the Revolution.
>
> Jn. Constable"

The latter note is of considerable interest, if true, because John Constable's information does not appear to be generally known, and is contrary to accepted accounts. It suggests that Raquette Lake is named after the Raquette River, rather than vice versa.

The opposing version of this story asserts that the snowshoes (called "raquettes" in French) were found at the lake, rather than the river, as recounted by historian Alfred L. Donaldson. He related that the snowshoes were abandoned on the southern shore of Raquette Lake by Sir John Johnson and his Tory folfollowers, when they were overtaken by the spring thaws while fleeing from the Mohawk Valley to Montreal in May 1776. The same story is told by historians Hochschild and Timm.[4]

It is impossible at this late date to determine which account is correct, but it seems probable that John, who recorded his note nearly a century before Donaldson's book, was apt to have been in personal contact with original sources of information.

Stoddard's 1881 Map of the Adirondack Wilderness was presented to John Constable by M.D. Ralph of Laran, Chateaugay Lake, Clinton County. Still in good condition, the map shows loving care and little use. John was an old man by the time it was issued, and his camping days were over. However, he enjoyed marking highlights of his many excursions in red ink upon the map, including locations where moose were killed, summer and winter campsites and the route of a road leading from

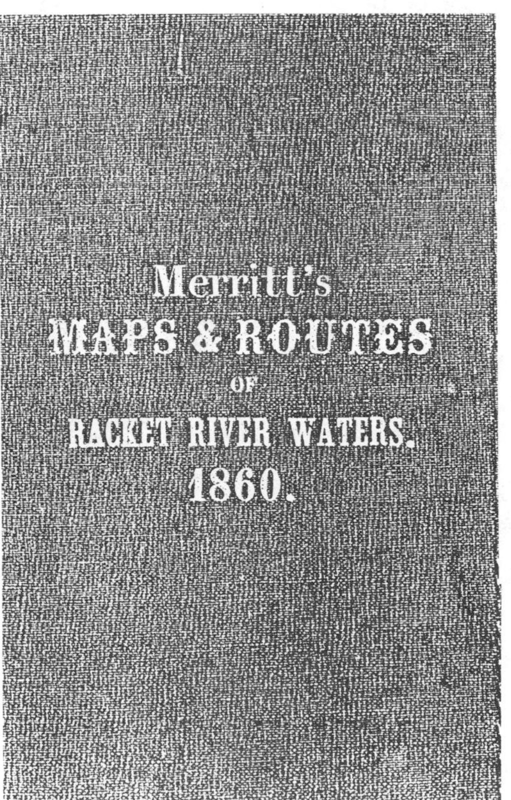

Merritt's 1860 book and map were presented to John by his cousin and brother-in-law, William Constable Pierrepont. (See a section of Merritt's map on page 103.)

The Raquette River
derives its name from
a large quantity of
snowshoes found upon
an islands near Potsdam
during the Revolution.

Mr Constable
1835.
1st excursion to the Raquette
Lake — W. C. Sr.
Jr. C
old Johnson
& Chase

Headquarters at head of 4th
Lake since 1833.

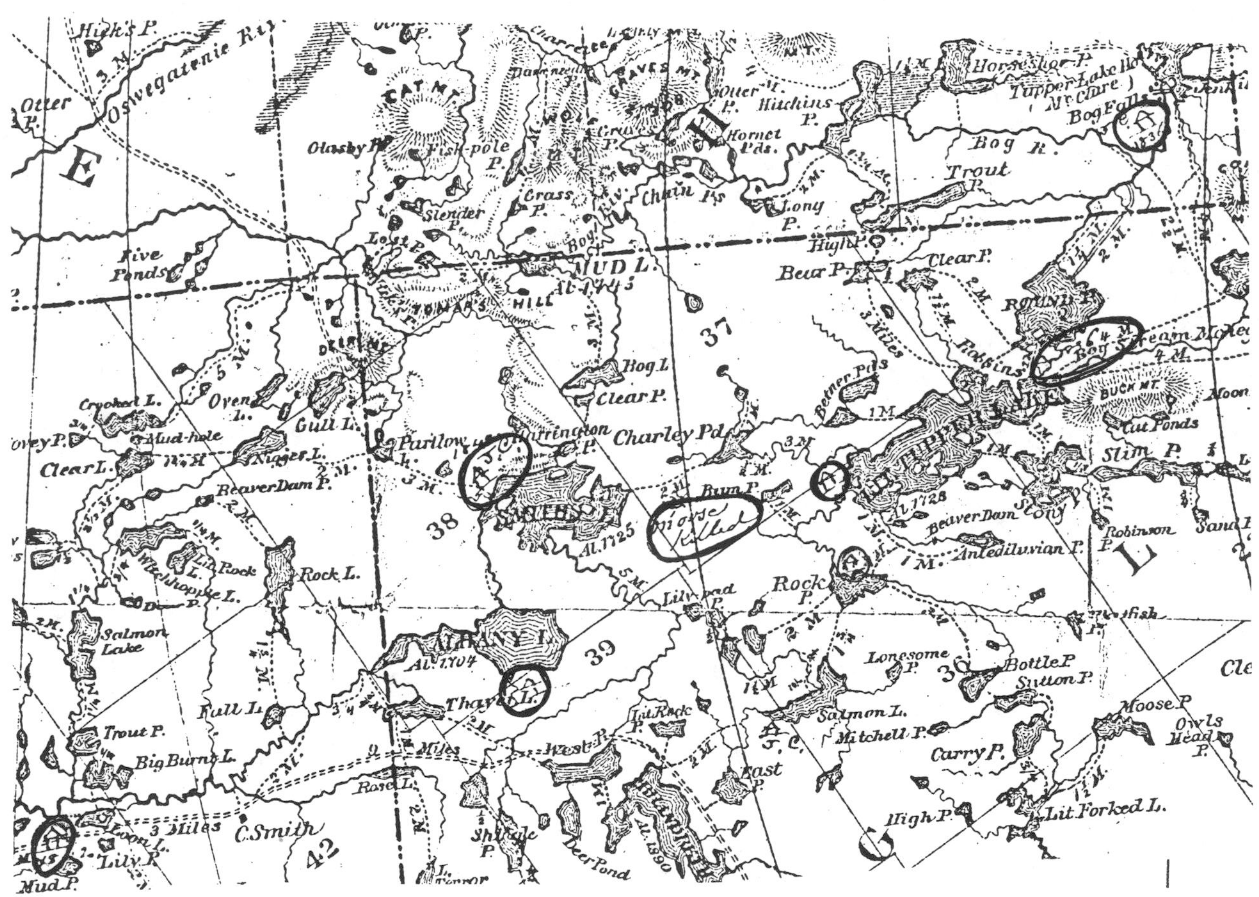

John noted locations where he had killed moose and established campsites on an 1881 copy of Stoddard's Map of the Adirondack Wilderness.

Westport on Lake Champlain through Elizabethtown, Keene, North Elba, Wilmington and Jay to Ausable Falls.

EARLIEST EXCURSIONS

John was twenty-one years old on his first trip to the Fulton Chain of Lakes in 1833. He followed the old Moose River Road from Boonville some 25 miles. This route was then a most difficult hike, impassable for wagons, through mucky bogs and forests, fording the Moose River. It terminated near the outlet of First Lake, where a few decaying structures were all that was left of former farming and mining ventures on John Brown's Tract. An old forge which marked the site of a flooded mine had become a landmark for passing trappers and settlers, giving rise to the name "Old Forge" for that area.

Only a few miles south, near the Moose River, was the abandoned manor house which had been built by John Brown's son-in-law, Herreshoff, in 1812 or 1813. In 1830, the Manor and adjacent lands were leased as a hunting preserve by Caleb Lyon and two other Lewis County residents,[5] all of whom were probably known by the Constable brothers, although not friends.

John established his camp headquarters—probably a substantial shanty—on the eastern end of Fourth Lake in 1833 and returned to the same site for several years thereafter. It also served him as a winter camp. There is no record of his companions on his first Adirondack trip but it seems likely that one or more of his brothers were with him and perhaps a guide or two.

FIRST VISIT TO RAQUETTE LAKE, 1835

In 1835, John and his older brother, Will, ranged around and beyond the Fulton Chain of Lakes, guided by the local trappers "Old Johnson" (Willard) and David Chase, who both lived in some of the abandoned buildings in the vicinity of the old forge.[6] On this trip the Constables first visited Raquette Lake and apparently fell in love with it, as they returned again and again in subsequent years.

Raquette and other nearby lakes were at that time completely virgin territory to white men, although Indians were still frequenters of the lakes and surrounding wilderness. The earliest settlers had not arrived yet, although a few hunters and trappers had visited periodically.

It is helpful to know when other early explorers first ventured into the area, in order to appreciate the historic importance of the Constables' wanderings. Their first visit to Raquette Lake in 1835 preceded that of Professor Ebenezer Emmons, State Geologist, by five years. They were also five years ahead of the Reverend John Todd and eleven years before the Reverend Joel Headley; these latter gentlemen were among the earliest authors of Adirondack books. The Constable brothers were 18 years ahead of A. F. Edwards, railroad surveyor, and some 40 years before the well-known surveyor, Verplanck Colvin, Superintendent of the Adirondack Survey.

The Constables were even ahead of Farrand N. Benedict (Professor of Geology at Burlington College in Vermont) who assisted the Emmons Survey Party in 1840 and left a more enduring memory in the region as an entrepreneur. He set about purchasing the whole area so that he could develop it and by 1850 owned all of Raquette Lake and its surrounding lands in Township 40.

Benedict foresaw with remarkable clarity the paths of destruction which he would eventually unleash upon the region. In 1854, an unsigned article was published, now generally attributed to Benedict. Entitled "The Wilds of Northern New York," it described the region in glowing

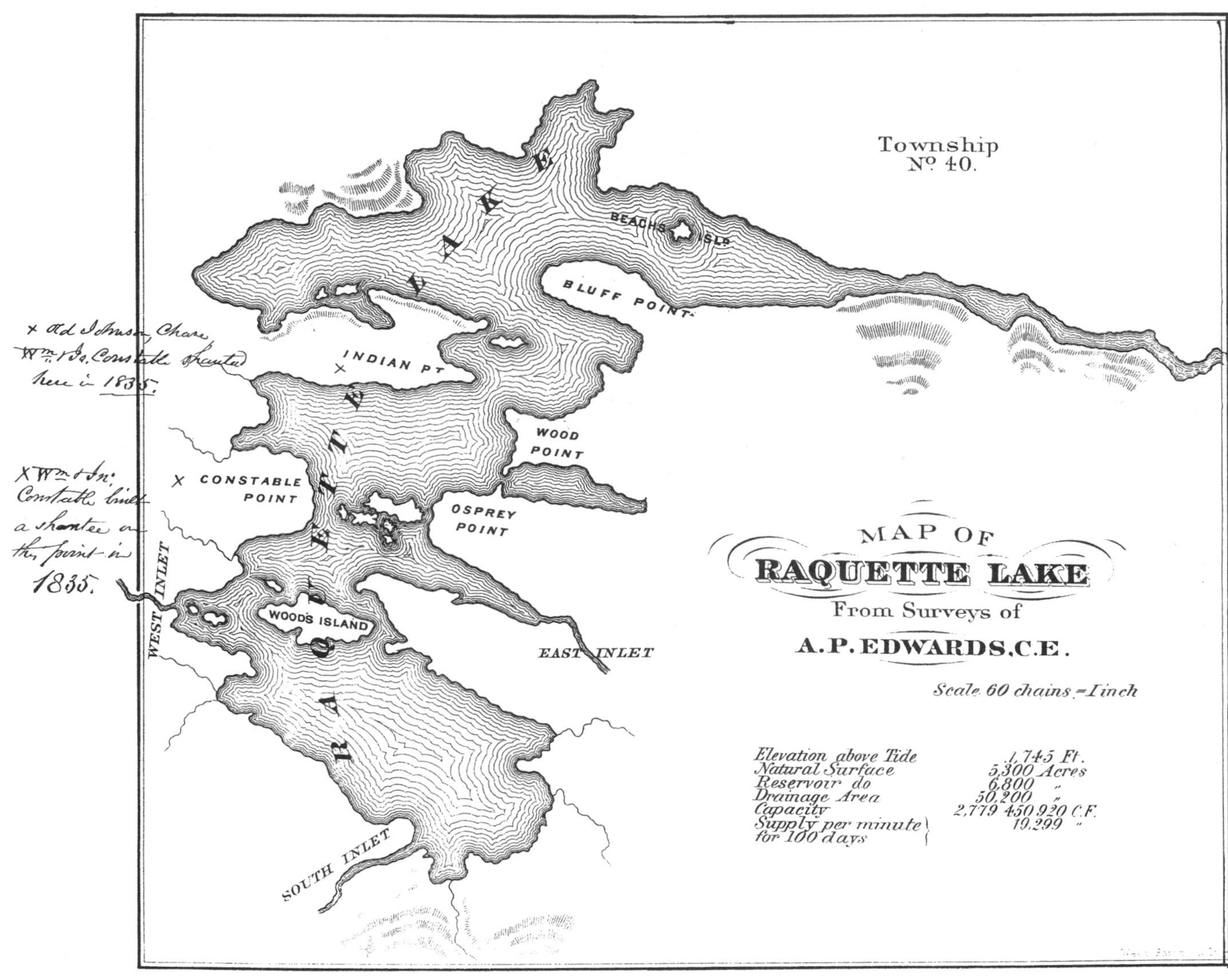

A. P. Edwards' Survey of Raquette Lake was prepared for a proposed route for the Saratoga and Sackett's Harbor Railroad Company in 1853. John Constable noted upon it: "Old Johnson, Chase, Wm. and Jn. Constable hunted here in 1835." "Wm. & Jn. Constable built a shantee on the point in 1835."

Professor Farrand N. Benedict
Geologist and Surveyor, owner, by 1850, of all lands surrounding Raquette Lake. (Courtesy of The Adirondack Museum)

terms, rhapsodizing about the scenery, the beauty, peace and healthfulness of the area and the bountiful fish, game and other natural resources. It concluded:

> ". . . in a few years, the railroad with its iron web will bind the free forest, the lakes will lose their solitude, the deer and moose will go to a safer resort, the eagle and raven leave their accustomed haunts, and men with an axe and spade will work out a revolution. . . ."[7]

However, such development was far in the future when the Constables were still exploring the lakes and mountains in the 1830s.

FIRST EXPLORATORY TRIP THROUGH THE ADIRONDACKS, 1836

In 1836, John undertook an extensive trip through the Adirondack waterways along with his youngest brother, Stevenson (then twenty years old), and his very good friend, Casimir de Rham. Among family memorabilia is a handsome brass compass which was presented to John on this occasion. It bears an inscription: "John Constable from Casimir de Rham, 1st June, 1836." Imported from England, the instrument is a dry compass with a balanced needle, made by Rubergall, an optician in London. The dial is divided into quadrants with precision markings.

The route of this 1836 trip can be followed from the notes John later wrote upon his 1881 Stoddard Map. The three young men penetrated as far north as Tupper Lake (then known as Mort Lake) and east as far as Blue Mountain. Along this course they camped at both ends of Fourth Lake, Rondaxe Lake (then called First Lake of the north branch of the Moose River), Big Moose Lake (then called Third Lake on the north branch), the Beaver River, Mud Pond (near Brandreth), Salmon Lake, Smith Lake (now Lake Lila), Albany Lake (now Nehasane), Rock Pond, Bog Falls (south of Tupper), Raquette Falls, Long Lake and Raquette Lake. This may be the first recorded circuit of these waterways.

1839 AND 1840 CIRCUITS

The Constables were among the earliest customers at Arnold's Inn, which was established by Otis Arnold in the abandoned Herreshoff Manor near the old forge. One of the earliest permanent settlers in the western Adirondacks, Arnold moved his growing family into the house in 1837 without the usual formalities of rental or purchase. They planted a few crops and added to their larder by fishing and hunting.

At first Arnold did not consider himself an innkeeper, but he was glad to supplement his income by accommodating visiting sportsmen.

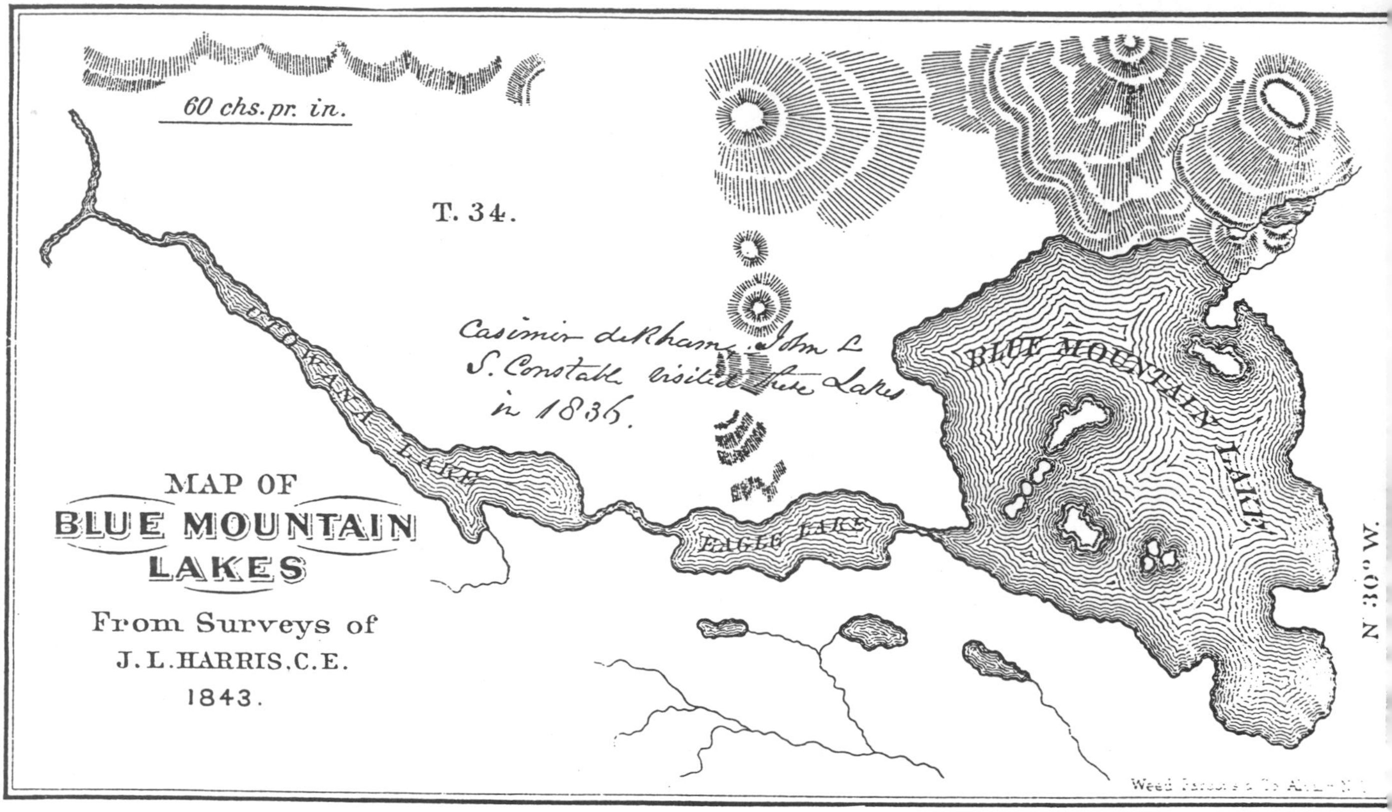

60 chs. pr. in.

T. 34.

Casimir deRham, John & S. Constable visited these Lakes in 1836.

UTOWANA LAKE

EAGLE LAKE

BLUE MOUNTAIN LAKE

MAP OF
BLUE MOUNTAIN
LAKES

From Surveys of
J. L. HARRIS, C.E.
1843.

N 30° W.

John Constable's note on the survey map of Blue Mountain Lake indicates that he first visited the lake in 1836, in company with his brother Stevenson, and their good friend, Casimir de Rham.

A fine English compass was presented to John by Casimir de Rham prior to their 1836 trip throughout the waterways of the Adirondacks.

It was not long before he discovered that keeping tavern and an informal hotel in that remote location was much more lucrative than farming and trapping. The Constables used the inn as a "jumping off place" for more extensive trips into the mountains.

In 1840, John again journeyed through the Adirondacks, following the Raquette River as far as Tupper Lake, but departing westward by following the Beaver River toward Watson and Lowville. On his 1840 map, he noted houses which afforded hospitality on Long Lake, as well as notes on the course of the Beaver River and lakes encountered along the way. Although he was thus becoming familiar with faraway lakes and streams, John was still unsure of the routes of the three branches of the nearby Moose River, according to another note on this same map (refer to pages 31 and 39).

1843 TRIP TO RAQUETTE LAKE

The first fully detailed account of a Constable camping trip was printed in a New York weekly sporting journal, *Spirit of the Times*, on February 3, 1844. The article, reproduced here, related the 1843 adventures of a trio which included two brothers who were designated John and Stanley but who were clearly John and Stevenson Constable.

This article contained one of the earliest descriptions of the central Adirondacks to appear in the popular press. Its significance can be better appreciated when put into historical context; this was a time when the region was still generally unknown.

WHO WAS BOB RACKET?

Unfortunately, the identity of the author, who accompanied the brothers, is unknown. He concealed his name by using a *nom de plume*, calling himself "Bob Racket." Pen names were a common affectation of sporting writers in those days; this pseudonym produced a mystery which is still unsolved. A second article by "Bob Racket," describing another Constable trip, appeared more than a decade later, in 1855. (It is discussed and reprinted in Chapter Four.)

Several Adirondack scholars have speculated about Bob Racket's identity, including Professor Warder H. Cadbury of the State University at Albany, the late Kenneth Durant (expert on guideboats and early explorations), the late William K. Verner (one-time curator of the Adirondack Museum and later director of the Schenectady Museum) and Ted Comstock (former proprietor of Wildwood Books in Old Forge).

None of these authorities have solved the mystery; they concluded only that Bob Racket was a close friend or relative of the Constables, and he lived in or had connections with New York City.

The author's ostensible purpose in writing was to inform readers about the beautiful lakes in Herkimer and Hamilton Counties and the abundance of fish and game. The article is spiced with witty descriptions of the high spirits which characterized Constable activities. They did everything enthusiastically, always "leaping" (rather than stepping or climbing) in and out of boats while trading jokes, puns, and exuberant Indian war whoops. Despite cold, wet and hunger, there was never a complaint; discomfort and danger evoked only greater bonhomie.

More significant is Bob Racket's evidence of the expertise which the Constables had developed in all types of woodsmanship: trip-planning, load-carrying, boat-handling, hunting, fishing and general self-sufficiency in the wilds. The author portrayed himself as a relative neophyte, often put under the guide's charge while fishing and hunting, whereas the brothers were totally independent.

Following is the 1844 article, reproduced with its many peculiarities of punctuation and spelling so typical of that age:

"To the Editor of the 'Spirit of the Times':

Dear Sir—

There is a chain of nine lakes in Herkimer and Hamilton Counties in this State, which for beauty of scenery and abundance of game, are probably unequalled in the United States, and I am only surprised they are so little known to the sporting gentry of New York. For their benefit I will give you a rough sketch of a trip to them, undertaken last summer in company with two other gentlemen.

Eight of these beautiful sheets of water are called 1st, 2d, 3d lake, etc. and the last and most northerly is called *Raquette* lake, (the French term for *Snow shoe*,) and is so called from the fact, that a large quantity of these shoes were found on one of the islands, with which the lake is studded. [Readers may note the discrepancy with other accounts of these snowshoes.]

Our party consisted of two brothers, (whom I shall call John and Stanley), Higby the Hunter, and myself.

We started on the 26th July from Constableville,* rode 13 miles in a wagon to the edge of the forest, where we were obliged to leave it, taking with us two pack-horses to carry our provisions to 1st lake (a distance of 20 miles,) we preferring 'Shank's mare,' on account of the roughness of the route, (which was but an Indian trail,) and to be ready for any game that might spring on our pathway. Our provisions consisted of

16 lbs. Rice
42 " Meal and flour
10 " Butter
4 " Fine Salt
4 oz. Salaeratus (baking soda)
1 " Pepper
10 lbs. Loaf Sugar
10 " Fat Pork
2½ lbs. Green Tea
2 bottles "Eau de vie"
1 " Pickles
1 " Currant Jelly

with Fire apparatus, Compass, Hatchet, Belt-knife, Air-pillow, and Spy-glass for *each*, with guns, fly-rod and rifle of course.

Our tramp through the forest was very fatiguing, as the night previous it had rained incessantly, filling the lowlands with water, rendering the walking very slippery, and leaving the bushes so wet, that the effect on us was the same as if it had continued to rain, for the sun never penetrated the thick canopy of leaves over our heads.

I had heard of, and experienced the attacks of mosquitoes on the meadows of Long Island, where they were said to be 'as thick as mud,' but never could I believe it possible that the air could support them in such swarms as they attacked us on entering the forest of 'Brown's Tract.' They bid defiance to veils and gloves, insinuating themselves under the one and penetrating the seams of the other. The only 'let up' to them was, when halting, we made a 'smudge' of dry leaves and wet moss, and enveloped ourselves in the smoke, (which is the only thing they appear to dread) so that our troubles though great were sure to 'end in smoke.'

Commencing our tramp at 9 in the morning, . . . we reached a small clearing, where lives an old hunter, named Arnold, (with a family of eight daughters and one son,) at 5 in the afternoon, a distance of 20 miles, (although equal to 30 turnpike miles) pretty well fagged out myself, although John and Stanley being more experienced woodsmen suffered less. We shot on the way 4 partridges and 8 pigeons. However, I could stand on my legs well enough to catch a fine mess of speckled trout for our supper, from a stream which washed the foot of the hill where the hunter's hut was situated.

In 15 minutes Stanley and myself caught with a fly 35 of the 'jewelled fish,' weighing from 8 oz. to 1½ lbs, but we had more *bites* with the *mos-*

* To reach Constableville or Turin, you leave the railroad at Rome, and take the stage. Distance 25 miles north.

quitoes than with the *flies*. Oh! how they did put it to us; our hands and faces were covered with blood from the massacre we had committed.

Our accomodations for the night were not princely; John and the hunter slept on the floor while Stanley and myself occupied a rude bed, but had it been even less comfortable, the fatigue of our day's journey would have converted it into a bed of roses.

At 6 the next morning we were *en route* again, having three miles to walk to reach the first lake. The weather was delicious, and the bracing mountain air with the beauty of the scenery soon made us forget the toils of the preceding day.

We soon reached the lake, where we found our boat (snugly hid in the reeds) which was to convey us to our camping ground 25 miles further. This boat was built of cedar by Higby himself, in the woods, with no other tools than a hatchet, drawing knife, hammer, and nails, was made as light as possible, 90 lbs., in order to carry it from lake to lake (portages of 1 to 3 miles) and yet was capacious enough to carry all our party with dog, guns, rods, provisions, etc.

As we moved up the lake, I could not sufficiently admire the beauty of the scenery, which very much resembled that of the Scotch lakes. I will not attempt a description as the reader (if curious) can imagine the effect of a happy combination of mountain, forest, and lake, wild as when first created, and without any appearance of the traces of civilization. Favored with a fine westerly breeze we soon reached the termination of 4th lake, (distance 12 miles) without a portage, as the communications from 1st to the 4th are navigable. Here, however, we had to transfer our packs, etc. from the boat to our backs, each carrying about 50 lbs., and Higby the boat, which he accomplished by means of a yoke rigged across the gunwales, turned downside up, with his head inside.

In this way we trudged about 2 miles over trunks of trees, through swamps, up and down hill, until we reached 6th lake. We here made a 'smudge,' for we never could halt an instant without doing so, or run the risk of being devoured by mosquitoes, moose-flies, or punkies (an insect resembling a gnat but more piquant)

Otis Arnold and his wife established a simple inn in the abandoned Herreshoff House near the old forge.

and prepared to launch our boat. We here noticed fresh moose and deer tracks in abundance, giving promise of goodly sport in perspective.

Again embarked, we paddled slowly along, hoping to get a crack at some ducks and loons which were in sight, but they were not such *geese* as to come within gun-shot.

The scenery of this lake and Seventh is wilder than the others, being more shut in by the mountains. The water is uncommonly limpid; you can see bottom distinctly at 30 feet.

In two hours we reached the termination of 7th lake, four miles, where we disembarked again for another portage, so you perceive that

> 'Our's the wild life of *forest* still to range,
> From toil to rest and joy in every change.'

although I must confess there was not quite so much '*joy*' in the *change* of carrying the boat as having the boat to carry us.

A mile now brought us to 8th lake, at the termination of which (three miles) another portage of 1½ mile brought us to the inlet which empties into Raquette lake, where we arrived at half past 6 P.M. having seven miles further to reach the shanty of the hunters, Wood and Beach, which was to be our diverging point.

The sky had for some time assumed a threatening aspect, and now gave every indication of an approaching storm; but thinking we could arrive at our destination before it commenced, on consultation we concluded to push on. The Inlet is 5 miles long, which we floated down slowly in order to shoot bittern, but being so late none flew.

As we issued forth into the lake, large drops of rain, and the increasing blackness of the sky announced that the storm was about to burst; and so it did with a vengeance.

This lake you must know is the shape of a man's hand, having 5 inlets and as many bays from a mile to four miles wide, and its circumference along shore must be at rough guess some 50 miles. 'Twas one of these bays (about 3 miles wide,) we had to cross, with our frail bark laden almost to the water's edge, and with only one life preserver among us.

It was now quite dark and we could only see our course as revealed to us by the lightning which was almost incessant, followed by peals of thunder which rolled through the mountains echoing and re-echoing with terrific grandeur. The rain came down in torrents, so that we nearly stripped ourselves to preserve our provisions from getting wet. John was in the stern, alternately steering and baling with one of Higby's shoes, (which was not half so efficient as

First, Second, Third and Fourth Lakes of the Fulton Chain
Panoramic view from Bald Mountain.

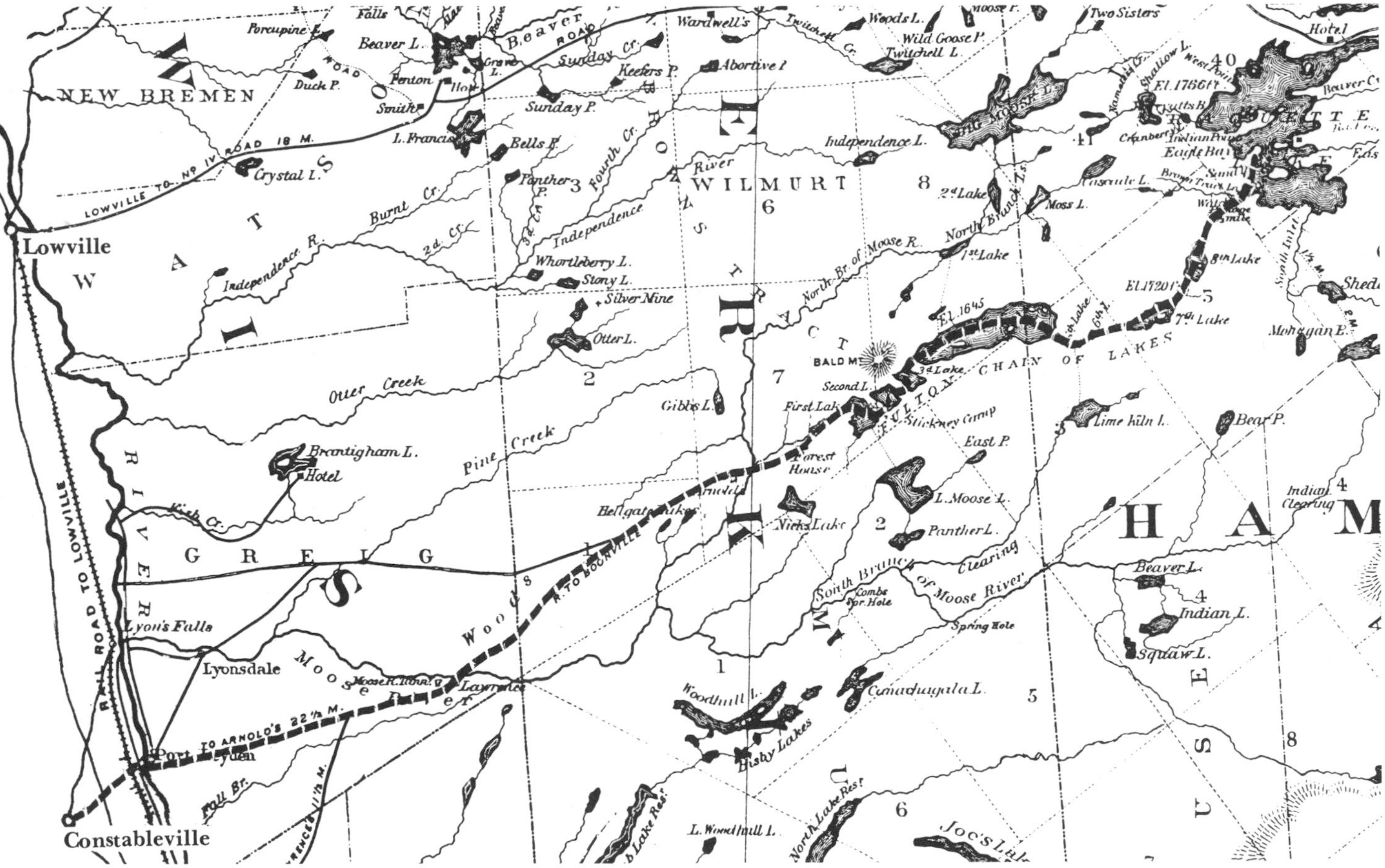

The route from Constableville to Raquette Lake followed by the Constables in 1843, drawn by author upon an 1876 map by W. W. Ely, M.D.

(Courtesy of the Adirondack Research Center of the Association for the Protection of the Adirondacks, Schenectady, New York)

a horseshoe) Stanley and myself amidships sitting on the bottom of the boat and Higby rowing.

'Hadn't we better put about, Higby?, asks John, 'we'll be swamped if we don't!'

'We'll be swamped if we *do*,' replied the hunter, 'keep her head to the waves, and as near her course as possible.'

'But I can't see the waves nor the clearing,' answered John.

'Well, do your best, for we are as near one shore as the other and must *keep on*. Ah! There's a bright flash—now you see the break in the woods—that's the point—keep her there! Fire a gun, Stanley; perhaps Beach or Wood may hear it and bring a torch to the shore.'

Snap—snap—both caps wet,— recapped—bang—bang— but the report was lost in a peal of thunder.

'Oh! Thunder!' cried I. 'Try another;' another, and still another were fired, but with the same success, as the thunder rolled continually.

The wind now began to blow in gusts, and created rather too much sea for our little cockle shell, as every now and then a wave would swash over the gunwale, nearly filling it.

'Bale away, John,' cried Stanley, 'and at the same time mind your course.'

'What *boots* it to bale with this old *shoe*?' responded John, who could not let an opportunity slip of perpetrating a pun even under such circumstances—'The water gains on me in spite of all I can do.'

'By Eolus,' exclaimed I, 'We'll be swamped! If this wind don't hold [let] up we must prepare for a swim, and lucky he who reaches shore such a night as this!'

Providentially the wind lulled, as it was only a gust, so that by constant baling with caps and shoes, we managed to keep afloat.

We now commenced shouting the Indian war-whoop, as much to keep our spirits up, as in hopes of making the hunters hear us, for the thunder was now less frequent, although the lightning was more vivid. 'Ah! there's a light moving on the shore,' shouted Stanley; 'tis they! —'tis the hunters! They hear us! pull away, Higby; aye, that's it; twenty more such strokes and we are safe.'

No sooner had our keel grated on the sand than we leaped from our boat, feeling thankful that we were once again on terra firma. Drenched to the skin, we entered the shanty, where we were welcomed by Wood and Beach, with a rousing fire before which we *basted* ourselves for about an hour, in order to dry our clothes. In the meantime the hunters were preparing a supper for us, consisting of smoked venison, trout, boiled rice and maple-sugar molasses, to which 'tis unnecessary to say we did ample justice.

After supper we threw ourselves upon deer-skins before the fire, and so 'turned in' for the night, where we 'slept without rocking,' as we had just had enough to last some time.

The owners of this shanty (which was built mostly of hemlock-bark) were two old hunters who had lived here about eight years, the one about sixty years of age, with grey hair, ruddy complexion, and athletic limbs; the other about fifty years old, a cripple (having lost both of his feet in consequence of their being frozen one winter when coming home from the clearings), with dark hair, weather-beaten visage, and robust body. The latter, although obliged to move on his knees, was about as active as his companion, frequently carrying 70 lbs. on his back, and in winter had rather the advantage of him, as with a thick covering of moose-hide, his knees answered the purpose of snow-shoes, without which they cannot hunt when the snow is on the ground. 'Tis rather curious that their names, Wood and Beach, should be so appropriate to the lives they lead. At sunrise we leaped from our deer-skin beds to prepare for the first fruits of our toil—viz., trout-fishing.

After breakfast Stanley and myself took our fly-rods, and jumping into a canoe, paddled ourselves to the N.E. inlet, about two miles distant.

Were I endowed with the power of description, I would descant in glowing terms upon the beauties of this lake, as I first beheld it when gliding across it that morning. Not a breath of air ruffled the surface of the water, which was as clear as when it first gushed from the rock, so that every feature in the picturesque mountains which lined its shore had a perfect counterpart in the liquid mirror that washed their feet. There was scarce a noise, save the occasional cry of a loon, or the dripping of the water from our paddle, to mar the appropriate stillness of the scene, and I could not but exclaim involuntarily, 'This must be Nature's sabbath-day, and this her place of worship.'

No sooner had our 'flies' touched the water than its surface appeared alive with the finny tribe, and in about two hours we killed forty-three of as fine brook trout as every graced the board of an epicure, the smallest weighing ¾ lb., and the largest 2½ lbs.

Had the mosquitoes, moose-flies and punkies, been less active, we should have caught more fish, but they 'laid into' us so strong, that in spite of spirits of turpentine and sweet oil (with which we besmeared our hands and faces), we were obliged to say enough, and shoot into the middle of the lake to get clear of them.

After dinner we made preparations for our 'floating,' which is the hunter's term for hunting deer at night. The 'modus operandi' is thus: —in the first place you make of birch-bark a lantern of the shape and size of a drum of figs, with one side cut out to throw the light ahead, leaving the boat in the shade; the light is supplied from two large candles (2 inches diameter), made of deer-tallow. This is placed in the bow of the boat, just high enough to clear the shooter's head, who sits close behind it, —the hunter taking his station in the stern to paddle.

In the second place you put on all the clothing you have been able to bring with you, not forgetting to furnish one of your pockets with a 'pistol' [flask], as the nights are rather cold and the fog from the fresh water is very penetrating, which you feel the more, as you are obliged to sit perfectly motionless and without speaking a word, from the time you commence 'floating' until you shoot a deer, which *may be* until daylight.

Thus equipped, with my shot-gun well loaded —each barrel with 12 buck-shot—and Higby with his rifle, we started across the lake for the south inlet (distant about seven miles), just as the sun was setting. At the same time John and Stanley started for the east inlet. Arrived at the mouth of the inlet, we went on shore and made a fire, as much to protect ourselves from the attacks of our enemies (mosquitoes) as to warm ourselves thoroughly for the 'float.'

Would that I could convey some idea of the impression that scene made upon my mind. Our fire now crackling and blazing until its flames almost reached the tall pine tops, threw its lurid light far across the surface of the lake, which lay at our feet calm as a quiet conscience. Then I felt the loneliness of our situation, and how entirely dependent we were upon our own resources. My mind naturally recurred to the times when our forefathers first settled the country, and who probably had trod upon the very sod where we now rested, easily imagining the difficulties and privations they must have undergone in pioneering their way through this vast wilderness. Then I thought of the persecuted savage, whose council fire may have been lighted on the very spot where ours now blazed, and who had been forced to yield, step by step, to the avarice of civilization, the soil in which his fathers slept, and which he had received an inheritance from Nature's God. No man of any sensibility could look upon a scene like that without being similarly impressed.

The last rays of the setting sun had disappeared from the west, when lighting our 'Jack,' we jumped into the boat, and glided cautiously up the inlet, Higby paddling without taking his paddle out of the water, and so slowly as not to make a ripple at the bow, for the slightest noise of water is sure to startle a deer. Moving as we did so noiselessly along, without a sound to disturb the death-like stillness of the hour, enveloped in fog and darkness, with the exception of the line of light which our 'Jack' threw out ahead, I could not help comparing our situation to Shaun on the River Styx.

We had not proceeded far before I beheld in the long grass two balls of fire of about the size of a walnut, three inches apart, which I knew to be the *eyes* of a deer, reflecting the light from our lantern. As Higby directed the boat slowly and cautiously in the direction, I began to tremble all over from intense excitement; in fact had what the hunters call the '*Buck-ague*' which all novices at 'floating' are sure to be seized with. When near enough to distinguish the body of the deer (say three rods), I raised my gun as deliberately as I could with the ague I had on me, and aiming for his eyes, fired.

'Do you see him, Higby?'

'No! But I think I hear him struggling in the grass! We'll take a look for him.' So getting out into the grass, with the water up to our knees, we looked in every direction without finding any traces of him. 'Where did you aim for?' asked Higby.

'Straight for his eyes,' I replied.

'Ah then, you have shot *over* him, for I forgot to tell you that at night objects loom up so that you must aim about twelve inches below your mark. However, better luck next time.'

So getting into our boat again, and keeping along the northern side of the inlet, in about an hour I saw another pair of eye-balls, but before I could get a shot at them, the owner was off, snorting and puffing like a high-pressure engine, to alarm his comrades at the approach of danger. However, we soon got sight of another, and this time did not let him off so cheap. Following the advice of the hunter, I aimed for his neck instead of his eyes, which was the better mark, and fired. The poor animal gave one bound, and fell as if he was shot, and so he was, sure enough, right through the head. Having cut his throat and marked the spot (by tying knots in the grass), we left him, so as not to encumber our boat in case we should find more, intending to fetch him in the morning.

I heard and saw two more that night, but could not get another shot, so we 'made tracks' for the shanty, and reached there just as day was breaking. John and Stanley having got home about an hour before us with the same success, having shot a fine buck.

We turned in and slept til nine, when we started again for the trout fishing to another inlet. We (Stanley and myself, John preferring deer-stalking,) caught this time, in about three hours, 65 lbs. of the finest and *thickest* trout I ever laid eyes on, and all with the fly (brown and green hackle). In this case all *under* 1 lb. we threw back to their native element, and the above weight is what we took home. The largest weighed 2 lbs. 2 oz., and was such a peculiarly-shaped fish (being very thick and short and small-mouthed) that I cut his profile out of birchbark and brought it home with me, having it now in my possession.

At night we 'floated' again, but with no success, having seen only one deer, without being able to get a shot at him.

The next day we prepared for a 'hound hunt,' which is always sure to result in the death of a deer. To accomplish this, we each chose our station at different points of the lake, commanding the most extensive view, and setting the hounds in the woods, wait until the deer 'takes to the water.'

Higby and myself took our station at a point projecting into the lake commanding a view of the opposite shore, about two miles distant, where he supposed the animal would be most likely to 'take water.' John and Stanley were lying in ambush on another point, 1½ mile distant. After waiting in anxious expectation for about an hour, during which time I was continually sweeping the lake with my spy-glass, I heard the baying of the hounds on the opposite shore, and turning my glass in the direction, saw something moving in the water, resembling two ducks. I motioned to Higby who, taking the glass, immediately said '*That's him!* Lie close, now, until he gets out into the lake, and then we can cut him off from the land.'

Ten minutes elapsed before we put out in our boat in full chase for our victim, while in the opposite direction we espied 'the brothers' about a mile off, pulling for dear life (or rather for the deer death—excuse the pun), having seen him also, although not as soon as we did; which gave us an advantage, so that we came up with the deer before they were within hailing distance. The poor creature swam nearly as fast as Higby could row, but soon getting tired, I ended his persecutions by putting a bullet through his head just under his ears, which caused death so instantly that he would have 'sunk to rise no more' had not the hunter caught him by the ear just as he was going down. Tying a rope round his neck we towed him ashore, when I performed the usual operation of cutting his throat, etc.

Deer Feeding at Raquette Lake
Sketch by Jervis McEntee
From "The Lakes of the Wilderness" *The Great Republic Monthly*, April, 1859.

and putting him into the boat, made for the shanty.

This was without exception the most glorious day's sport I have ever had! Its novelty, the beauty of the scenery, and the little fatigue attending it, rendered it indeed, to my taste, the very perfection of hunting.

The following day we devoted to 'Salmon Fishing,' having previously bated the 'grounds' with speckled trout, of which we had caught more than we could eat in a week.

To take these, (Salmon trout) you are obliged to fish in water from 40 to 60 feet deep, with heavy cod-lines, and hooks about 3 inches long, and of peculiar shape, baiting them with a small fish, such as dace, minnows or roach. The depth of water is so great that you can scarcely feel them bite, and it requires a powerful jerk to hook them, so that in a couple of hours we were heartily tired of it, having only caught two, one weighing 10 lbs., the other 17 lbs. A month earlier in the season, immense quantities of these salmon are taken, weighing from 3 to 25 lbs., and although their meat is very rich in color, it is not so to the taste; we therefore preferred devoting our time to 'fly-fishing,' the fish and sport both being better.

To give a minute account of every day's sport, I find, would be rather monotonous. I will therefore conclude this 'sketch' with a description of a *Moose Fight*, which occurred with Stanley, and Higby the hunter.

On the morning of the 4th August, about daylight, we were aroused by the barking of the dogs and the yells of an Indian war-whoop, which we soon discovered proceeded from a boat on the lake, making towards the shanty.

In a few minutes we distinguished the voices of Stanley and Higby, who we imagined took this means of notifying us of some signal success, (as none of us had been very fortunate in 'floating' for the last two nights) such as killing three or four fine bucks; but we little dreamt of the actual cause. On their landing, we found their clothes were drenched with water, and their first exclamation was—

'We've killed a *Moose*! Build a fire, Wood, or we'll shake our teeth out, for this time we've got the "*Moose* ague" of the worst kind; not the "Buck-ague."'

A fire was quickly made, and as soon as they got *thawed out* a little, so as to be able to speak, Stanley recounted the adventure as follows, as nearly as I can recollect:—

'When about five miles up the east inlet, on our way down, I espied the eyes of a large buck (as I thought) not four rods from us; but what was my astonishment on approaching, to find him take to the water, and make for the boat. Neither of us, however, spoke a word, but waiting until he got within a rod of us, I "let slip" one barrel at him, aiming between the horns, which were immense—looming up at night like two pine trees. This had no effect but to make him bellow with pain, and did not change his course. I now discovered we had something *more* than a buck to contend with, and determined to reserve my last barrel until certain it would take effect; so 'twas not until he was within two feet of the boat that I let him have it right between the eyes. With this, he sent forth such a roar as to "make night hideous," and plunging forward upset our skiff, "spilling" us both into the river. Higby made for the shore, and I for the boat, which was floating down with the current; and fearing the moose would attack me in the water, I kicked away as lustily as I could; pushing the boat ahead of me in the direction of Higby's voice (for it was as dark as Erebus, our "Jack" being of course extinguished). I found the hunter somewhat alarmed, (probably on my account,) but more mortified that the beast should have escaped us, for we now heard him bellowing through the woods as he "made tracks" from us. "There's one consolation, however," says he; "the crittur must die, for not even a moose can carry *very* far two such charges of lead as you favored him with, planted in his 'look-out house.' Didn't you notice a *gurgling* sort of noise when he roared? That was blood in his throat; for from the direction you fired, the shot must have reached his wind-pipe. I am sure we'll find him in the morning not far off, so let's mark the spot and make the best of our way for the shanty." I fortunately had picked up one of the paddles and leaving our guns, lanterns, and everything else at the bottom of the river, we started for home, which I thought we would never reach, as we were so chilled with our wet clothes that even the exertion of paddling nine miles could scarcely keep our blood in motion; but thank God here we are—so pile up the wood—give us a bowl of that hot tea—and then let's off in pursuit of our enemy, for the day is breaking and we've no time to lose.'

Thus Stanley concluded his account of the moose-fight, and although the ducking had chilled his blood, you perceive it had not cooled his ardor.

After breaking our fast with a little boiled rice and maple sugar molasses, we started off in pursuit of the wounded moose, each of us taking a boat, with a hunter and dog, and in about two hours came to the spot indicated by knots tied in the grass where the encounter had taken place.

On landing, we soon struck his trail, by the quantity of blood which lined the bushes, which was so great that we concluded, of course that he must have soon dropped from exhaustion.

In this, however, we were disappointed, for after tracking him for a mile and a half, we lost his trail in some mossy ground, on the edge of the thickest swamp that I ever saw, where he probably had sought shelter.

We made several attempts to penetrate the thickets (which even the dogs could not do,) and not being able to discover where he entered, were at length obliged, most reluctantly, to give up the chase, all most sadly disappointed, as we had fully expected to have found him either dead or dying, from the large quantities of blood which lined his track; which, if we had not seen, we would have thought it was a hoax played off upon us by Stanley and Higby, but from the size of his foot-marks and the length of his stride, there was no doubt but that the animal wounded was a bull moose of the largest kind, weighing not less than 1,000 lbs.

We spent the remainder of the day in fishing up our guns, etc., and catching trout, which in this spot were very large and abundant, two of us taking in about an hour and a half 56 lbs. weighing from 1½ to 3 lbs. each. We returned to our shanty at about sunset, and after a hearty supper, retired to our deer-skin couches, pretty well fatigued with our day's operations.

Two days after this adventure we retraced our steps for 'the clearings' where we arrived on the 7th Aug., having been in the woods just twelve days travelling in that time 131 miles as follows:

13 miles	from Turin to edge of forest	in wagon
20 "	to Harisof's [Herreshoff's] House or Arnold's	on foot
3 "	from do to 1st Lake	on foot
12 "	to head of 4th Lake	in skiff
1 "	Portage to 6th Lake	on foot
4 "	to head of 7th Lake	in skiff
1 "	Portage to 8th Lake	on foot
3 "	to head of 8th Lake	in skiff
1½ "	to Raquette stream	on foot
4 "	down the river to Raquette Lake	in skiff
3 "	across the lake to shanty	in skiff
65½ "	from Turin to Raquette Lake	
65½ "	back again	
131 miles.		

Game taken:—
1 Moose wounded but *not* taken.
5 Deer.
1 Mink.
2 Ruffed Grouse.
4 Spruce [Grouse].
1 Cock of the Woods.
25 Pigeons.
170 lbs. Brook Trout—2 person, 20 hours fishing
20 lbs. Salmon Trout—2 persons, 2 hours fishing

If any of your readers should desire further particulars about the hunting grounds of Brown's Tract, they will be cordially furnished by

Your obd't. servant,
BOB RACKET
New York, Jan. 30th, 1844."

The foregoing article ranks in Adirondack annals as one of the finest accounts of an early hunting trip. Three items in the narrative deserve further embellishment, to emphasize their historical value or because references to them occur in later chapters: Salmon Trout, Higby the Hunter, and Wood and Beach.

SALMON TROUT

Every account of a Constable foray into the wilderness is replete with references to catching large numbers of "salmon trout." The term is not familiar today in the Adirondacks, so readers may wonder whether this species of fish has been extirpated. An explanation is found in the *First Annual Report of the Commissioners of Fisheries, Game and Forests*, printed in 1896 [p. iii]:

> ". . . The Game Law of the State provides a close season and other regulations for a fish under the name of Salmon Trout. We have no salmon trout in any waters of the State, and the fish should be called by its proper name, Lake Trout. . . ."[8]

HIGBY THE HUNTER (1809-1890)

Higby's major claim to fame, until now, has been citations by Kenneth L. Durant, author of two books about Adirondack guideboats. In his first book, *Guide-Boat Days and Ways*, Durant's chapter on "Beginnings" includes one paragraph quoted from the foregoing article in *Spirit of the Times*:

> *"Higby the Hunter - His Boat - 1843*
>
> We soon reached the First Lake of the Fulton Chain where we found our boat (snugly hid in the reeds) which was to convey us to our camping ground 25 miles further. This boat, which was built of cedar by Higby himself, in the woods, with no other tools than hatchet, drawing-knife, hammer, and nails, was made as light as possible, 90 pounds, in order to carry it from lake to lake (portages of one to three miles) and yet was

> capacious enough to carry all our party with dog, guns, rods, provisions, etc. . . . Higby [carried] the boat by means of a yoke rigged across the gunwales, turned downside up, with his head inside."[9]

The above is among several descriptions of progenitors or earliest-known models of Adirondack guideboats.

In his next book, *The Adirondack Guide-Boat*, which was co-authored with his wife and published posthumously, Durant again refers to the above paragraph, calling it "the earliest specific report we have giving some details about a portable boat."[10]

However, Higby the Hunter, himself, is also noteworthy among Adirondack guides despite the fact that he is relatively unknown. A very resourceful and capable woodsman, he guided from the 1830s to the 1880s, ranging throughout the Adirondacks. He was most familiar, however, with the areas around the Fulton Chain, Raquette and Blue Mountain Lakes and the Beaver River. Accompanying almost all of the Constable trips, he was a friend as well as guide for two generations of the family. (See photo at the beginning of this chapter.)

No first name or other identification has been mentioned, but it has been possible to establish his identity by studying census records, histories, maps, a Higby Family genealogy and records kept by Charles Bunke, historian of the Town of Watson near Lowville.

Higby the Hunter was William R. Higby, born in May 1809, a son of William Wey Higby. His father and several uncles were part of a group from Middletown, Connecticut who had all moved to Lewis County in the late 1790s at the behest of Nathaniel Shaler, William Constable's land agent. Most of them settled in Turin and Shalerville and slowly they dispersed throughout the county. In 1807, there were ten adult males named Higby in the town of Turin.

William R. Higby was married to Fannie Dean in 1831. They moved to the tiny settlement of Watson on the Black River sometime in the late 1840s.[11] That probably accounts for the fact that later Constable trips often reached Raquette Lake by a more northerly route which went through Watson and along the Beaver River, rather than up the Moose River and Fulton Chain.

A nice description of Higby is given in Jervis McEntee's diary, which is at The Adirondack Museum Library. McEntee was an art student who rambled through the central Adirondacks on a sketching trip in 1851 and later attained some renown as a member of the Hudson River School. He encountered Higby at Albany Lake (now Nehasane Lake) in 1851:

> ". . . Higbie [sic] pleased me much. A man of fifty, stout, sedate, and yet kind and affectionate as a child. He came up to my idea perfectly as a Jimmie Woodsman, and the more I saw of him, the better I was convinced of his kindness . . . and his skill in all matters connected with the glorious woods life. In a little bag he carried innumerable little tools such as screws, screw-drivers, awls, etc. and he was not at all disconcerted on discovering that he had left his candles and mould at the Stillwater, for he had tallow with him and using a branch of alder he made two as fine ones as could have been made when men have better tools to work with. I liked the old man very much . . ."[12]

At the time McEntee was writing, Higby would have been only forty-three, not fifty, but he was undoubtedly weathered by his outdoor life. He was young enough, however, at age fifty-five, to enlist in the Union Army during the Civil War:

> "Watson . . . [is] the home of Higby the Hunter —volunteer at fifty-five . . ."[13]

Higby returned home after the war and

resumed guiding; he is listed as a "Beaver River Guide" by E.R. Wallace. He also continued building boats, according to a laconic note in a diary kept by his son, Almeron, in 1876. An 1876 map of Watson indicates the location of Higby's home, near his son's. Both were still standing in 1988; Almeron's is now a local tavern. An old boat-building workshop, which they may have shared, has been converted to a garage and stands at the village crossroads.

Almeron Higby, often known as Al, also did some guiding. He accompanied Nathaniel Sylvester and several others on a climb up Blue Mountain in 1858. In the following year he married Eliza Puffer, a neighbor from Watson; her father and brothers were also guides. Almeron is mentioned again in the final chapter of this book. (Some references to Almeron misspell his name with an "in" ending; the spelling used here is derived from the Higby family genealogy.)

WOOD AND BEACH

Bob Racket's narrative was the first of several sporting memoirs to mention the pair of hunters, Wood and Beach, who were the first settlers at Raquette Lake. Every writer who visited during the 1840s and 1850s also told of this aptly named pair. These included Ebenezer Emmons (State Geologist) in 1840; the Rev. Joel Headley in 1846; Charles W. Webber in 1849 (a sporting naturalist who wrote for *Spirit of the Times*); Jervis McEntee (the art student) in 1851; State Engineer A. P. Edwards in 1852 and art journalist William J. Stillman in 1855. From their writings we can derive a more comprehensive picture of the hunters, their shanty, and their singular lifestyle.[14]

William F. Wood was born in Vermont; his first known appearance in the Adirondacks was about 1832, when he would have been thirty-four years old. At that time he was living with two other trappers on the Joy Tract near Old Forge. In 1833, Wood bought 208 acres of land in the remote area between Nehasane and Smith Lakes. He probably had trapped and camped upon it, but there is no indication that he ever lived there.

Writers disagree about the year of Wood's notorious accident, in which he lost both feet. Although some historians believe it was as late as 1850, our reference from the Constables' trip in 1843 indicates that it occurred some years previously. This is corroborated by other visitors: Emmons was the earliest and he dated it as several years prior to his 1840 visit; McEntee stated it happened in or about 1835; William J. Stillman placed it at 1838 and Headley indicated it was several years prior to 1846.

There is general agreement about the circumstances and effects of the accident. It occurred on a cold winter night while Wood was returning from the settlements to his home near the old forge. While crossing the Independence River, which was partially frozen, Wood slipped into the water. Some reports indicate that he was drunk at the time.

Although both legs were frozen, he managed to climb out and take shelter in a hunting lodge, but could not build a fire and dry off, because his matches were wet. There he lay alone for three days, and was nearly dead when found by the famous trapper, Nat Foster. When it became necessary to amputate his frozen legs below the knees, the grisly service was performed by Wood's Indian friends, who also nursed him back to health and provided him with heavy leather knee pads to assist crawling. Over the ensuing years, William Wood adapted so well to this disability that he was able to continue hunting and trapping and could travel alone through the woods in any season.

View on Raquette Lake (1840)
Engraving by C.H. Burt after painting by John William Hill (Courtesy of The Adirondack Museum)

The cabin and clearing shown in this view undoubtedly belonged to Matthew Beach and William Wood, as they were the only residents at Raquette Lake when Hill visited there in 1840. The peak in the background is West Mountain, which rises directly behind (west) of Indian Point and overlooks Raquette Lake. J.W. Hill accompanied the first Emmons expedition in that region, as staff artist, and some of his work was used by Emmons to illustrate his Survey of the District. This view was first published in 1849 in Joel T. Headley's *The Adirondack or Life in the Woods.*

By 1839, if not earlier, Wood had teamed up with Beach and they settled at Raquette Lake. In that year, the two attended the second annual town meeting of the Town of Long Lake and were elected as assessors, commissioners and inspectors of schools. Wood was also designated a Justice of the Peace. Because of the scarcity of residents, most men had to accept at least two offices.

They built a small cabin on the western side of the lake at Indian Point, and their occupation of that point was legalized ten years later when 25 acres were deeded to Beach by Farrand Benedict. Their cabin was described picturesquely by a visiting journalist, Charles W. Webber, in 1849:

> ". . . [They built] a typical hunter's lodge of bark and graced it with the antlers of many deer." It

was located ". . . a few rods from the edge of the lake and of such peculiar and original construction that few would imagine it, at first sight, a human habitation. . . . [The hut] was scarcely more than a hunter's bark shanty of large size, excepting there was a huge fireplace of spruce bark and a rough floor . . ."

Joel Headley described their life style and how well Wood had overcome his handicap:

> ". . . It is rather a singular coincidence that the only two inhabitants of this wilderness should be named *Wood* and *Beach* . . . These two men have killed hundreds of deer since they settled down here together, and a great many moose. Their leisure hours they spend in preparing the furs they have taken, and in tanning the deer skins, of which they make mittens. They need something during the long winter days and evenings for employment. When the snow is five feet deep on the level, and the ice three and four feet thick on the lake, and not the sign of a human footstep anywhere to be seen, the smoke of their cabin rises in the frosty air like a column in the desert—enhancing instead of relieving the solitude. The pitch pine supplies the place of candles, and the deep red light from their humble window, at night, must present a singular contrast with the rude waste of snow, and the leafless forest around them.
>
> When a quantity of these mittens are made up, Beach straps on his snowshoes, and with his trusty rifle in hand, carries them to the settlements, where they meet with a ready sale . . ."
>
> ". . . [Wood] has used his knees as a substitute for feet; and strange as it may seem, he follows his line of traps for miles through the wilderness, or with rifle in hand, hops through the woods in pursuit of deer. He may be seen plying his oars, and driving his little bark over the lakes and along the streams; and when he comes to a portage, the upturned boat will surmount his head, and takes its course to the adjacent waters. His is a case that proves that there are instances in reality, 'where truth is stranger than fiction.'"

Wood's remarkable adaptation and his stamina were also described by Alvah Dunning, a later Raquette Lake guide:

> ". . . [he] once made his way along—probably in the 1850s—on his stumps from Raquette Lake to Elizabethtown, over a route 75 miles or more in length, carrying his own boat and pack."

As years passed, the clearing around Wood and Beach's crude shanty was improved and expanded to about 40 acres, on which they raised vegetables for themselves and for visitors, as well as hay for their cattle. They also established an orchard of berry bushes and fruit trees.

In the early 1850s, Beach and Wood had a major disagreement which ended their sharing a domicile. Wood moved out of the cabin and set up residence in a storage hut only 50 rods (275 feet) away. He lived there until 1860, raising and training hunting dogs; he and his dogs were frequently hired by visiting sportsmen, including the Constables. He continued to trap throughout the winter, selling his skins in the settlements, until he finally moved to Elizabethtown, where he died in 1868. His final years at Raquette Lake were not as lonely an existence as might be supposed, because his younger brother had also settled on the lake with a large family.

This brother, Josiah Wood, had moved to Raquette Lake in 1846 from Vermont with his wife and six children. They built a log cabin on a peninsula on the eastern side of the lake and another four children were born after their arrival. In 1850, the children ranged from one to eighteen years of age. Josiah too was an independent sort of man; he told a visitor in 1855 that since they had passed the anti-liquor law he "couldn't be hired to go back to the States."

The other member of this odd pair of trappers, Matthew Beach, was born in Massachusetts. He was 11 years older than William

Wood's Cabin on Rackett [sic] **Lake, 1851**
Pencil drawing 11″ x 13″ by Jervis McEntee
(Courtesy of The Adirondack Museum)
Since this hut appears to be a much less substantial building than the one pictured by Hill in 1840, it seems that the quarrel which prompted Wood to leave Beach's cabin had already occurred by the time McEntee made his sketch in 1851.

Wood. As a young man, he had spent some time in the Saranac area, and then settled at "Beach's Lake" (often spelled B*ee*ches, now known as Brandreth Lake). An island in the northern part of Raquette Lake is also named after him.

A good description of Beach was written by Charles W. Webber in 1849:

". . . [He is] an old, white-haired veteran, stalwart and hearty, whose step is still elastic and eye bright as ever . . . with a true, hunter-like air, and . . . appeared indeed no ordinary woodsman. . . . He has picked up much information in one place or another—no doubt no small amount from naturalists who, while visiting that country for geological exploration, have made that hut their headquarters. Of that company, the learned Professor Emmons of Albany stands conspicuous. . . ."

Five years later, Stillman wrote:

". . . [He is] a man in the neighborhood of four score years of age, but vigorous and looking to be not over sixty. . . . The rude cabin which he first built has grown gradually into a comfortable house, with fifty or sixty acres of land in tolerable cultivation. . . . He was a volunteer at the Battle of Plattsburgh, and I drew him into some narrations. . . . Mr. Beach lives here contentedly, without a wish beyond Raquette Lake . . ."

After separating from Wood, the aging Beach sold his property to Amos Hough, a farmer from Long Lake, with provision that Hough and family would live with and look after him. He died in 1862.

This long digression about Beach and Wood and Wood's brother is included here because they were the only other residents of Raquette Lake for many years after the Constables became regular visitors. They were frequently hired by the Constables and enjoyed neighborly relations.

John Constable ended his bachelor revels soon after the trip described in *Spirit of the Times*. In July 1844, he married his first cousin, Julia E. Pierrepont (twelfth child of Anna Marie Constable and H. B. Pierpont) and over the ensuing years they had four sons of whom the elder two, Casimir (born in 1845) and James (1847), also grew up to love camping in the Adirondacks. The younger two died in early childhood.

No records exist of any Adirondack trips by John or his brothers during the remainder of the 1840s. The heyday of the Constables at Raquette Lake started in the following decade.

June 1850.

W. C's. orders. for the first Ladies Expedition to the Woods.

This jaunty title for the Constable family's 1850 camping trip was handwritten by William Constable III. It accompanied letters to his brother, John, and sister, Anna, at Constable Hall concerning trip preparations. (Courtesy of John P. Constable Jr.)

William Constable III
(1811-1887)
This portrait hangs in the Library at Constable Hall.

CHAPTER THREE

1850: The First Ladies Expedition to the Woods

In the summer of 1850, William Constable III exuberantly organized a family vacation which he dubbed "First Ladies Expedition to the Woods." The party included five men and seven women who trekked into the central Adirondacks and then camped for three weeks in open leantos at Raquette Lake. They repeated the experience often in subsequent years, but their expeditions were not recorded in Adirondack history, until now.

Therefore, Adirondack historians have misidentified the first ladies to cross the Adirondacks on a camping trip as two members of Governor Seymour's party in 1855. Those women were his niece and the Lady Amelia Murray, a maid of honor to Queen Victoria, who afterwards published memoirs which included a description of the trip.

Alfred L. Donaldson asserted:

> "Indeed, Lady Amelia can undoubtedly claim the distinction of being the first of her sex to make a pleasure-tour through the Adirondacks."[1]

Harold Hochschild, a meticulous historian, wrote in a similar vein:

> "The first lady to make a pleasure tour through the Adirondacks, or at least to record one, was an English spinster, the Honorable Amelia M. Murray. . . ."[2]

These authors would have been surprised to learn that ladies of the Constable family and their friends preceded Governor Seymour's party by five years.

Information about the first Constable expedition is obtained from two letters written by Will in New York City to his brother, John, and sister, Anna, in Constableville. He outlined plans and preparations, included a list of provisions, and issued "orders" in mock military style.

Corroboration that this trip actually took place as planned is furnished by Jervis McEntee's diary. (This young art student, who camped at Raquette Lake during the following summer, mentioned Constable exploits which were common knowledge at that time.)

Seven women participated in the expedition: Anna Constable, cousins Matilda and Annie McVickar, Cornelia Lent (a relative of Will's wife), Jane and Mary Major (family friends) and Sarah Richards (who married their brother James three years later).

The men included all four brothers: Will (William III, then thirty-nine), John (thirty-seven), James (thirty-six), and Stevenson (thirty-four), as well as Will's seventeen year old son, William IV, (usually called Willy or William Jr.) and Andrew Major (probably a brother of two of the ladies in the party). Ages are mentioned here to emphasize that some of them were already middle-aged, despite the jocular youthful tone of Will's letters. Higby the Hunter, as usual, was chief guide for the party.

Advance preparations at Raquette Lake were made by John and Stevenson Constable with Higby, who preceded the group by two weeks. They arranged transport and overnight accommodations en route, and supervised construction of two large leantos at Sand Point on the western shore of the lake—the same site where Will and John had first camped in 1835. Will was then in the process of buying 50 acres of "the point" from Farrand Benedict, who owned most of the lands surrounding Raquette Lake; he subsequently bought another 50 acres.[3] For years thereafter the site was known as Constable Point but today it is called Antlers Point.

Will's instructions to John indicated that both were familiar from previous trips with all the local residents and sources of supplies. They ordered lumber, rented boats, and hired Josiah Wood to assist Higby in building the shanties; he and his family lived directly across the lake from Constable Point and were obviously well-known by the Constables, as their packing list contained "a box of old clothes for the Wood children." Eleven-year-old Alonzo Wood was hired as an assistant to Higby the Hunter for the duration of "The First Ladies Expedition."

The entire group assembled at Constable Hall, ready for departure on July 16th. The ladies, apparently undaunted by their cumbersome long skirts, had received specific instructions in the amount of luggage they could take along, and the camping necessities they would need, such as long gloves to protect against biting flies.

Anna had gathered the necessary provisions in advance. Although they planned to supplement these food supplies with fish and game to be caught after arrival at Raquette Lake, the size of the party and amount of supplies necessitated two wagons.

Their route on this occasion lay north of the Fulton Chain of lakes. They followed local roads 35 miles through the Black River Valley and Lowville to Watson, and thence to Orrin Fenton's Hotel at the Settlement at No. 4, where they spent the first night.

The second day's travel was harder and longer—37 miles along the "old military road" which roughly paralleled the Beaver River from No. 4 to Beach's Lake (now called Brandreth) and finally led to North Bay on Raquette Lake. This road was seldom used by wagons and was in terrible condition; swamps, mud-holes, rocks and fallen trees all impeded passage, so that walking was often more comfortable than riding, although neither was easy. (In later years an extra day was allowed for this part of the journey.)

When the party finally arrived at Raquette Lake, John and Stevenson and guides were waiting with boats to transport them to Constable Point. When Will anticipated this arrival, in his letter, his tone became jaunty as he instructed John to "then resign all command to your superior," who was clearly William, himself. (It became customary on such trips for Will to designate himself as "Captain," and John as "Lieutenant.") The full text of both letters and the list of provisions follow with indecipherable parts indicated by __?__.

William Constable's Orders For The First Ladies Expedition to the Woods.

"List of Party & Things for
Raquette Lake, July 16th, 1850 to leave
Constable Hall at 8 o'clock a.m., rain or shine.

This sketch of Constable Hall was drawn by William Constable III in 1854. (Courtesy of John P. Constable Jr.)

William Constable
William Constable, Jr.
Anna Constable
Cornelia Lent
Jane Major
Mary Major
Andrew Major
Matilda McVicar
Stevenson Constable &
John Constable (to join Party at Raquette July 17th, 1850, at point where the road strikes the lake. 3 miles from __?__)
James Constable
Miss R. [Sarah Richards] &
Annie McVickar (perhaps they will join the party)

Each lady can take Pillow, blanket, thick shawl, carpet bag, bathing dress, veil, leather gloves, to be long to protect the wrists, gaiters strong and loose, India Rubbers, bag of towels, soap, etc. etc. and underclothes for say 10 days."

Letter of June 19, 1850
from Will to his brother, John

"My dear John,

You have not answered me about Extra Names & Miss Richards going to Raquette, etc.

You will leave Home by the 1st of July. Leave for me a memorandum of anything you wish attended to.

I wish our large waggon [sic] and harness and

pair of strong horses for ½ month. Waggon is perfect. Order hole in top fixed. If you hire horses, the owner to be at risk, we to use them as we would our own. The horses are to be kept in good pasture at Long Lake until we return. I wish Peter Evans and his horse and waggon hired for 4 days to go with things to Raquette and right back with our own waggon, and to come for us, as we can get back with our own waggon. Tell Fenton we wish beds, supper and breakfast for say ten persons the night of the 16th of July, you may [stay also] the 1st. John, do not fail to reach the Raquette on the night of the 15th. You will at once hire Josiah Wood to assist in building 2 shantys on Sand Point and have plenty of wood cut and piled at each. Our shanty will be near two old cut white birch logs, cut I think by us on our first visit. The Ladies Shanty will be 6 or 8 rods nearer the point. You will see a small stick stuck down about 5 feet long near the place. Allow no trees or brush to be cut near the place except dead ones or those you think unsafe. Be careful of our trees as we expect to buy 50 acres of the point. You will hire 3 of the best small boats and see that they are perfectly *tight*. (Beach and Wood can use their own large boats.) Should you not be able to get all the boats you wish at the R. [Raquette], send at once to Long Lake to Wm. Austin. He has very good ones to hire. Also send to Long Lake to William Cary for 6 pine boards 1¼ inches thick. He will plane them and deliver them at the outlet of R. [Raquette] for $2 for table and seats. *Make* them strong.

Josiah Wood we will not want when the party arrives, but his son we will hire during our stay to live and sleep at home and come over early to assist Higby as all the wood will be cut. I think we can do with Wood. I will get him on occasion to bait 5 buoys for us.

On the afternoon of the 17th of July you will proceed with 3 small and one large boat covered with hay to the Raquette Bay where the road from Fenton's first touches the lake. You will, with the men in your command, hold yourself in readiness at 7 oclock p.m. to assist in embarking the Forces and baggage you will find there, leaving a supply and guard to protect the horses which will remain all night. You will then resign all command to your superior.

I wish you to bear in mind that it is proscribed for any general to take the field with such a large force under his command without being assisted in detail by all the officers under his charge.

The forgoing orders are however not positive, but much is trusted to your discretion.

Forage (for the troops) nearly ready on arrival at the encampment, I think, would not be unacceptable?

You will also, without loss of time on the receipt of this, report to me if the Bridge over the Stillwater (commonly called Twichel Creek) has been repaired, and if the road beyond has been cut out, so that troops and heavy ordinance can advance with safety.

Would it not be prudent to convert P. Evan's single waggon into a team waggon and pair of horses in case our carriage should break down. Tell Anna I have looked and asked all over for long gloves and the cheapest I can get are $__?__ per pair. Cannot she do without and take short ones and sew a piece around the wrist, as the other girls are going to do. I have just received James' letter and shall write Miss R. [Richards]. What about Extras from Home?

Will"
[Signature Obscured]

Constable Point at Raquette Lake
Painted by Arthur F. Tait (1819-1905) circa 1862.
Oil on board, 4½″ x 12″
(Courtesy of The Adirondack Museum)
The point was surrounded by a sandy beach with a gentle slope, ideal for campers.

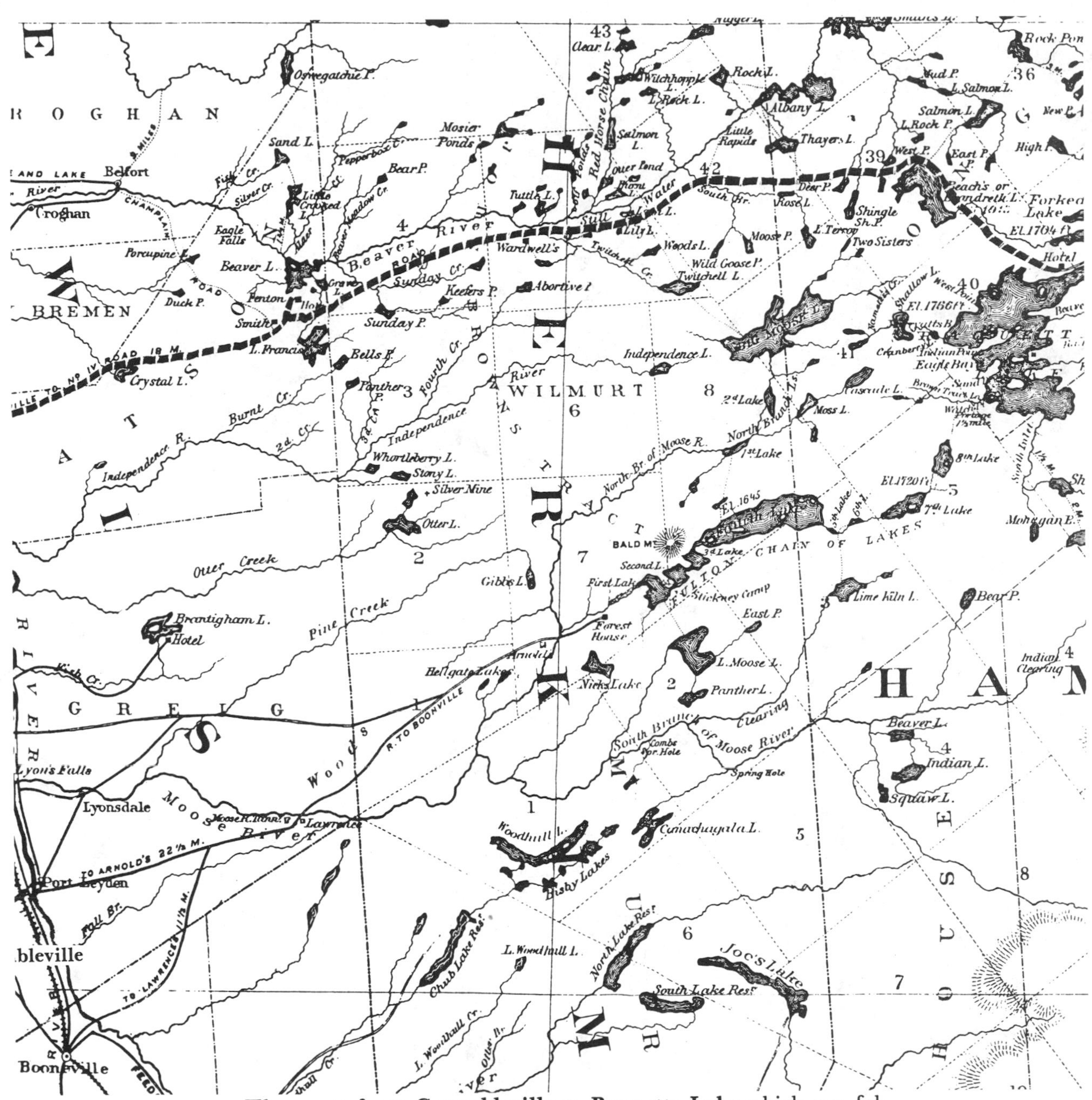

The route from Constableville to Raquette Lake which was followed by the Constables in 1850, drawn by author upon an 1876 map by W. W. Ely, M.D.

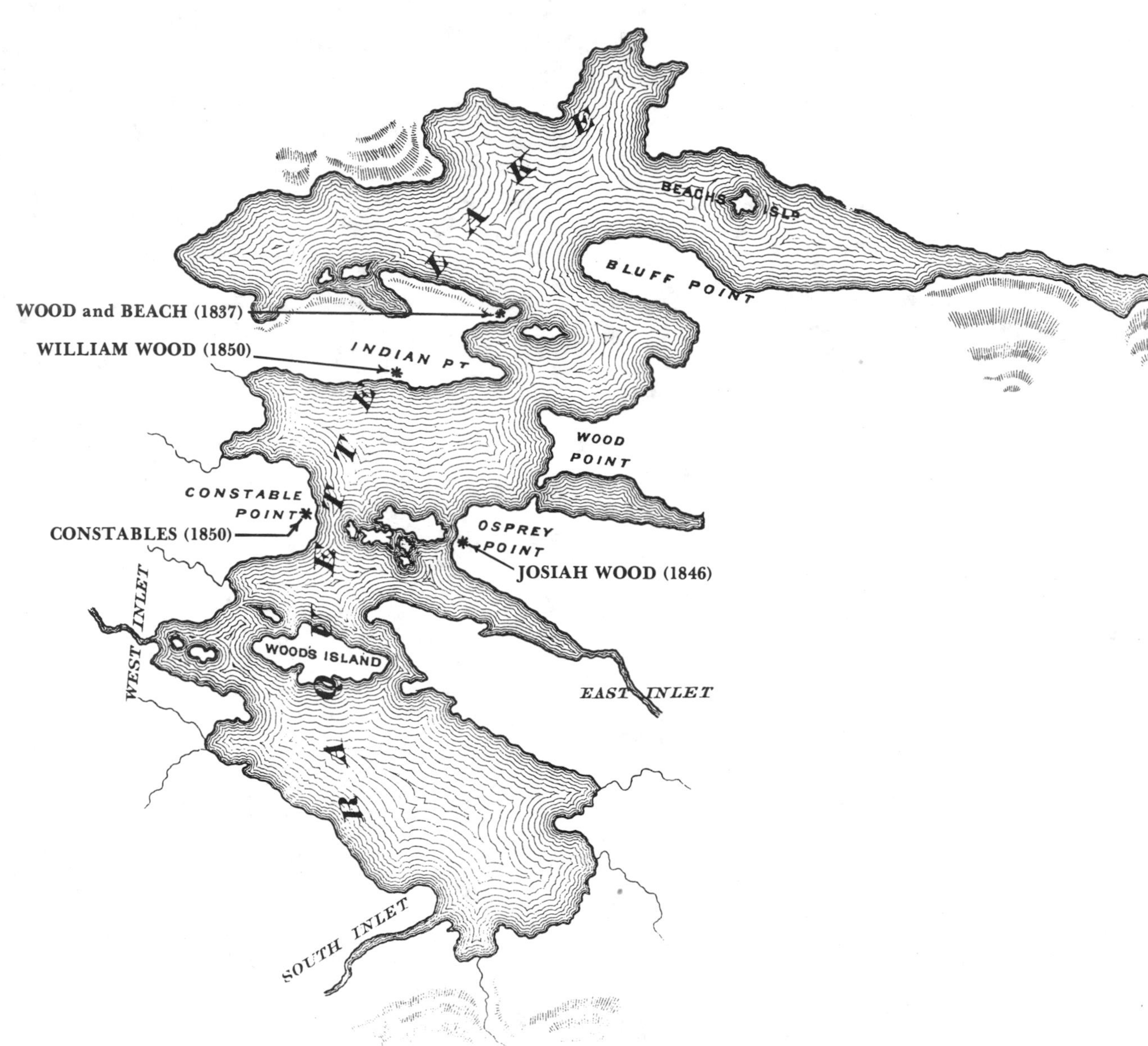

Raquette Lake Settlers. The only settlers on Raquette Lake until 1855 were William Wood, Matthew Beach and the Josiah Wood family. Their sites are noted by author on a copy of A. P. Edwards' Survey Map.

Letter from William Constable III
to his sister, Anna

"June 19, 1850

My Dear Anna,

I send you the list. You can get what you please ready before I come up. Shall be with you on Thursday, the 11th of July at 5 p.m.

[*Note:* Extra column of figures on left indicates a later change in quantity of some goods after the original list was compiled.]

Cork screw!!
Dutch oven, tin
Candles and candle stick
½ barrel of Flour
26 25 lbs. of Butter Crackers, Keg
50 " " Butter. Keep in ice house
15 " " Pork. Bag cellar
27 20 " " Rice
6 5 " " Tea. Tin canister
25 25 " " Sugar. Keg or tin canister.
5 5 " " Salt. Box
2½ 2 " " Soda and acid. Jars.
¼ ½ " " Pepper. Tin pepper pot.
2 2 Nutmegs in grater
3 dozen Lemons in Box
1 jar of Pickles
1 box of Raspberry sirup
Currant jelly
2 Bottles of Brandy
2 Umbrellas

Box of old clothes for "Wood children"
Fishing pole with gear, etc.
Fireworks, Lamp oil and wick
Oil for horses to prevent flies.
4 Bushels of Oats.
Buffalo [robe] to cover things in waggon
1 ax

1 dozen plates, tin or earthen
½ " dishes
½ " glass tumblers
½ " tea cups and saucers
½ " spoons
½ " large iron spoons
1 teapot, tin. John C's iron grill
1 Frying pan. I have at Raquette.
1 pan for mixing bread
1 doz. knives and forks
2 tablecloths and "brown" dish towels
Wicking towels, etc. etc.
Lamp with Anna
Pickles with Anna
Currant Jelly " "
Raspberry syrup " " in office
Lemons in ice house
Nutmeg grater with Anna
Cork screw
Buffalo robe upstairs if you require it but
__?__
Towels files or get from Mother, also
More clothes for Woods girls
There is the large fishing rod and reel
Bring all tackle and hooks.

Mr. Ellis will take onto the porch from the cellar when you want.

Firkin of butter sunk in icehouse.

We Shall Expect you at the Raquette the 18th, July, 1850.

. . . *Eric Coe* is to have his horses shod the 15th and deliver them to you on the 16th July. I have made no bargain but he knows exactly where they are to go and is perfectly willing. The horse will go with *Charley* before one wagon. The mare go and return with Peter. Send and see him when you come up.

Coach and old cloaks upstairs."

Tait's Leanto at Constable Point
Oil on board, 4½" x 12"

It too was painted circa 1862. The leanto was probably built on or near the same site as one of the Constable Leantos.

Unfortunately, it is not possible to provide a daily account of the trip which followed all the elaborate preparations, as no description was written by any of the participants.

However, a few details were furnished by Jervis McEntee's diary; he and his friend traversed the same route through the wilderness during the following year (1851) and also camped at Constable Point:

> ". . . I went over to look at some shanties in which we proposed staying. There were two built in the very best possible manner, and were made by Mr. Constable last summer for the accommodation of himself and a party of seven or eight ladies who spent a month there . . ."[4]

"THE INTREPID FEMALES" OF BLUE MOUNTAIN

In a later edited and published version of his diary, McEntee expanded upon the earlier note and highlighted another feat by the ladies of the Constable party in 1850 - the climbing of Blue Mountain. That peak, rising 4,139 feet high, dominates the view from Raquette Lake, particularly from Constable Point. McEntee wrote:

> ". . . We spent a fortnight here [Raquette Lake], and left it with regret. During our stay we occupied one of two comfortable bark lodges built and owned by the Constables of Constableville, who spent the previous summer here with several other gentlemen and a number of ladies, who, it is said, enjoyed the life exceedingly and accomplished many fearless expeditions, one of which was the ascent of Blue Mountain."[5]

This reference to the ladies' ascent of Blue Mountain solves a puzzle which has long bothered Adirondack historians. Both Alfred L. Donaldson and Harold Hochschild referred to the notched tree which had adorned the summit of Blue Mountain during the 1850s, on which the first women who ascended the mountain had etched their names. Both historians regretted that no written record endured, so they could not identify the first women to scale the peak. Nevertheless, that accomplishment elicited praise from Harold Hochschild:

> "The roster of these intrepid females has unfortunately vanished."[6]

McEntee's note now clears up the mystery.[7] He and other writers also furnished descriptions which help us to envision some of the Constables' travel experiences at that time.

FENTON HOUSE AT NO. 4

The inn at No. 4, where the party stayed at the beginning and end of the 1850 trip, is of historical interest, as it was one of the major gateways to the Adirondacks from the west. Fenton's forest hostelry, near Beaver Lake, served travelers and vacationers for over a century.

Orrin Fenton was one of the first settlers at No. 4, arriving in 1826. He, his wife and 18 children were the only residents of that part of the township for many years. At first he supported his growing family by farming, fishing and hunting, but so many sportsmen and vacationers asked for lodging when passing through the area, that he finally put his hospitality on a paying basis. Making a virtue out of necessity, he declared his home an inn[8] and it quickly established a favorable reputation.

Jervis McEntee wrote of his overnight at Fenton's in 1851:

> "We arrived at Fenton's about ten o'clock, where we fed our horses and partook bountifully of an excellent dinner, the which we had been anxiously looking forward to, for Fenton's fame for

The road to Fenton's was still unpaved and deeply rutted in the 1890s, as shown in this photo. (Courtesy of Edward Comstock Jr.)

The expanded Fenton House pictured here in the late 19th century, started as a farmhouse. It was rebuilt and enlarged by Charles Fenton, one of Orrin's sons, and grew into a popular inn at the edge of the forest. From the platforms erected upon the roof, guests could look over Beaver Lake and surrounding countryside. (Courtesy of Judge George R. Davis of Lowville)

good dinners is obvious in the Black River Country."[9]

The name of the settlement, "No. 4," is itself a curiosity. It should not be written without the abbreviation or the arabic number, as it derives from its designation as the most prominent part of the fourth township of John Brown's Tract. First known as "The Settlement at No. 4," in common usage the name became contracted to just "No. 4," and this short form became official when a post office was established at Fenton's about 1876.[10]

During the Civil War, Fenton's hotel served as a recruiting station. When old age and infirmity forced Orrin Fenton and his wife into retirement in 1864, they sold their home reluctantly. A few years later, their son Charles bought back the family property and reopened the hotel. He made improvements and several enlargements over the next few decades. One of the unusual features which Charles Fenton added was a pagoda-like tower, from which guests could see the countryside for miles around, as well as most of nearby Beaver Lake. By the time Wallace published his Adirondack guidebook in 1872, Fenton's had become a popular woodland resort:

> ". . . We arrive at the Fenton House, which, with its new and capacious enlargement, affords entertainment to 75 to 100 guests, and is a most suitable resort for those not desireous of camp-

Log Road in Hamilton County, 1844
Oil on canvas, 27″ x 34″
by Regis Francois Gignoux (1816-1882)
(Courtesy of The Adirondack Museum)

This undesignated road shows the corduroy construction used in marshy areas. It might be a section of the Old Military Road or Catamount Road, which was one of the very few in Hamilton County at that time.

ing out, and yet who would enjoy all the advantages in the way of 'the line and the chase,' that first class sporting grounds afford . . . That explains why No. 4 has become such a popular rendezvous - and especially for ladies."[11]

After Charles died in 1899, management of the hotel was taken over by his daughter, Cora Fenton Parker, until 1938. Then ownership passed outside the family, but it continued operations until 1965, when a fire leveled the main buildings.[12] The site of the old hotel is still clearly visible.

THE OLD MILITARY ROAD

Even today, the road east from No. 4 is unpaved sand, heavily rutted, and crested with stones which add to its bumpiness. It was originally constructed during the War of 1812 to form a conduit for military supplies between Sackett's Harbor on Lake Ontario and Crown Point on Lake Champlain. Sometimes it was called "the old military road" or the "Albany Road." Nineteenth century travelers have described its condition with curses; however, the description most contemporary to the Constables' 1850 trip was written by Jervis McEntee in 1851:

> "The Catamount Road threads the wilderness from Carthage on the Black River to Crown Point on Lake Champlain, a distance of one hundred and twenty-five miles. This road, *en passant*, is simply a path cut through the woods, with an attempt at bridging streams and morasses with corduroy. . . . It seems practically useless, as there are often whole years during which it is not traveled by a single team throughout its entire length. Fishing and hunting parties frequently avail themselves of it in hauling their provisions to Racquette Lake, but the labor of traveling it is more than many care to undergo."[13]

In the next chapter, we have a detailed account of Constable troubles on this road, during a later Ladies' Expedition.

John Constable's notes on section of Stoddard Map around Big Moose Lake: John noted the site west of Big Moose Lake at which he had killed two moose in 1851, as well as the location of a winter camp at the inlet of Big Moose Lake and a camp site on the west bay of Big Moose Lake. These notes were written after 1881 on his copy of Stoddard's Map of the New York Wilderness. The shape and size of the lake drawn by Stoddard is not accurate.

CHAPTER FOUR

Adventures in the 1850s

SUMMER OF 1851

A second "Ladies Expedition" followed during the next summer. Although the Constables left no record of this trip, another source indicates that four ladies participated on this occasion. It was late August, about one month after Jervis McEntee had occupied the Constable leantos, that the family returned to the site themselves.

This information comes from a student employee of Farrand Benedict, who had been hired by his professor to assist a survey party at Raquette Lake throughout the summer of 1851. His name was Abner Leavenworth, and he kept a diary which includes one note of particular interest on August 22nd:

> ". . . As it was a rainy day, we did not work. a.m. went on an errand to the Constables at Sand Point. Mr. C. has been in the habit of visiting this lake since 1832. [Leavenworth is mistaken; 1835 was their first visit.] He has his family with him and others to the number of 10. There are 4 ladies. Last year six [ladies] went out. They looked healthy and seemed to like the woods much. They camp in snug log and bark shantys. Mr. C. is about to buy the point. . . ."[1]

It is probable that family camping trips became an annual event after William III took possession of Constable Point; however, the participation of ladies during the summer did not preclude the men from taking their usual bachelor hunting trips.

NAMING OF THE BIG MOOSE REGION

John had a particularly successful hunt in the fall of 1851, from which the Big Moose region (a few miles north of Fourth Lake) later derived its name. Details are recounted by the late William Marleau, forest ranger, in his book, *Big Moose Station*:

> ". . . On a hunting trip up the Independence River, he [John Constable] surprised and killed a bull and cow moose out in the headwaters swamp in September, 1851. Constable and his companions butchered the two animals and spent the next three or four days making jerky from the meat so they would be able to carry it down the long trail through the heavy spruce and balsam flats to the settlements. . . .
>
> "After butchering the two animals, Constable hung the bull's big horns in the crotch of a large

soft maple tree on the edge of the swamp. The flaming foliage performed a perfect frame outlined against the golden tamarack background. The horns remained in the maple tree for many years as the tree gradually grew around and eventually covered the central core of them. The early surveyors, guides, trappers and sportsmen referred to the area as 'the Big Moose Swamp.' Shortly after the railroad was built, [1893] the tree fell over. But the name stuck and the railroad station built there was called Big Moose Station."[2]

Until the 1850s, Big Moose Lake was called "Third Lake" to indicate its position in a chain of lakes on the north branch of the Moose River. Its proximity to the Fulton Chain's "Third Lake" often caused some confusion, so the new designation, "Big Moose," was also extended to the lake.

Sometime during the 1870s, it was also called "Sherman's Lake," in honor of General Richard U. Sherman who often fished there. (He was not the famous general of the Civil War, but was President of the Bisby Club, which was one of the forerunners of the Adirondack League Club near Old Forge.)

Verplanck Colvin, the great Adirondack surveyor, miscalled the lake "Great Moose Lake," but that name was never used widely and the "Big Moose" name finally prevailed for the lake, village and railroad station.

1855: "A MONTH AT THE RACKET"

In 1856, an extensive account of a Constable family sojourn at Raquette Lake was featured in *The Knickerbocker*, a New York monthly magazine, serialized over three issues. A reference to the fall of Sebastopol indicates that the trip took place during the previous summer.[3] "Bob Racket" is again denoted as author—the same pen name used in the account of the 1843 trip, recounted in *The Spirit of the Times* in 1844, and reprinted here in Chapter Two.

It is generally believed that both articles were written by the same author, as there are strong stylistic similarities and a repetition of some subjects and phrases. If the author of the second account did not write the first one, he is guilty of plagiarism, as the moose story is retold in nearly the same words! In any case, William's affirmation that the moose story was told to him by his brother Stevenson bolsters identification of the participants on the 1843 trip. Whether The Lieutenant—John Constable—is actually Bob Racket is not proven, but seems likely.

The writer displays the same exuberance as in the earlier article, apparently a family characteristic. Once again the campers enthusiastically triumphed over discomforts and adversities. Once more the middle-aged participants whooped and hollered and vied with each other in athletic prowess. Again they cultivated pseudo-military and romantic nomenclature in exaggerated chivalric fashion. Through all their diversions and adventures, they clearly had a wonderful time.

On this occasion the participants were six men and four women, with guides Higby and Puffer. Identification of the campers is obscured by their romantic adoption of *noms de chasse* in all references to each other. The ostensible reason given for this procedure was to avoid the formality of using "Mr." and "Miss" or the familiarity of Christian names when addressing each other. Such an explanation implies that all members of the party were not related or intimately known to each other—and continues to confuse readers and historians.

Among the men, it is reasonably certain that William Constable III was again the *Captain*, and John Constable was *Lieutenant*. It is possible from references to "the son of the captain" to identify *Hawkeye* as William Jr. (IV), then twenty-two years old. The other three men, called *Schenedau, Wingemund* and *Red Jacket*, may have included brother James, as well as cousins or friends. (During the story-telling episode, it becomes clear that brother Stevenson is not with them this time.) John's sons were, as yet, too young to have joined the party, but possibly his wife, Julia Pierrepont, was one of the women.

The ladies were known as *Onkahye*, *Metoah*, *Pocohantas*, and *Manita*. The last-named is the only one who can be identified with certainty. She was William Constable's daughter Jane, always called "Jennie" in the family, and was then eighteen years old. There is no hint of who the other ladies were, from which generation, or whether any had been on previous expeditions. Since Anna was not yet married, it seems likely she was one of the party.

The text of the three articles follows, with their original punctuation and spelling.

A Month at the Racket
(First Installment)

(September, 1856)

"'Why don't you write an account of that famous expedition?' said Uncle Robert to me one day, while relating it for the fifteenth time to some feminine relatives; 'for by so doing you will save a great deal of wind, and probably spare your conscience a little, for I have heard you tell it at least half-a-dozen times, and the number of deer killed seems to increase with every relation. I've no doubt that you might (with a little embellishment) make an article interesting enough for a magazine . . . '

Acting on this suggestion, my dear Mr. Editor, I have been induced to draw the following sketch of a 'Month at the Racket,' made up chiefly of extracts from my journal and contributions from a lady of the party, and should you or your readers derive any gratification from its perusal, 'tis Uncle Robert you must thank, for without his timely hint, I should never have thought of writing for a magazine.

There is in the centre of this State, (New-York,) within a few miles of our very doors, a district of country as great a wilderness as you can find this side of the Rocky Mountains. It is one vast region of mountains, lakes, and rivers, which, for their number and beauty, are unsurpassed by those of any portion of the United States. It is known on the map as Hamilton County, but should be styled the 'County of the Lakes,' from the infinite number of these inland seas, which are scattered throughout it, each communicating with the others by means of rivers, ever and anon assuming the form of rapids and cataracts, foaming and tumbling along, until they find their way to the Atlantic, both by the St. Lawrence and Hudson Rivers. The Black, Moose, Sacondaga, St. Regis, Racket, and Indian rivers take their rise here, flowing through Lakes Pleasant, Indian, Racket,* Piseco, and Long Lake. Although many of these lakes have been visited by a few adventurous hunters, yet there are some whose echos have never been awakened by the crack of a rifle, or their waters disturbed by the 'cast of a fly.' This country was formerly known as the hunting-ground of the St. Regis Indians, and is yet worthy of the name; for nowhere east of the Mississipi can you find a section of country of the same size so abounding in large game as this same Hamilton county.

It is fifty-six miles long by twenty-eight wide, and contains six hundred and eighty thousand eight hundred acres of land, of which only nineteen hundred are cultivated. The number of inhabitants at the last census was nineteen hundred and forty, scattered through seven towns, of which Lake Pleasant is the principle. With this geographical preface, I will now proceed to the promised sketch.

'T was on the twenty-fifth July we started from Constableville for this 'Eldorado' of the hunter. Our party consisted of fifteen, namely: six gentlemen, four ladies, two hunters, and three drivers, who were to convey us in two carriages, with a wagon for our baggage and provisions. The roads were so bad, and the difficulty of pro-

* Racket Lake is 1745 feet above tide-water.

curing means of conveyance so great, that our captain would allow each one (ladies included) only twenty-five pounds of baggage, stowed into the smallest kind of a carpet-bag.

Our first day's journey brought us to Fenton's (thirty-five miles) which was the last clearing on our route. Here we dismissed one of the carriages, as the road had become so rugged that walking was decidedly the easier mode of conveyance.

With one lady on horseback attended by a cavalier, three in the carriage with the captain, and the rest on foot carrying their guns and rifles, to be ready for any game that might spring on their pathway, we started from Fenton's at an early hour, in order to reach our first camp (twenty-three miles) before night-fall. In consequence of the recent rains, the road was in many places almost impassable, and so heavy that our wagon frequently 'got stuck.' We however reached Stillwater (half-way) at two, where we found the bridge in such a state as to oblige us to unhitch our horses, and draw the wagons over by hand. It now commenced raining again, just as we were preparing to take our lunch, which we dispatched in a hurry, as we had prospects of a dark and stormy night overtaking us before we could reach the foot of Albany mountain, where our camps had been built for us. With the assistance of Jimmy Cain,* we got our horses and vehicles safely across the river, and hitching-to made another start.

The road we now found still worse than the 'other side of Jordan,' which we had thought as bad as could be. We however plunged and wallowed along, the ladies with difficulty keeping in their carriage, yet raining too hard for them to walk, until darkness overtook us, about three miles from camp, when we heard a sharp crack from the baggage-wagon, with a cry of 'There goes the axle!' As the rest of the party were walking far ahead, I found myself alone with the ladies in this dilemma, being obliged to drive, while our driver walked ahead to pilot us, as we could not see the horses' heads. My first thought was, that we must pass the night in the carriage, as there was no possibility of passing the baggage-wagon, from the rocks and trees that hemmed us in on all sides. As we had the provisions with us, our case was not so bad as it might be. However, on examining the axle, (which was of wood,) I found the crack was *lengthwise*, and did not weaken it so much as I at first supposed; so lashing it with some stout cord, we ventured on, and soon met some of the party with pine torches coming in quest of us, the captain being somewhat alarmed at our non-appearance.

At half-past nine, without further accident, we reached the foot of Albany mountain, where we were joined by the rest of our party, who with blazing torches and shouts of welcome, conducted us through the wet bushes, over mossy stumps and trunks of fallen trees to the camps, about seventy yards distant, where two rousing fires soon dispelled the gloom of darkness and of rain in which we had been enveloped for the last three hours.

After a hearty supper in the ladies' camp, of hot tea, cold ham and bread, we left them to their first sleep in the woods, and retired to our own camp, about ten rods off, and throwing ourselves down in our wet clothes, on a bed of fresh hemlock boughs, with our feet to the fire, slept as soundly as on a bed of roses.

Morning of 27th.—Still raining, but with prospects of breaking away.

Breakfast over at eight, we resumed our journey. The rain having ceased the ladies preferred walking to being tossed about as they were yesterday; but as the leaves were still dripping and the roads slippery with mud, they concluded to take the bruising instead of the wetting.

We reached Beach's Lake (seven miles) at twelve without any accident, although within an ace of overturning the ladies' carriage several times. Here we were kindly furnished with three boats by Dr. Brandreth, who owns the lake and township, in which we rowed ourselves four miles on our journey, a most delightful change and a great relief to the ladies, who were pretty well

* This JIMMY CAIN is a miserable specimen of humanity, who, according to his own account, has been living at this spot for the past seven years, in a wretched shanty, with no companion but a dog.

bruised by the tossing and twisting they had received in their carriage.

On arriving at the south end of the lake, we halted to refresh ourselves, with which design the gentlemen plunged into the cold and limpid waters, while the ladies sought a shady spot by some running brook to prepare our lunch.

This is a beautiful sheet of water about four miles long by a mile wide. The shores are mountainous, the waters limpid, and fish abundant, chiefly lake-trout. At two we again started, all much refreshed and cheered by the bright weather, and the prospect of soon reaching the end of our journey, for Racket Lake was only four miles distant. The road was now much better then any we had passed over, so that we accomplished the distance in about two hours.

Although we had accomplished no great pedestrian feat, (walking only twenty-two miles the day before, and twelve that day, with four miles of rowing,) yet I assure you I was pretty well worn out with anxiety and fatigue, and rejoiced with an uncommon joy at the sight of our forest-home in the distance.

We here found our old friends Higby and Puffer, the hunters, who had been sent ahead to build our camps and clear the roads from fallen trees, with whom we exchanged a hearty welcome. We lost no time in transferring ourselves and baggage to the boats they had brought for us, five in number, and, pushing forth into the lake, were more than compensated for the fatigue we had undergone, by the beauty of the scene.

The sun shone brighter than at any time on our journey. Not a breeze ruffled the surface of the lake, so that every mountain and island was reflected in its bosom with a distinctness that made it difficult to define the substance from the shadow. The shouts of the men, the merry peals of laughter from the ladies, found a ready response in the echoes of the mountains, as if welcoming us to our home in the wilderness.

As we turned a point, or shot by an island, a solitary loon would start up, and with its melancholy but musical note seemed to ask why we thus profaned its solitude.

A row of five miles brought us to Sand Point,* which was to be our abode for four weeks. You can imagine with what eagerness we all (especially the ladies) examined the camps, and the preparations the hunters had made for our accommodations during this long sojourn.

The camps were built of hemlock bark, entirely open in front, and about two feet high in the rear. That for the ladies was within three feet of the lake, with a screen of evergreens between it and the gentlemen's, which were about fifty yards off. The floors were of fresh hemlock-boughs, which were to serve also as beds. For pillows, the gentlemen had their carpet-bags; and the ladies, cushions stuffed with moss.

Our first thought after satisfying our curiosity was to satisfy our hunger, which was 'immense.' Higby soon 'got us up' a nice dinner of broiled venison, nice and hot rolls, with a capital cup of milkless tea. You must know that tea in the woods is much better *without* milk than *with*. 'Cause why? You can't get it.

The sun had set ere we had concluded our repast. The twilight was spent upon the lake, and when darkness came a full moon soon dispersed it, so that it was a matter of doubt with some of the more romantic of the party, whether to spend the night upon the lake, or in the camps. An hour longer, however, decided the question, when fatigue prevailed over romance. With our camp-fires brightly burning, we arranged our respective beds, and the captain appointing a watch to replenish the fires, we turned in and slept a sleep that 'knew no waking' till morning.

* This is called SAND POINT from its terminating in a little sand spit of beautiful white sand, and belongs to our captain, who purchased it some years ago on account of its beauty of location and possessing a spring of most delicious water. It gushes out from beneath, or I might say from the very rock itself, and settles in a natural basin of white sand, fringed with moss, which served as our refrigerator. Its temperature is forty-one, and contains considerable fixed air, but no mineral properties, and is almost as light as Congress-water. Such a spring in an accessible district would build up a 'fashionable watering-place.'

To give an account of how every day was passed, would occupy more space in your pages than the subject would warrant; therefore I will merely give the general routine of our proceedings, with a few extracts from my journal as written on the spot.

The first thing done on the following morning by the captain, was to establish a strict camp discipline, assigning to each one a certain rank and particular duties, also giving to all the party a *nom de chasse*, by which title we were always to address each other, thus avoiding the formality of mistering and missing one another, as well as the familiarity of using the Christian names. These were as follows:

Gentlemen.—The Captain [William Constable III]
Lieutenant [John Constable]
Hawkeye [William Constable IV]
Schenedau
Wingenund
Red Jacket

Ladies.— Onkahye
Metoah
Pocahontas
Manita [Jennie, daughter of Wm. III, sister of Wm. IV]

The boats were named the 'Loon,' 'Fawn,' 'Star-light,' and 'No-you-don't,' this last an Indian name, in Anglo-Saxon meaning you can't come it.

As the only provisions we took with us were fifty pounds of pork, one barrel flour, fifty pounds of rice, fifty pounds of sugar, fifty pounds of butter, six pounds of tea, and four gallons of molasses, we of course were to depend chiefly on the products of the chase for our subsistence, so that the first order of the captain was for the lieutenant to take the 'Fawn' and go with Puffer to the East-Inlet [now called the Marion River] to fish, and at the same time to procure a stove, which had been left at the rapids by the late engineering party [a railroad survey party headed by A. F. Edwards]. The order of course was promptly obeyed, and although the distance rowed was eighteen miles, in six hours we returned with a fine mess of trout and a most capital cooking-stove, for which latter piece of good luck we were indebted to Mr. Spofford. The fish (some of which were over two pounds) with some corned venison, rice and hot rolls, gave us a sumptuous dinner for the first day.

The rest of the party spent the day in improving the accommodations of the camps, by putting up shelves, clearing pathways and cutting wood.

Dinner over, at seven orders were issued to prepare for a 'float,'* assigning the duty to Hawkeye, (who was considered the best shot of the party,) and Puffer, the hunter, who never pulled a trigger that a deer did not fall.

July 30th.—Weather clearing. Last night, on account of rain, and too much wind for the 'Jack' to burn, no deer were killed, therefore no meat for dinner. Went to South-Inlet and caught fifteen pounds of trout fortunately, else should have had to dine on flour-victuals 'entirely.'

'Come, Lieutenant,' says the captain to me after dinner, 'we must man two boats for a float to-night, for a buck we *must* have, or we'll starve. The ladies already begin to murmur at this vegetable diet, and I myself don't relish it over-much. You, Hawkeye, try your luck again to-night with Puffer; while you, Lieutenant, take Higby with you, and if you don't furnish venison for the table tomorrow—'

'You may take *me* for a buck,' said I, finishing his sentence.

Off we started, followed by the prayers of the ladies that we might be indeed successful, (for they were really getting apprehensive that we might be obliged to live entirely on fish and bread,) Hawkeye for the East-Inlet and I for the South.

Arrived at the mouth of the Inlet (four miles) we went ashore and made a 'smudge,' to protect ourselves from the mosquitos, while preparing our 'jack' and arranging our seats for a long sitting.

While awaiting the approach of darkness, I

* This is the hunter's term for killing deer at night, with a lantern or 'Jack' in the bow of your boat, while paddling along the shores of the lake or up the inlets, where the water-lilies abound, on the leaves of which the deer feed at night.

Floating for Deer
by Theodore R. Davis
From "Sketches in the Adirondack Region," *Harper's Weekly*, November 1868. (Courtesy of The Adirondack Museum)

could not but be impressed with the loneliness of our situation in that immense wilderness, and how entirely dependent we were upon our own resources. My mind naturally recurred to the poor persecuted Indian, whose council-fire may have been lighted on the very spot where ours now blazed, and who had been forced to yield, step by step, to the avarice of civilization, the soil in which his fathers slept, and which he had received an inheritance from Nature's GOD. While thus musing, the twilight disappeared, and lighting our 'Jack' we pushed forth up the Inlet, with murderous intent upon the innocent deer."

(Second Installment)

(October, 1856)

"To say the least of it, 't is an ignoble way of hunting, thus to steal upon the poor animal, while in the security of his solitude he was seeking his nightly food. I must confess that my conscience rather smote me, as our boat glided with its spirit-like motion over the water, and with feelings somewhat akin to a mid-night robber, every noise, even the splashing of a duck, or the jumping of a frog startled me, as if conscious that my deeds were evil. But as necessity knows no law, these feelings soon left me when I remembered the promise I had made and the parting injunctions of the ladies.

We had not proceeded a mile up the inlet, when Higby, hearing a noise in the grass, turned the boat in the direction whence it proceeded, and there I saw, within ten yards of me, as fine a buck as ever carried horns, with his eyes flashing back the light of our lantern, like two reverberators.

Crack went my rifle, off went the deer, bounding and snorting like a high-pressure engine, alarming his companions who, joining in the chorus repeated by the echoes, made the hills resound again as if alive with frightened deer.

'What did you aim at?' cries Higby.

'At his eyes, of course.'

'Ah! there was your mistake. I forgot to warn you that at night objects loom up so, that you should always aim at least six inches below your mark. However, better luck next time.'

Having re-loaded, we proceeded on. But now up-rose the moon, whose brilliant light outshone our feeble 'Jack,' thus revealing to the watchful deer the presence of a foe, and although we heard many, we could not approach near enough to have another shot during the whole night; so, with mingled feelings of mortification and disappointment, and the prospect of another day on flour victuals, we returned to camp, having rowed and paddled fifteen miles. Hawkeye came in shortly after us, from the East-Inlet with no better success, owing to the brightness of the moon, as he had heard plenty, but they were too wary to allow an approach within rifleshot.

30th. [sic; it should be the 31st]—Raining. Captain goes with Onkahye and Puffer to the South-Inlet to fish. Returns at four with twenty-two pounds of trout, just enough for one meal. The ladies entertained us this evening in their camp with dramatic readings.

A Drive

1st August.—Was awakened this morning by the barking of hounds, and then the voice of our captain was heard. 'Come up, my men, and get ready for a 'drive'.* William is here with the dogs . . . not a ripple on the lake, and a cloudy sky 'proclaims it a fine hunting morning.'

To bathe, breakfast, and man our boats, was but the work of an hour.

'Now, my men, are you all ready? nothing forgotten? Rifles all loaded? ammunition, spy-glasses, life-preservers, all on board?' 'All!' was the ready response from each. 'Now, Lieutenant, you with William and the hounds, take Metoah in the 'Fawn,' and station yourselves at Burnt-Point. You, Hawkeye, in the 'Loon' with Red Jacket and Pocahontas, row to mouth of South-Inlet, near to the fallen hemlock. Wingenund, you with Schenedau and Manita in the 'No-you-don't,' will take your station on the East side of

* This is the hunter's term for driving deer into the lake with hounds and shooting them in the water.

South Inlet, Raquette Lake
Photo by S.R. Stoddard

South bay, opposite to Burnt Point. I with Onkahye and Higby, in the 'Starlight,' will watch on Pine Island. Now, attention to the orders. He who *first* sees the deer, alone has the right to shoot him; therefore, each one must keep a sharp look-out, scanning every portion of the lake within range of his glass, as the deer is as likely to break water five miles from where the hounds are put out, as any where. Let not the fascinations of the ladies entice you from your duty, as a feast or famine depends on your watchfulness. On no account must the deer be shot, until all the boats have come up. No boat must leave its station until the deer is seen, or the return gun is heard, which you, Lieutenant, must fire, in case the dogs take the back-track. Now, off to your stations, and remember, the watchwords are: vigilance and caution.'

The army of Napoleon never listened with more attention to an address from their idolized commander, on the eve of some great battle, than did our little band to these words, as they fell from the lips of our noble captain, while laying on our oars, eager to start on our first 'drive.'

Not a breeze was stirring, nor was there a single cloud to temper the rays of an August sun, as our little fleet shot out into the lake, each boat striving to pass the other, until heading for our respective stations so changed our courses as to make further contention useless. The cheers of the ladies, the shouts of the men, and the baying of the hounds, made such a chorus as probably never before waked the slumbering echoes of those forest hills.

In about an hour each boat reached its station, there to await patiently and watchfully the exciting moment when the persecuted deer should 'break water.'

Two, three, four hours sped their course, and the mirror-like surface of the lake remained unbroken, save by the splashing of the fish-hawk, as he darted after his prey, or the ripple of the loon, as he glided from one island to another, and whose long necks often times we would mistake in the distance for the antlers of a stag.

At last I descried the captain's boat pushing off from Pine Island and rowing with great speed in a northerly direction, whence, turning my glass, I saw a magnificent buck, plowing the lake like a steamer.

In a moment we were in our boat, rowing and paddling with all our force, while the other boats were seen putting off, having discovered the movements of the captain nearly at the same time. Now came the exciting moment. 'Pull, William, for your life; the other boats are gaining on us—ah! that's it—a few more strokes like that and we'll be up with our prize; there! he heads this way! what a noble fellow he is! what antlers! how his brilliant eyes flash as he wildly turns, seeking for some avenue of escape between our boats: poor fellow! he little thought that, escaping from his brute pursuers he was to fall into the hands of a greater enemy—man. Give way, William, he is making for the shore, we must intercept him, or he is lost: there, that's it: now he turns. What a magnificent sight, as he ploughs the water with his head erect, and his antlers towering like two young saplings; his eyes glowing like beacons, and his nostrils distended like a thorough-bred racer.

As the boats approach, the captain's voice is heard. 'Come on, my men; pull lustily; he shall not be shot until you all arrive. Lieutenant, as you are the first to come up with the deer, 't is your privilege to shoot him, but wait for the signal from me.

Then a cry was heard from Metoah: 'Oh! Lieutenant, I beseech you, do not let Hawkeye shoot him; how can you, when he looks so imploringly out of those sad and expressive eyes, so eloquently appealing for mercy; how can you have the heart to kill him? for my sake, spare—'

The last words were lost in the report of my rifle, thus ending the entreaties of my fair companion with the life of the deer.

Attaching a rope to his antlers we towed our prize to the camp, the other boats following in our wake, making a sort of triumphal procession, although Metoah remarked it was to her more like a funeral procession.

We reached camp in time to have it dressed for dinner, and *such* a feast, I hope, dear reader, you may often experience. You would naturally imagine that, being cooked so soon after killed,

A Swim for Life
by Thomas Moran (1837-1926)
First reproduced in "Adirondack Days" by Henry Vane, *Harper's*, October, 1881. (Courtesy of The Adirondack Museum)

the venison would not be tender, but I assure you that nothing could be more delicious.

'Come Schenedau,' cries the Captain, 'to the spring and fetch us two bottles of champagne, for this day we must offer a libation to Diana for the successful termination of the chase.' The bottles were brought, 'all dripping with coolness and covered with moss,' and the wine almost as cold as if 'frappé 'd á la glace.'

In making the libation to the goddess, instead of pouring it on the table, as was the custom of the ancients, we adopted the more modern one of pouring it down our throats, at the same time drinking to the health of our friends in the clearings.

I will here give an outline of the discipline of the camp, so that you may judge how necessary order and system are to the harmony of a party like this.

We rose at seven, bathed, (airing our clothes at the same time, for we always slept in them,) cleaned our rifles, washed out the boats, and ready for breakfast at eight. As the ladies' camp was only four feet from the lake, they had only to step out of their bed of boughs onto a beautiful beach of white sand, where, under the shelter of an arbor vitae that projected over the water, they took their bath, Narcissus like, making a mirror of the lake, but not, like him, becoming enamored with the reflection.

'Twas their duty to set the table, which they did by turns.

After breakfast the Captain would issue the orders for the day, assigning to each man a special duty, one to go to the inlets for fly fishing, another to the 'Buoys' for hand-line fishing, a third to hunt small game, such as partridges, rabbits, etc., a fourth to keep guard at the camp, and so on.

The ladies always accompanied any of the party when so disposed, otherwise they would occupy themselves in reading, sewing, or walking in the woods. Dinner at five, (having only two meals a day,) after which all hands were generally ordered to assist in clearing a path around our territory, 100 acres. At this, there would sometimes be a little murmuring, but never an open rebellion. At sun-down a supply of wood for the night was carried to the two fires, after which we were at liberty to occupy our time as most agreeable to ourselves, which, of course, was generally with the ladies, either in their camp, or on the lake, until it was time for 'floating,' (nine o'clock,) at which each took their turn, two floating every night.

Saturday, 4th August.—Rain, rain; went with Puffer to Brown's Tract Inlet, with rifle and rod. Saw no deer; caught about fifteen pounds of trout, average one pound. Mosquitoes awful.

Clear at five, Hawkeye floated up the East-Inlet, and killed three deer, while the Captain with Higby killed four in the South-Inlet.

Storm on the Lake

6th August.—Cloudy, with strong symptoms of rain. Spent the morning in camp. Took an early dinner and started at five for the East-Inlet, taking Pocahontas with me to gratify her desire to see a deer shot at night. We started thus early, in order to fish at the upper 'spring hole' and float down. No sooner were we fairly out upon the lake than we saw unmistakeable signs of an approaching storm. The whole western horizon (which had been shut from our view while in camp, by the density of the woods) was hung as with a pall; the stillness of the air, the cries of the loon, all announced a speedy outbreak of the elements.

'Shall we proceed or return,' I said to Pocahontas, 'you see the indications of what we may expect, and that before long.'

'Go on,' was her heroic reply, 'I never like to 'put back.' I am well protected by this India-rubber blanket from the rain, and by this life-preserver from accident. So you must act precisely as if I were not with you.' On we went. We had not reached the mouth of the inlet (three miles) when Puffer cried, 'There it comes,' and looking back, we saw, about a mile off, the surface of the lake whitened by the pattering rain, as it came dashing on before the gust. 'Sure enough, there it comes, and with a vengeance. Be careful and let it strike us astern and there is no danger.'

In a few moments it overtook us and sent us flying on our course. We were in hopes that from its violence it would not last long, and by sundown would clear off, and give us a fine night for floating, so that we continued on to our fishing-ground five miles further, which we reached at seven. Fished an hour, catching about twenty pounds of trout, when, finding there was no abatement of the rain and every appearance of a settled storm, with too much wind to allow our 'Jack' to burn, Pocahontas reluctantly consented that we should make the best of our way back to camp, which we did forthwith.

On reaching the mouth of the inlet, the clouds seemed to gather themselves from all quarters of the heavens, as if preparing for a grand finale. We had scarcely reached the middle of the lake, when their floodgates were opened and down came a torrent of rain, (to which the previous shower was a mere circumstance,) accompanied with lightning and thunder, and such a gust of wind, that I thought our little skiff was doomed. The darkness was so intense that we could not discern each other, save during the flashes of lightning. The lake appeared like an immense ocean of ink, so black was everything around us. The wind blew a perfect hurricane, kicking up a tremendous sea, which, washing over the gunwales, threatened every moment to engulph us. 'Keep her head to the sea, Puffer, and try to hold your own,' I cried, 'for to make headway against it is impossible. It is too violent to last long, and if we can only keep afloat ten minutes longer we are safe.'

Whether from confidence in her pilot, or her life-preserver, I know not, but in all this war of elements my fair companion was perfectly fearless, and seemed to enjoy the awful grandeur of the scene in proportion as the storm increased, and so should I, *perhaps*, had I not felt the great responsibility of so valuable a life in my charge.

It was indeed sublime to witness such vivid flashes of lightning, increased in intensity by the dark curtain which surrounded us, and to hear the peals of thunder, taken up by the echoes of the mountains and repeated until another peal burst, making a continuous roar of heaven's artillery. By constant bailing we managed to keep afloat, and as I predicted, in twenty minutes the clouds broke away, the wind lulled, and we could discern the outline of the opposite shore. In a few minutes more the rain ceased entirely, the sea went down, so as to enable us to head for camp, where we arrived at about eleven o'clock, thanks to Providence and Puffer.

We found our friends on the beach all anxiously looking out for us, and much alarmed for our safety. Our clothes were not only wet through, but our very skin was saturated, from having been so long rained upon. After a cup of hot tea and a thorough basting before a rousing fire, I 'turned in,' and murmering thanks to God for our preservation in sleep, soon forgot the dangers we had passed.

Raquette Lake

A view of Blue Mountain from Constable Point on Raquette Lake was sketched by Jervis McEntee in 1851. It was published in an account of his trip entitled "The Lakes of the Wilderness" in *The Great Republic Monthly*, April, 1859.

West Mountain, Raquette Lake
by William Richardson Tyler (1825-1896)
Oil on canvas 12″ x 20″
(Courtesy of The Adirondack Museum)

9th August.—Six of our party left us to-day to visit Blue Mountain to see the sun set and rise from its summit, taking Puffer with them and two boats. Floated with Higby.

10th August.—Rained in torrents all last night, much to the discomfort of the Blue Mountain party. Went to South-Inlet to get the deer I shot last night. Returning crossed the south bay, against a strong westerly gale and a very heavy sea. At dark, the party not yet arrived from Blue Mountain. Built a bonfire on the end of the point for a beacon to guide them, as the gale still continued and the lake was wrapped in darkness. At nine, the Captain getting anxious, ordered Higby to take a boat, with provisions to mouth of the inlet, thinking and hoping they would not venture to cross the lake this dark stormy night, but encamp on the other side.

Higby had been gone about fifteen minutes when our hearts were gladdened by a shout from off the lake, and presently one of the boats made its appearance with Red Jacket, Schenedau and the hunter, but no ladies. 'Where is the other boat?' we anxiously inquired. 'Why, has it not arrived?' replied Puffer, 'It put out into the lake some time before us, and we thought, of course, we should find them here. As Hawkeye pulls the strongest oar, and having the tightest boat, thought it best for the ladies to go with him, our boat having sprung a leak coming over the rapids, and as you see, is half full of water.' Our anxiety was now intense, for our fears were that, being so heavily laden, the boat had swamped, (being only built to carry three persons,) and that they were at this moment drifting about the lake at the mercy of the waves.

Our first impulse was to man all the boats and scour the lake in search of them, but before the last boat pushed off, the well-known warwhoop of Hawkeye rose above the gale, (which now roared through the pines with a most dismal moan,) dispelling our fears and bearing to a father's heart such joy as only a parent can feel, for both son and daughter of our beloved Captain were in that tiny skiff.

'Thank God we are safe,' was the exclamation of Hawkeye, as the keel of his boat grated on the sand. 'See to your daugher, father, for she has fainted, and give us all a little brandy, as we are wet through and through by the dashing waves.'

Sure enough, there was Manita lying in the bottom of the boat, with her head in the lap of Metoah, and Pocahontas in the stern a perfect picture of resignation. Would that I could convey some idea of that scene, as by the light of our blazing torches the father bore the lifeless form of his fair daughter in his arms, while we assisted the other ladies (who could scarcely walk from fatigue and want of food) to the camp. But I'll not imprison in words a scene that you can so much better imagine. The motion and the application of cold water soon restored Manita to conciousness, and a cup of hot tea so revived them all, that they began relating their adventures, which the Captain soon put a stop to, by ordering them instantly to bed, and in the morning would listen with pleasure to their recital.

11th August.—Raining; Captain brought home twenty pounds of trout today from East Inlet, fortunately, or else should have had another dinner on bread and pork, as we have shot no deer for two days. Puffer came into camp this afternoon with news that there was a bear in the neighborhood, as he found the carcases of the deer he had dressed drawn some distance from where he had thrown them, which could have been done by no other animal than old bruin. Set a trap for him.

12th.—Was awakened early with a shout from William Wood that the bear was caught. Leaping from our beds, we seized our rifles and rushed to the boats, while Hawkeye, with a gun and rifle in each hand, commenced dancing an Indian war-dance, so excited was he at the prospect of shooting a bear. 'Hold,' cries the Captain, 'not a boat stirs until the ladies are ready.' In fifteen minutes the whole party, in four boats, were on the way to the scene of action, which was on the shores of the lake, about a mile from camp.

Sure enough, there was one poor victim so exhausted with his struggles to escape from the iron jaws of the trap that he scarcely deigned to notice our presence, but kept up that weaving motion so peculiar to the bear, and appeared far less excited and alarmed than were his persecutors. Seeing that he was firmly held by the forefoot, we approached within a rod of him, and after viewing him a while and wondering what he would do if he should escape, Hawkeye performed the part of executioner by putting a bullet through his head. 'We'll have meat for dinner to-day, anyhow,' I cried. 'Yes,' said Metoah, 'for those who choose to eat it; I'll not, you may depend on that, if I starve.' '*Nous verrons*, my dear lady; you may be glad enough to get it before we are out of the woods.'

Today molasses gave out and reduced to an allowance of rice and of rolls, fearing the flour might give out also, as there appeared to be no satisfying our appetites.

Sunday.—Weather clear and cool. Breakfasted on bear's meat, and yellow rolls spoiled by too much soda. Dinner, same, with the addition of a little smoked venison and a few potatoes, hot from the Blue Mountain. Went to church with Onkahye on the top of 'Eagles' Crag, a hill that overlooks the lake, where we had an eloquent sermon from the 'stones and running brooks.'

To a rightly constituted mind, how much more effective and impressive is the communion with God's works in a vast solitude like this, when you see the undeniable evidence of His wisdom and power in all around you, than the best discourse that ever issued from a pulpit.

Camp smoked so, preferred sleeping in the hammock. As I lay with my face up-turned toward the stars which, now concealed, now revealed, by the waving tree tops, as if playing bo-peep with a mortal on earth, I could not but compare my situation with the multitude now thronging the watering places, cooped up in boxes twelve by eight feet, fed like sheep from a public crib, changing their dresses four or five times a day, with every change of scene in the fashionable drama of 'Who's the Dupe?' there enacted, all actors and actresses, no spectators; all artifice and energy, no nature and truth: while

> 'OURS the wild life of tumult, still to range,
> From toil to rest and joy in every change,'

with no limit to our lodging-room, the mighty forest for our hotel, for ever breathing the pure air of heaven, living a life of primitive simplicity, such as GOD intended man to live, and seeking our pleasures in such natural excitements as bring no reaction with them. There was no dressing every morning in a manner the most becoming, no putting the best foot forward, no mawkish sensibility of taste, no endeavor to excel, except in contributing to the happiness of others, but each one followed the dictates of his own natural impulses.

With these thoughts I fell asleep, and was awakened in the morning by the rain pattering on my face. Rain, rain!—when shall we have two consecutive days without rain?"

Third Installment

(November, 1856)

". . . question was, what shall we do now: have tableaux, charades, recitations, or tell stories? The Captain proposed the latter, to which we all assented, provided he would commence first.

As the suggestion came from him, he could not refuse, and therefore began as follows:

The Moose Fight

'You all recollect, in going up the East-Inlet, about four miles from its mouth there is a large bend, known as "Moose-Bend." This name was given to it by our valued and valiant friend Higby, from its being the scene of a terrible encounter with an enormous moose, one of the largest of his species, in which he and my brother Stephen were the heroes. The Lieutenant was of the party, though not in the boat at that time, and will vouch for the truth of the story, as I have it from my brother's own lips.

'They had floated all the way up the Inlet without seeing a deer, and were on their way back, when reaching this bend, they descried, as they thought, the eyes of a large buck not ten rods off, which, to their astonishment, took to the water and was making direct for their boat. Before they could recover from their surprise, the animal was nearly on them. Stephen fired, as he said, right between the horns, which, looming up in the obscure light of their dimly-burning "Jack," appeared like two huge hemlocks stripped of their leaves. This had no effect but to make him snort a little, not even changing his course; so, on he came, until within three yards of the boat, when Stephen let him have the other barrel. This time he sent forth a terrific roar, and plunging forward, upset their skiff, spilling them, of course, both into the river.

'Higby made for the shore, and my brother for the boat, kicking away lustily in the direction of the hunter's voice, for it was as dark as Erebus, their "Jack" of course being extinguished, apprehensive that the moose might attack him in the water, for they now knew it to be a bull-moose, and of the largest kind.

'They were both very much mortified that the animal should have escaped, as they now heard him bellowing through the woods at an awful rate, fairly "making night hideous."

'From the gurgling sound he made when roaring, they were satisfied he was mortally wounded in the throat, and that they would find him not far off in the morning, so they marked the spot by the stake, which you see yet remains, (although it is ten years since the occurrence,) turned the water out of their skiff, and supplying their lost paddle with one of the seats, (leaving their rifles and everything sinkable at the bottom of the river,) made the best of their way to camp, which they reached at day-break.

'John and our friend the lieutenant here, were startled from their beds by the shouting and whooping they made, and supposed they had killed at least a half-dozen deer: so you can imagine their surprise when they related their adventure.

'After warming themselves thoroughly, and taking a cup of hot tea, they all started off again, taking the hounds with them and two boats, feeling confident they would bring home a moose weighing not less than half a ton.

'In this they were doomed to be disappointed. After tracking him for over a mile, through bushes covered with blood, they came to a swamp, so thick and miry that even the dogs could not enter it. It was, in fact, impenetrable to any animal but a moose, and for that reason no doubt he had sought refuge in it.

'After making several ineffectual attempts to penetrate the thicket, they were obliged most reluctantly to give up the chase, all sadly disappointed, and Stephen mortified, as he could not understand why, when so near to him, he had not killed him instantly.

'Thus ended this famous moose encounter, and this is the reason why that spot is called Moose-Bend; and it is now for the Lieutenant to say how near I have stuck to the truth in the relation of it.'

'Too near by half, my dear Captain; not a word of exaggeration or of embellishment. Had *I* told it, I should have seasoned it with a *little* of the marvellous, such as a death-struggle in the water between Stephen and the moose, with Higby swimming to the rescue, just in time to save his life, by plunging a knife into the throat of the moose, etc., etc., or something of that sort, just enough to make it spicey . . .'

. . . a shout like an Indian war-whoop was heard from off the lake, starting us all on our feet. We rushed from the camp, seized our rifles, and ran to the shore to see what untimely visitor came thus to intrude upon our little band. What was our delight on recognizing the voice of an old friend, and when his boat reached the shore, out jumped Andrew Newcome into the arms of Hawkeye, who embraced him as a brother. We were all rejoiced to see him the more that we knew he must bring letters for the ladies, for we had now been nearly three weeks in the wilderness without any tidings from home.

Those who have been a long time at sea, when homeward bound, and speak a vessel recently from the port they are striving to reach, can judge of the anxiety and joy we experienced as we awaited the answers to the thousand inquiries we put to him in a breath.

Then came the reading of the letters, (for he brought some for all the ladies,) which fortunately contained naught but good news. Afterward the papers were glanced over. Sebastopol not yet taken. No deaths among our friends . . .

The excitement . . . being somewhat subsided, we repaired to the supper-table, which the ever-provident Higby had covered with all the 'delicacies of the forest.' 'Tis needless to say that our new-come visitor did most ample justice to it, for he had not eaten a mouthful since morning, had ridden thirty-five miles on horse-back and rowed five, performing in forty-eight hours from New-York what took us four days to accomplish.

20th August.—Clear, with a young moon. No floating to-night. Being our last night at the Racket, we manned all the boats and went upon the lake to take of it a last farewell. Bon-fires were lighted on the several islands and points in the vicinity of our camp, not of rejoicing, as they are generally demonstrative of, but to dispel the gloom that pervaded our hearts at leaving a spot that had been endeared to us by so many delightful scenes and so much unalloyed pleasures. What a calm and lovely night it was! The stars shown with unusual lustre, paling the youthful moon just struggling into existence as it sank behind the distant hills. Not a ripple marred the brilliant reflections of our bon-fires, which (as they burnt so near to the water's edge you could not distinguish the reflected from the real light) appeared like vast comets, floating with the stars on the surface of the lake, while Schenedau with his flute waked up the echoes of the silent hills, until the beauty of the original music was lost in the thrice-repeated notes the nymph gave back, as if overjoyed at an opportunity of speaking after the long silence to which she had been condemned by Juno.*

So enwrapped were we by the beauty of the scene and the consciousness that it was our last night of forest-life, that it was mid-night ere we retired to our camps to seek that repose so necessary to fit us for the toilsome journey on the morrow.

The morning of the 21st was the saddest of any yet experienced in the camp. Long and dismal were our faces when we assembled at breakfast to partake of our last meal on our rude pine table.

After placing the baggage, (which had been marvelously reduced,) we proceeded to demolish

---

* ECHO, one of the nymphs, was punished by Juno, for playing a trick upon her, by depriving her of all control over her tongue, neither able to speak *before* another has spoken, or to be silent when one has spoken.

Evening on Raquette Lake
Oil on canvas, 18″ x 30″
by James D. Smillie, 1874
(Courtesy of The Adirondack Museum)

our camps and dining-shanty. This was a melancholy but imperative duty, otherwise they would be used by other parties, to the destruction of all the fine wood in the vicinity, which, as I before mentioned, was the property of our respected commander. While the demolition was going on, we received a visit from our neighbors on the other side of the lake, Si Wood, wife and daughter, on whom we bestowed all our superfluous clothing.

At eight o'clock the Captain gave the signal for departure, and in a few minutes boat after boat pushed from the shore, and, forming a line, six in number, advanced in solemn procession toward the North-bay, leaving 'Sand Point' and all its delightful memories behind us, never perhaps to be visited by the same party.

The day was most lovely, and as we rounded the point, from each boat was discharged a 'farewell gun,' which, like a volley o'er a soldier's grave, was the loudest demonstration we could make of our grief at departure.

With the assistance of a fine southerly breeze we soon reached the point of debarkation, but what was our dismay to find no horses to convey our luggage to the wrecked wagon which had broken down three miles beyond Albany Mountain, to which (a distance of fourteen miles) we of course had to walk. We had no alternative but to leave the baggage behind us, careful, however, to take the provisions with us, which Higby carried in his pack.

We had not proceeded more than two miles when we met the teamster riding at a killing pace, having found the horses about four miles back on their way home. On reaching Beach's Lake, we had recourse again to the boats, for the use of which I would here thank Dr. Brandreth, especially in behalf of the ladies, who found great relief from them after walking four miles.

We reached Albany Mountain at five, without any accident or incident worthy of note. The Captain, with Higby, immediately went to examine the broken wagon, which lay about three miles further on, and returned with rather long faces, being doubtful whether it could be repaired so as to be strong enough to carry the ladies or even the baggage. This news, however, did not dishearten our fair companions in adventures, although much fatigued by their walk of twelve miles, and nine miles' boating.

25th. [sic; it should be the 22nd]—Broke up camp at seven. On reaching the wagon, found that Higby (who had been to work at it since sunrise) had succeeded in making it stronger than ever, and that too, without a nail, screw, or rope, using in their stead wooden pins and withes of birch.

Our troubles did not end here, for we had a balky horse, who would either not go at all, or else with such a rush as to stave every thing to pieces over the rocks and gulleys which constituted our road. The ladies soon found it was less fatiguing to walk, so they accomplished the remainder of the distance to Stillwater on foot, regaling themselves with raspberries which lined the road in great abundance.

We here made a halt of two hours to dine and bait the horses. All started again to walk, the Captain ordering me to remain behind to bring on the baggage, as it required the greatest care and skill to keep our unruly team from dashing the wagon to pieces. The teamster walked behind to pick up the articles that were constantly thrown off by the violent jerks and succussions [sic], which frequently came near plunging me headlong into the bushes.

I had proceeded in this way about three miles, when I met Puffer running toward me with the tidings that Onkahye had fainted and was lying in the road about a half-mile ahead.

On reaching the spot I found the Major bathing her temples with water, which in a few minutes brought her to.

After administering a few drops of the only medicine we took with us, (brandy,) she revived sufficiently to be placed in the wagon, and the Major taking a seat alongside of her, we proceeded on; the horses having exhausted somewhat of their fire, were rather more tractable.

About a mile further on we met the other ladies, who reluctantly obeyed the orders of the Captain, to ride; as there was evidence of an approaching storm, it was desireous to get to Fenton's before night-fall. This we accomplished without any other incident, just as the storm commenced.

We were rejoiced here to find some friends who had driven thirty-five miles that day especially to meet us.

After giving satisfactory answers to the multitude of questions with which we deluged them, we sat down to a most sumptuous supper, to which 'tis needless to say we did ample justice, as our walk of twenty-two miles had given us somewhat of an appetite.

23rd August—Left Fenton's at eight, in the rain; ladies in the carriage, (which was sent here to meet us,) and the gentlemen in the baggage-wagon.

Had not proceeded three miles before the carriage made a grand 'smash-up,' and was obliged to send one of the hunters back to Fenton's for his farm-wagon.

In about two hours the old gentleman himself made his appearance, with a nice strong *topless* wagon, not quite so comfortable in a pelting rain as if it had been covered.

Leaving Goodale (the driver) to take care of his horses and wreck, we continued on and reached Constableville at eight o'clock that evening without further accident.

Thus ended the famous expedition, to which Uncle Robert alluded, and to whom you are indebted for the *ennui* or pleasure derived from its perusal. It was productive not only of a vast deal of enjoyment to all the party, but conduced wonderfully to their health, especially of the ladies, who gained so much weight as scarcely to be recognized by their friends. With a *resumé* of the game killed, I conclude:

One bear; twenty-four deer; five hundred and forty-three pounds of speckled trout, beside a quantity of small game, such as partridges, pigeons, and rabbits."

The foregoing account of "A Month at the Racket" has both narrative and historical value. The vivid scenic descriptions and the story of the campers' adventures are enjoyable, as well as the self-conscious wit of the raconteur, although modern readers may be put off by his flowery style.

The description of ladies enjoying themselves in the Adirondacks about one hundred and fifty years ago—zestfully hiking, fishing, boating and camping—indicates that liberated women existed even in those days.

Readers may note one inconsistency in this account. At the end of the trip a "Major" suddenly appeared among the party, taking care of Onkahye when she fainted along the road. Since he was not mentioned previously, we must assume either that "Captain" was the intent and this was a mistake in nomenclature by the author, or that the newcomer or one of the other gentlemen had been given such a rank in addition to an Indian name.

A historically significant note appeared at the end of the camping trip in the laconic report that the Constables now demolished their leantos and dining shanty before departing, in an effort to keep others from camping on Constable Point. Unfortunately, this effort failed, as will be seen in later chapters.

Two more early Adirondack residents were mentioned in *The Knickerbocker* account who are of some interest: the hunter or guide Puffer and hermit "Jimmy Cain."

GUIDE ASA PUFFER

The Thomas Puffer and William R. Higby families were among the earliest settlers in Watson and were later related by the marriage of their children, as Almeron Higby married Eliza Puffer in 1859.[4] Asa Puffer, Eliza's brother, was one of four sons all of whom were noted as proficient hunters. Asa often assisted and eventually substituted for Higby in guiding for the Constable family; his name recurs in later chapters of this book. Puffer is listed as a Fulton Chain guide in Wallace's *Guide to the Adirondacks*.[5]

The best description of Asa was furnished by

Asa Puffer, the Guide
Sketch by Jervis McEntee
From "The Lakes of the Wilderness" in *The Great Republic Monthly*, April, 1859.

Jervis McEntee, who employed him during the summer of 1851, at a salary of $20 a month. As neophytes in the woods, he and his companion dubbed Asa "our mainstay and deliverer" and they developed a strong appreciation of his stalwart qualities:

> "Asa Puffer . . . inherited . . . a solid contempt for Seventh Day baptists . . . [He] stood high in the town of Watson, as a non-commissioned officer in the militia, [and] acted as agent for a tract of wild land, inhabited chiefly by deer, musk' rats, and mosquitoes. . . ."
>
> "Asa fell much below my ideal of a woodsman, being a short, squat man, with a broad chest, and somewhat dull and stolid countenance; yet . . . [possessed] knowledge in wood-craft, good judgement, and discretion in times of difficulty, and unvarying good nature and evenness of disposition. . . ."
>
> ". . . whatever comforts he might have, done up in a cotten handkerchief, consituted his entire outfit for a summer's sojourn in the woods. . . ."[6]

HERMIT JAMES O'KANE

There are several variations of the name of the hermit who lived at Stillwater during the 1850s. The Constables called him "Jimmy Cain."

"Jimmy Kane," differing in spelling but not pronunciation, was described by McEntee in vivid terms:

> "Taking him altogether with his huge frame, his sun-blossomed face, his old grey cravat and unctuous woolen shirt, he was decidedly an unpleasant looking chap . . . the odor of the cabin was in keeping with the personal appearance of its occupant. . . ."[7]

> "We arrived at the Stillwater, where we lodged for the night in the cabin of one Jimmy Kane . . . the unctuous and odorous Jimmy, shining with the grime of his lair, greeted us at the door with a broad smile of welcome.
>
> His cabin was situated in the midst of a tract which had been burnt over, and was strewn with the trunks of blackened trees, presenting a scene of grim desolation. Here he lived by sufferance of the hunters, who owned the lodge, and entertained all those who sought shelter with him. . . .
>
> Jimmy . . . was very indignant that we had brought no liquor with us, and reflected severely upon our prudence in venturing so far into the forest without a rum jug. . . ."[8]

Fuller information about Jimmy is given by historians Sylvestor[9] and Stephens,[10] from which the following summary is derived.

Jimmy O'Kane (a third spelling) arrived at Stillwater about 1844 and lived there for some 12 years, near the confluence of Twitchell Creek and the Beaver River. He eked out a living by fishing, trapping and hunting and by the charity of hunters, who usually gave their leftover supplies to him when concluding their trips. He owned several boats which he rented to sporting parties, most of whom rowed up the

Beaver River to Albany and Smith Lakes (now called Nehasane and Lake Lila).

As he grew old and feeble, and no longer able to catch deer, he subsisted mostly on fish and smaller game. When Nathaniel Sylvestor last saw him in May 1857, he was sick from exposure and what was later diagnosed as cancer of the stomach.

On New Year's Day 1858, Jimmy was found dead in his shack by passing hunters; he was 70 years old. A few days later, a group of men from Watson struggled through deep snow for 30 miles to bury him on a hill overlooking the river, at a site he had previously chosen. His gravesite was marked with a crude wooden sign at its head and a wooden paddle at the foot.

Schoolboys: James and Casimir Constable
(Courtesy of John P. Constable, Jr.)

CONSTABLE TRIPS AT HOME AND ABROAD

Because the records of Constable trips, gathered from so many sources, are incomplete, it is impossible for us to know how often members of the family visited Constable Point or made other forays into "the woods"—as they called the Adirondacks.

We do know that John Constable could not have participated in such trips during 1857 and 1858, because he was abroad with his family. His purpose in traveling to Europe was to oversee the education of his two sons, Casimir (twelve) and James (ten), who attended a boarding school in Switzerland. John and his wife lived at a pension nearby at Vevey, and despite the beauty of the Swiss mountains, they were very homesick—both for Constable Hall and for the Adirondacks. John wrote often to his mother and brothers, expressing these sentiments, as well as envy at a fall trip which Stevenson and Will had taken:

> May 30, 1857: "We visited Lakes Como, Lugano, and Maggiore. They are beautiful . . . I would certainly give Raquette the prize against any lake I have yet seen . . . [Here] mountains are too far, it is too hot . . . no fishing . . ."
>
> June 15, 1857: "I feel restive and anxious to be at home . . ."
>
> August 10, 1857: "Homesickness has become a disease . . . if I take a walk, I am at once carried back to our lovely hunting grounds, and the contrast destroys the pleasure I might otherwise derive. . . . Sleeping or waking, our thoughts are homeward."
>
> Sept. 22, 1857: "Dear Stevie . . . Lord, how I have dreamt and dwelt upon you and Will in the woods. It has entirely spoiled my trip hereabouts —as the crowds and connections contrasted

> strongly with the solitude and sentiment of our lovely camping ground. Now is about the season I should love to be there. . . ."[11]

An entry in a hotel register discloses that Stevenson and Will made a spring trip to Raquette Lake in 1858, along with young William IV. They spent one night at a new, primitive hotel, the Raquette Lake House, on May 20th.

Also during 1858, a report was printed from a group of sportsmen who were visiting Tupper Lake, which gave evidence of a previous Constable presence: ". . . We found a comfortable bark shanty, large enough to accommodate 20 men, which our guide told us was 'Constable's Camp'—owners not at home, we took possession."[12]

When John and his family returned from Europe, he hastened to take them to Constable Point at the first opportunity, which was the summer of 1859. Young Casimir and James, along with their cousins Harry and William Delancey Pierrepont, had been attending a boarding school at which they had become friendly with William G. Low and his half-brother, Gus (Augustus).[13] These schoolmates joined the family expedition to Constable Point; our only record of the trip comes from memoirs by William G. Low:

> "Our camp was on a point belonging to Mr. Constable, in a grove of pine trees, with a spring coming up from under a huge rock. Here we spent two or three weeks delightfully. We had plenty of venison and trout, though Mr. Constable would not allow more deer to be killed than was needed to supply us with food. . . . We attended service on Sunday at a house on the lake, going to it in our canoes. We certainly had to thank Mr. Constable for a delightful and, to us, new experience."[14]

This documentation of the Constables' hospitality indicates, once again, their inclusion of children in family camping trips, companions for each generation.

Their joyful pattern of family vacations continued for many years, but during the next decade a new factor—tourism—was to enter the picture, impinging upon their private paradise.

Constable Point, Raquette Lake
Painting by Charles Themanen, 1865
Oil on canvas 11″ x 11″
(Courtesy of The Adirondack Museum)

CHAPTER FIVE

The 1860s: Passing Campers and Rise of a New Generation

Constable Point was an ideal campsite on Raquette Lake, because of its sandy beach, fine spring and beautiful view of Blue Mountain. Unfortunately, it was almost irresistable. Despite the Constables' efforts to discourage strangers from camping there when they were not in residence, the site was used by many other visitors. Some left little indication of their stays, except perhaps by littering or tree cutting, but a few artists and writers recorded their experiences there.

ALBERT BIGELOW

Albert Bigelow, a writer for the sporting magazine *Forest and Stream*, camped at Constable Point with some friends in 1859. He described a curious event which an elderly member of his party had also experienced twenty-five years earlier, on the same site. Bigelow wrote:

> "While we were on the way he told us that at his first visit a fish hawk had its nest near the camping place and a grand bald eagle also had one, and that every day of his stay there, the fish hawk would come out to get his fish for himself and probably his family, but that Mr. (or Mrs.) Bald Eagle was there always soaring in a lofty circle waiting for him. When the hawk, having seen his fish, made his fierce and sudden drop for him, the eagle made his circle smaller so as to keep well over the fish hawk's drop. Then the hawk would come struggling out of the water with a good trout or other fish, wriggling in his talons. The hawk, while trying to get out of the water and a hold on the air with his wings, and seeing the old 'Wall Street' eagle with his eyes on the fish he had marked for himself, screamed and whistled louder and louder and aimed for his nest in the woods, although he knew it to be useless with Mr. Eagle right over him lower and lower until the hawk, just as the eagle was almost on his head, dropped his fish, while the eagle, continuing his rapid drop, seized the fish before it struck the water. He said this play continued every day while he camped there. . . .
>
> We made our camp where his camp had been and stayed there about ten days, and every day either the same old fish hawk or one of his descendants and perhaps the same old bald eagle went through the same performance. It was interesting to see the daily repetition. . . ."[1]

ARTHUR F. TAIT

In 1860, and for several years thereafter, Arthur F. Tait camped at Constable Point with

Above: **An Early Start**

Below: **Camping in the Woods, A Good Time Coming**

Painted by Arthur Fitzwilliam Tait (1819-1905)

Lithographed and published by Currier and Ives, 1863

(Courtesy of The Adirondack Museum)

friends. During this period he was collaborating with Currier and Ives on a series of sporting paintings suitable for print reproduction. He made numerous sketches of their campsite at the Point from which a number of paintings were derived.

Two of his famous oil paintings, *An Early Start* and *Camping in the Woods - A Good Time Coming*, depict Constable Point during his stay there in 1862. In the former, which shows a hunting party getting underway, Tait is believed to have used his patron, John C. Force, as a model for the handsome, well-dressed sportsman in the foreground.[2] The latter painting was described by Warder H. Cadbury in his recent book on Tait:

> "In *A Good Time Coming* (1862) Tait portrayed his shanty on Constable Point at Raquette Lake. . . . The natural focus of camp life, the fire, is kindled against one log atop another at the back to reflect a welcome warmth into the bark-roofed shelter. Certain details catch the eye: smoke-blackened cooking buckets hang from poles on forked sticks, while freshly caught trout sizzle in the frying pan and the coffee pot simmers in the hot coals. . . ."[3]

Shanties shown in Tait's drawings and paintings appear to be smaller and less substantial than those described by the Constables.

Many of Tait's paintings included deer, deer hunters, fish and fishermen. He was an enthusiastic sportsman as well as a sensitive observer. Black and white reproductions of his paintings do not do justice to his artistry, because his strong use of color so enhances his subjects.

Tait shot a moose in 1861 while floating on the East Inlet in the same area where Stevenson Constable and Higby had encountered one in 1844. Tait's experience was similar; although badly wounded, the animal evaded trackers and escaped. However, two or three weeks later it was killed by William Wood, the crippled hunter, who found it was emaciated because its jaw had been broken by Tait's shot. In Wood's words: "It had a broken jaw, and was very lean."[4] This later proved to be one of the last moose killed in the Adirondacks.

The summer of 1869 was the final time Tait camped at Raquette Lake, although he revisited it often in later years from campsites or hotels in the vicinity.

CHARLES THEMANEN

In 1865, an obscure artist named Charles Themanen camped at Constable Point. Our only knowledge of him is an oil painting of his crude leanto there, which has found its way into the collection of the Adirondack Museum. The shanty appears to be a small one, probably indicating that he was alone with his guide, or a member of a very small party.

"ADIRONDACK" MURRAY

The Reverend William H.H. Murray spent six weeks at Constable Point in 1866 camping with a friend, their wives, and guide John Plumley of Long Lake. That summer one of Tait's friends revisited Raquette Lake and may have seen the Murray party there. He complained:

> "There was such a mob (men, women and boys) on Raquette, that I do [did] not go to Constable Point. . . . One day (last Sunday) there were 18 persons on Constable Point and a minister among them performed church. Think of this and shudder!"[5]

Murray returned often to Raquette Lake in subsequent years, camping on Osprey island, which came to be known, for a period as "Murray's Island."

Raquette Lake and Murray's Island
Lithograph from E. R. Wallace's
Descriptive Guide to the Adirondacks.

CONSTABLE CHILDREN CAUGHT A BEAR

Although no family records have been found pertaining to Constable trips to the Adirondacks during the decade of the 1860s, other sources indicate that they continued to visit often, as a younger generation came of camping age.

An exciting episode occurred about 1863 when some of the children encountered a swimming bear at Smith's Lake (now Lake Lila). Several years later, the story was recounted around a campfire at Smith's Lake to visiting writers, H. Perry Smith and E. R. Wallace, who included it in their book which was issued in 1872:[6]

> "A family named Constable were camping on the lake at that time, among the members of which were two girls, aged respectively fourteen and sixteen years, and a little boy of ten or twelve. This youthful trio started one morning to row across Eldridges' Bay . . . to take up a set line. Before they had gone half the distance, they discovered an object moving in the water, which they supposed to be a deer. Upon approaching it, however, they soon learned, from unmistakeable growls, that it was a huge black bear. Then began a desperate struggle for its capture. The little party had no fire-arms of any description, and the battle was carried on with the oars only, and with these the girls pounded old Bruin's head vigorously, while the boy managed the boat with the paddle. The great beast made frantic efforts to board the little craft, but was repeatedly driven back to his bath by the well-aimed blows of the oars. Finally, either by the constant hammering on his cranium, or by a little extra muscle applied to one blow, the old fellow rolled over on his side and breathed his last. The brave girls clutched their hands into his hair, and the boy paddled the boat back to their camp with their trophy, to the unbounded astonishment of their father."[7]

Unfortunately, the narrative does not iden-

Smith's Lake (1883)
Painting by Levi Wells Prentice (1851-1935)
Oil on canvas 26″ x 48″
(Courtesy of The Adirondack Museum)

tify which Constables were involved, and a study of the children's ages yields only speculative information. The boy involved may have been John's youngest son James, or John's brother James' son, Stevenson II.

However, there were no girls of appropriate ages in the lineage of any of the families directly connected to Constable Hall. There were two such girls, however, among their neighboring cousins who may well have accompanied their relatives on such a trip. Their father was William Constable McVickar, son of Eweretta Constable McVickar and her husband James.

OTHER CONSTABLE TRIPS

In any case, the tale indicates continuing family camping trips into the Adirondacks. Additional evidence is a reference in Stephens' *History of No. 4*, written in 1864:

> "Constables' 'Shanty' at No. 4 and their 'Point' on Raquette Lake, 40 miles beyond, and the names of ladies on the 'Notched Tree' on top of Mt. Emmons [Blue Mountain] . . . reveal who are frequenters of the attractive regions of the Adirondac . . ."[8]

Other indications of Constable expeditions come from old hotel registers. One was the Lawrence Hotel at Moose River crossing, which served travelers coming to the lake country via the Moose River and Fulton Chain. It enabled them to break the arduous journey between Boonville and First Lake. Lawrence's register lists several Constable stopovers; the first was on September 3, 1864, when Will and Stevenson spent one night accompanied by several friends from New York City and a liveryman from Boonville.

Later that same year, John and Stevenson took a long winter hunting trip, described in a letter which John Constable wrote to his son Casimir, at Harvard. The letter is noteworthy for three reasons.

Most significantly, John revealed a problem in the family finances which indicated that the days of living as a gentleman-farmer were ending. Income yielded by Constable estates was no longer sufficient to support their accustomed lifestyle. John warned of the coming necessity to "work for a living."

Secondly, the letter included a fine account of the winter trip, with all its hardships and hazards, excitements and disappointments. It is the only account we have of a winter trip, and the only signed account of any Constable trip, acknowledging authorship. Stevenson was apparently the prime mover on this expedition; John joined him for only a portion of the time.

Thirdly, the unabashedly affectionate tone of the letter indicated a warm relationship between John and his sons showed that he was able to impart to his boys the great joy he felt in wilderness excursions.

JOHN AND STEVENSON'S WINTER TRIP, 1864

[*Note:* There are several indecipherable words in this handwritten letter, which have been indicated below by question marks. Additional paragraphing has been inserted to facilitate reading.]

Letter by John to his son, Casimir

"Sunday, 8 (?) or 18th December, 1864

Clear & brilliant day, excellent sleighing.

I have just driven Aunt Anna and dear Mother up from the church, and will now write to you my darling son to let you know of my safe return and good health.

Mother sent me your and dear Jamie's letters three times whilst I was in the woods and which were brought in by Higby or Puffer. You cannot tell what a relief and pleasure they were to me as I read and reread them by my camp fire after a hard day's hunt . . .

I suppose you hear regularly from dear Jamie who has now chosen his course, and one I highly approve of, for there is every prospect that each one of us will soon be forced to work for a living. If it were not for dear Grandmother and Mother, I could meet the crisis with a smile, but as it is, I sometimes feel inclined to __?__ those who have forced this state of things upon us.

We had, as I always have, a pleasant time in the woods. Plenty to eat and a good appetite to enjoy it. I relish the grandeur and the soothing calmness of God's primeval forest more and more as I shrink from this cold and selfish world. How I wish I could lead you into one of our balsam swamps when the trees are bending over gracefully from a recent heavy fall of snow. One who has [not] experienced, cannot conceive how fearfully oppressive the solemn silence is. The crack of the rifle which at other times reverberates for miles, scarce reaches the ears of one a 100 yards distant, and to yourself has a dull leaden sound.

Uncle Stevie was glad to have me. Mr. Higby soon joined us and it was like old times. We constructed a nice strong sled and as the hard wood was exhausted near our shanty, we cut out roads at a distance and on a noisy day not fit for hunting, Higby and Puffer would cut and Uncle Stevie and I would draw several cords of wood . . .

We would put on two back logs 2 foot diameter and with a good sharp *point (?)* stick make a fire to gladden one's heart.

Puffer took out my box before we went in—it weighed about 350 pounds—upon a sled constructed for the purpose, with his horses. It is a distance of twelve miles or more from the last of the back settlements, through swamps and over . . . hills. Requires three days to go and come. He and his 2 sons left the horses on the other side of the river in a balsam thicket with straw for their bed and hay & oats for their supper, the latter in 2 troughs cut out of half logs on the

Deerstalking in the Adirondacks in Winter
by Winslow Homer
Wood engraving 7¼″ x 9¾″
Printmaker and publisher unknown
(Courtesy of The Adirondack Museum)

spot. They then fell[ed] a tree and passed on to the shanty—about 300 yards distant. Heard the wolves during the night, which is common.

But, when the boys recrossed they found the horses had broken loose and gone. Puffer himself had gone hunting. The boys, thinking of course the horses had returned home, but in a few miles met the horses headed towards the shanty—and wet with fright. The wolves had evidently caused them to break away, and had hounded them all night, and were at the time growling and gnashing their teeth. The boys, having no gun, were anything but comfortable.

But they [wolves] are cowardly brutes and fear a man. They reached home safely. In a few hours more I have no doubt they would have attacked the horses. Their power consists in the strength of their jaws. They will eat up a deer from tail to muzzle leaving nothing but the hair. Now the strongest dog cannot break the thigh bone of a buck.

The first morning after I arrived, as we were about to start out on a hunt, the pack opened in full cry, evidently coming up on both sides of the river driving a deer. We ran in different directions to get stations on the shore. Puffer could see the bushes shake opposite to him, and the wolf, scenting him, stopped howling and barked like a large dog. He passed Uncle Stevie, still hidden by the bushes, but I had the good luck to catch sight of him and blating [bleating] like a deer stopped him long enough to open a little hole through his jacket—which sent him flying. We crossed over [and] found hairs from both ends but were unable to follow, there being no snow. He was shot through the stomach and would die in his first bed.

A deer (if you pressure him) with such a wound will travel all day, but if left alone will soon lie down and you will find him dead the next day. The large pack of wolves disturbed our hunt seriously. The deer were very wild and scarce.

Another day, when on my return to shanty—about three miles distant—my eye caught something black, which proved a large bear rolling down the opposite hill. I stopped him by blating, and shot him through the centre. You know they

John Constable III
(1813-1887)
This portrait hangs above the mantle in the Drawing Room at Constable Hall.

John Constable's Snowshoes are on display at Constable Hall.

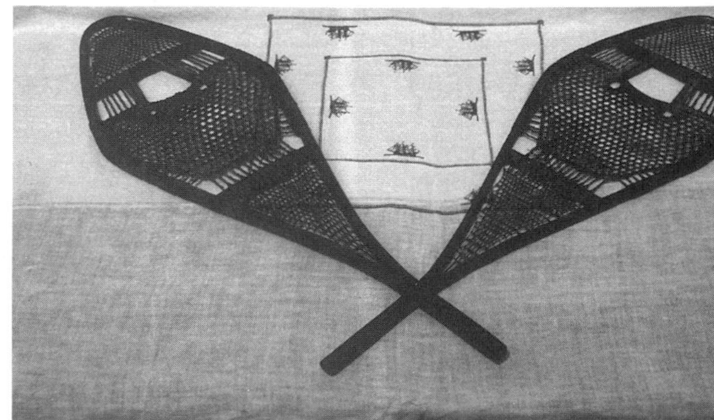

are very tough and die hard. I followed him a short time, but as it was nearly dark and I had three and a half miles to reach shanty—left him to die and follow him in the morning.

But, alas for my luck. It commenced raining and it continued to all night and next day, so that we had a needless hunt with a good soaking. Weather they say here was 12 degrees below zero, whilst we were wading creeks and wet to the skin. But we made ourselves comfortable at night with a grand fire and hot venison stew. Had good coffee for breakfast, hot bread & butter & fried deer's liver or Hare or Partridge, etc. etc.

We four killed 15 deer, but my share might be represented by X . . . I wish I could embrace you. Ever your attached

Father"[9]

CASIMIR'S COURTSHIP

In 1867, another large family party took place at Raquette Lake. In preparation for it, a major effort was made to improve the infamous wagon road from No. 4 to Raquette Lake. A woodsman, named Charlie Phelps, was hired by the Constables to "cut out" the brush from Fenton's to North Bay of Raquette Lake, then to transport their goods by wagon to this point, and finally to transfer them to boats and deliver them to Constable Point.[10]

That was also the year in which a small sawmill began operating at Constable Point, one of several on the lake "used mostly for the convenience of camp owners."[11] Apparently civilization—with all its advantages and disadvantages—had started its encroachments. Probably they now used sawn lumber to construct shanties, rather than cutting more trees on the Point.

The 1867 expedition is the last large family party of which we have a written record, and it also included other guests who came and went at intervals during the vacation.

One visitor may have been Clinton Hart Merriam, the noted naturalist, who was a good friend of John's. One indication of this is the register from the Lawrence Hotel at Moose River Crossing, which noted on August 1 that "Mr. Constable, Mr. Merriam and two sons" stayed overnight. It fails to distinguish which Constable it was, and whether the sons were Constable's, Merriam's or one of each. Presumably, they were on their way to Constable Point, where they either preceded or joined the larger party.

Our best account of the party derives from a letter written to Casimir by his good friend, Dr. James Levick of Philadelphia. Casimir at this time was twenty-two years old, and had spent three years at Harvard earning a Bachelor of Science degree in 1865, and then staying on for an additional year of studies.

Dr. Levick attended the first part of the family party at Constable Point, but had to leave before it ended because of professional obligations. His lugubrious missive indicates that William IV, his sister Jennie, and Casimir were present, along with their fathers—William and John—and other unidentified persons.

Family traditions were still in practice, now carried out by the younger generation. Two Indian names were used—Eagle Plume and Garetta (in a part of the letter not reproduced)—and military titles were still in evidence: while Casimir served as Second Lieutenant, his father, John, was still "first luft." William III was still Captain. The men still loved to use the romantic nomenclature of chivalry, fancying themselves cavaliers, serving their ladies.

"Philadelphia
1109 Arch Street
September 5, 1867

My dear friend Casimir:

As I sit, this evening, once again in my office, and in the midst of 'the haunts of men,' I have again and again thought of you and your delightful party on the Raquette. It is unnecessary for me to say that I have wished to be with you—I *hated* to leave you, and not a day has since passed that I have not looked for the life, social and physical, that I there led with you. It is now between 8 and 9 o'clock p.m. and, childlike, I have pleased myself by fancying how you are situated, what you are doing—thinking about, etc., etc., etc.—The day with us has been a hot and oppressive one—one of the hottest of the whole season, occasionally mixed up with showers. There may have been rain with you, but I suspect you have escaped the heat. Just now you are having a blazing fire in front of each shanty, and in one of these shanties there is a group of fair young ladies and at their feet their devoted knights. A few minutes since, the ever-thoughtful host and watchful *Captain* has left his company in charge of his 'first luft' [lieutenant] and has walked over towards the table and the kitchen, looking after hot water and wondering to himself if that Philadelphia doctor wouldn't like to join him in a hot toddy—"not one of those sugar and water mixtures of the 'first luft,'" but 'a real stiff glass of his own making?' (That he would, my gallant host, most gladly!)

. . . Like a queen among her subjects, winning homage from every heart, sits our friend and hostess *Mrs. Constable*, always more thoughtful of others than of herself,—so womanly that we can not believe this is her first year of womanhood and yet—so youthful that we can scarcely believe she is Madame. Just as the mountain air braces our spirits and infuses fresh vigor into our frame, without our being able to tell what there is in it different from other atmospheres, so her very presence, by a catalytic action, almost unconsciously exerts its refining and purifying influence upon all about her. Close by her side is her handsome cavalier, a worthy looking lad for such a queen. With what true chivalry has he every night left his slumbers to kindle the fire, and to guard from harm his sovereign lady and her fair maidens. May God grant that the fire in their hearts may always burn as brightly as it now does and that while his strong arm may ever be near to protect her from harm, that harm may never threaten her. . . .

William Constable IV
(1833-1887)
This portrait hangs in the library at Constable Hall opposite one of his father, William III. He was the second William Jr., and was known familiarly as "Willie."

Casimir Constable
(1845-1905)
The oldest son of John Constable III was called "Cassie" by family. He inherited Constable Hall in 1887.

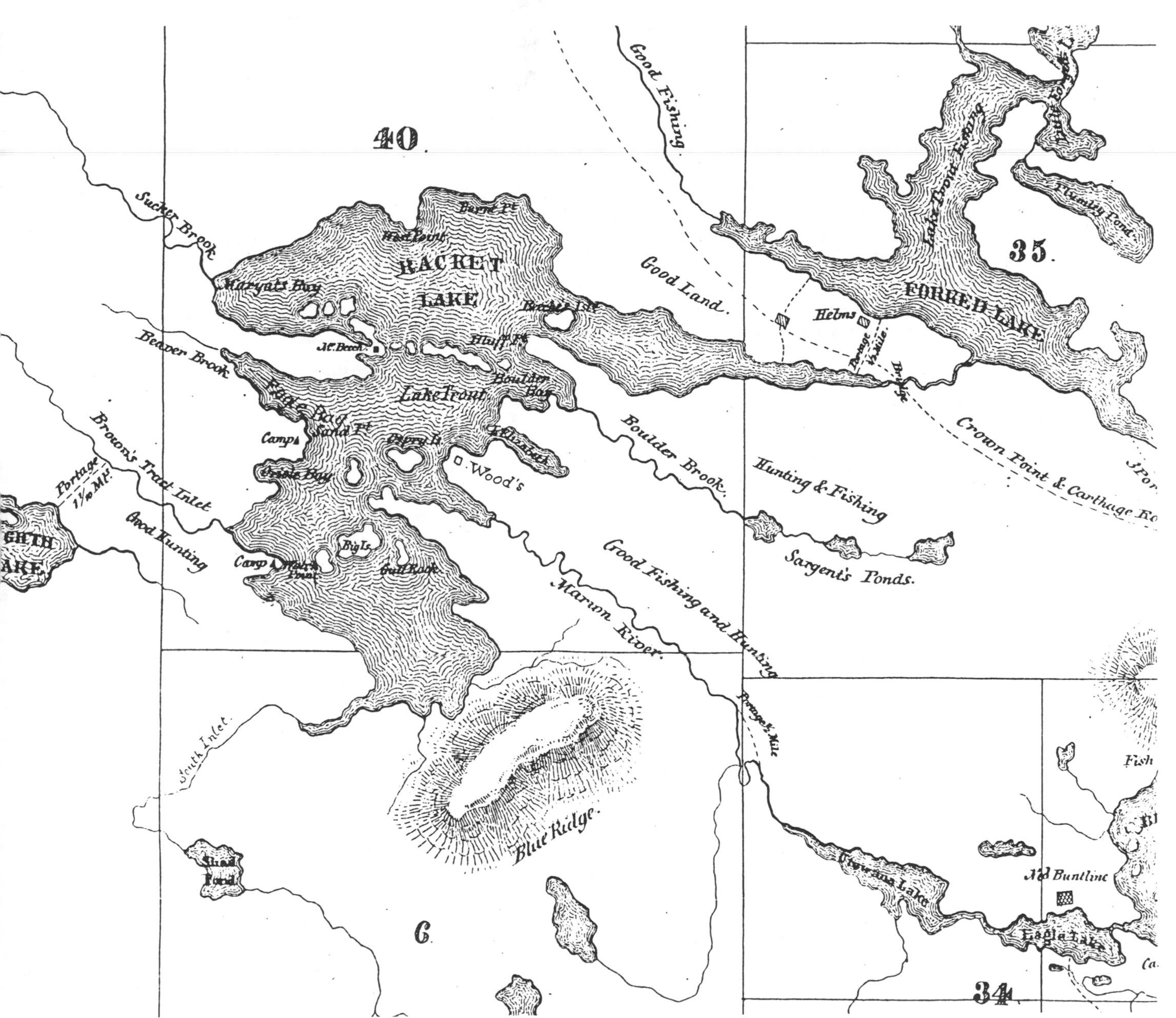

Merritt's 1860 Map of the Headwaters of the Raquette River
Notations portray the whole area as a mecca for hunters and fishermen.

[Omitted here is a discussion of attributes of two other young ladies and two men who are unidentified, and do not seem to be family members.]

In the extreme left of the shanty, with her *'first love'* now at her feet, now at her side, now moving around elsewhere, but never getting out of range of those bright eyes, half sits half-stands, our brilliant friend, *Miss Jeannie*. What a sharp first __?__ she keeps up with the lieutenant, and how pleasantly he wards off every shot or gilds every arrow before he returns it! Brave, chivalrous fellow that he is, take care, Miss Jeannie, that none of those arrows ever wound as fierce and manly a heart as ever beat. Ah my dear *Cassy*, it would have taken even duller eyes than mine not to have seen and that very soon, that in truth *'the ground was preoccupied'* long before I was permitted to survey it. That indeed there was no need for me to spend my time in vain 'dangling.' And she was a very kind friend who prevented my poor old heart which so long had been in a semi-dormant condition from waking up again to the beating of its earlier and happier days, only to fall back wounded and torn into a hopeless and helpless lethargy!

May heaven bless and protect Miss Jeannie, but to other hands than mine will the privilege of that protection be committed in this world.

Affectionately your friend,
James J. Levick"[12]

From the closing paragraphs of the letter, it is apparent that Casimir and his first cousin, Jane (Jeannie or Jennie as she was always called) are flirting with each other, if not actually courting. Indeed, they did marry, but not until 1882, 15 years after this letter was written! Jennie was eight years older than Casimir, and —according to family stories—she loved him jealously for many years prior to their marriage, and frightened away any other young ladies in whom he took any interest. Eventually, her love was reciprocated.

It is almost certain that William IV was the newlywed whose bride reigned over the assemblage, although his marriage date, gleaned from family records, does not correspond exactly.

In the years after college, Casimir followed his father's dictum about earning his own living, becoming a mining engineer who specialized in the processing of iron ore. In this connection, he traveled extensively throughout Europe and was instrumental in introducing the Bessemer process of steel-making into the United States. During his travels he collected old books, including some extremely rare first editions which were added to the library at Constable Hall.

He also enjoyed working with his hands, and installed a small forge in the workshop at the Hall. He and his brother James, who became an architect, were each responsible for later improvements and additions at Constable Hall.

Casimir was highly cultivated, intelligent and meticulous, and was distinguished by particular precision in his manner of speaking and writing.

Although Casimir confined his Adirondack trips primarily to summers, his father and uncles continued enjoying the mountains in all seasons.

Old hotel registers again yield records of the Constables' passage during the final year of this decade. On May 11, 1869, guides Rueben and Nelson Cary of Long Lake stayed at the Raquette Lake House on their way to Brown's Tract to meet William Constable III and his son, William IV. (For several years previously, Rueben Cary had been one of a series of operators of the Raquette Lake House—a very primitive sportsman's camp at the time.)

Later the same summer, on August 8th, James and Stevenson Constable overnighted at the Lawrence Hotel, Moose River Crossing, with Asa Puffer as guide. They came out of the woods nearly a month later, returning to Lawrence's on September 3rd.

The summer timing of this last trip suggests

that they might have joined a larger family party at Constable Point, which may have come in by the northern route, carrying the stores in wagons. In any case, they probably spent some time at Raquette Lake.

THE IMPACT OF MURRAY'S BOOK

In 1869 the Constables undoubtedly witnessed the famous rush of summer visitors which had been unleashed by publication of "Adirondack" Murray's new book *Adventures in the Wilderness* (alternately titled *Camp-Life in the Adirondacks*) which was issued in the spring of 1869, and became an instant best-seller.

Partly autobiographical, part guidebook and part fiction, the book romanticized camping in the wilds. Many readers reacted by stampeding into the mountains in search of good health and wholesome adventures, although most were grossly unprepared and ill-equipped for such expeditions. Fortunately, most of them only reached the periphery of the mountains, as there were not enough guides, boats or

"Murray's Fools" Scrambling from Train to Steamship
From *Harper's New Monthly Magazine*, August 1870.

Murray's book, *Adventures in the Wilderness*, and his public lectures on the same subject, popularized the region and initiated such a rush of neophytes into the woods that the exodus was lampooned and participants were labeled "Murray's Fools."

The Reverend W. H. H. "Adirondack" Murray

accommodations for them all to penetrate the interior.

Some of the heartiest among them, however, did reach Raquette Lake, violating its woods and waters with constant noise and revelry. They filled every available campsite and hotel room. The Raquette Lake House accommodated twice the number of guests as in the previous season, i.e. 400 visitors as compared to less that 200.[13]

Constable Point was terribly afflicted by this overflow of humanity because Murray had the audacity to instruct his readers to trespass upon it!

> ". . . go to Constable Point and quench your thirst at the coolest, sweetest spring of pure water from which you ever drank."[14]

Although we don't know how many visitors availed themselves of this advice, it certainly had an adverse impact upon the Point.

Unwittingly, perhaps, Murray provoked an overwhelming stream of new tourists to the region, which resulted in destruction of the wilderness solitude they all had come so far to enjoy.

CHAPTER SIX

The 1870s: Time of Rapid Changes

The 1870s were a period of enormous change and development throughout the Adirondack region, as its attractions were acclaimed by many writers, artists and other visitors.

During this decade, Verplanck Colvin began his famous surveys, and the creation of an Adirondack State Park was first proposed. Detailed guidebooks for the region were published by both Wallace (from 1872) and Stoddard (from 1874), with new editions issued every year to update listings of guides, accommodations and transport schedules.

"Adirondack" Murray's book continued to be immensely popular, despite some negative reactions from disappointed neophytes and public satirists. His lecture tours excited even greater interest, inspiring thousands of additional visitors. Murray condemned sportsmen who "would foolishly monopolize the wilderness for their own exclusive amusement and benefit," and he prophetically predicted a widespread multiplication of hotels and cottages to accommodate the crowds.[1]

Adirondack Railway Station, North Creek
(Courtesy of The Adirondack Museum)

As masses of people now required transportation to the North Woods, mass transportation developed to meet the need. Dr. Thomas C. Durant was the first to build a railroad from the periphery into the interior of the region, when he completed the line from Saratoga to North Creek in 1871. Stage coaches fanned out from the railroad in all directions, linking various settlements. New hotels multiplied on mountains and lakeshores.

Travelers bound for Raquette Lake could take the train to North Creek, stage to Blue Mountain Lake and then hire boats to row or paddle down the Eckford Chain of Lakes; there were only small portages between Blue Mountain Lake and the Marion River, which was the east inlet of Raquette Lake. In 1878, William West Durant started steamship service on this route, with a short-haul railroad traversing the mile-long carry.

Casimir Constable was one of the first of the family to avail himself of the new, fast access by rail. Unfortunately, no details of his visits have survived, but it is known that he made eight trips to Blue Mountain Lake and environs between 1871 and 1874. This information comes from a note in his handwriting on an envelope, stating that it held accounts of these trips.[2] Unfortunately those contents of the envelope have been lost; the only item found inside was Dr. Levick's letter from 1867 (reproduced in the last chapter).

It is significant that Casimir designated his destination as "Blue Mountain Lake," rather

Steamer Service on Blue Mountain, Eagle and Utowana Lakes
Photo by S. R. Stoddard
The *Utowana* started service in 1878; in 1879 the steamer *Killoquah* began connecting service on the Marion River and Raquette Lake. Passengers walked ¾ mile over the Marion River Carry (then called the Bassett Carry) until a small railroad was built in 1900.

than Raquette Lake. He clearly welcomed bypassing the arduous trip of several days from Constableville through the wilderness.

The trip to Raquette was now becoming easier, however, by older routes, as well. Abner Lawrence had opened an inn at the Moose River Crossing, half-way from Boonville to First Lake of the Fulton Chain, and considerable improvements were made to the road itself by proprietors of a new hotel at "the Forge." This was the Forge House, erected in 1871 on a hill overlooking Forge Pond, operated by Sanford Sperry; he had previously succeeded Otis Arnold as inn-keeper at Herreshoff's old house. The new hotel contained 13 guest rooms, beds in the attics for guides and servants, and such civilized amenities as a dining room, parlor and bar.[3]

Lawrence's Moose River Inn

The Forge House

Perched on a hillside facing Forge Pond, the inn was a popular hostelry for sportsmen and travelers on the Fulton Chain of Lakes.

CONSTABLE CAMP AT BIG MOOSE LAKE

James Constable was one of the first guests to stay at the new Forge House,[4] but there is no indication of which James—John's brother or son. In either case, the hotel register indicates that he spent one night there in July 1871, accompanied by James H. Peabody, a friend from Philadelphia. They were bound for the North Branch of the inlet to Big Moose Lake, a favored spot for trout fishing. It is probable that they also visited a new family cabin which had been erected recently on the lakeshore.

The Constable camp at Big Moose Lake is mentioned in Wallace's first guidebook (1872), in his description of the lake:

> "This most beautiful and secluded sheet (4½ x 1 [mile]) furnishes, it is said, the best June fishing in the Wilderness, and there is no scarcity of venison here. The Constable families, of Constableville, N.Y., and New York City, so long identified with the woods—most enthusiastic admirers of forest life—have constructed a model cabin on the shores of this lake."[5]

No other writers have mentioned this Constable cabin and it has not been possible to determine its precise location. One indication may be the shanty drawn by John on his 1881 Stoddard Map (reproduced at the beginning of Chapter Four). He drew a shanty at the end of

Aerial View of Big Moose Lake
(From *Up Old Forge Way* by David H. Beetle)
This view from the western end of the lake shows the several bays which contribute interest, solitude and beauty to its shoreline. West Bay is on the left and the Inlet is to the right of the upper center.

West Bay, near where the Big Moose Chapel stands today. On modern maps the shape of the lake is somewhat different from Stoddard's, so only a rough approximation is possible.

The Big Moose area was a favorite of the Constables, even before John had killed two moose there in 1851. He had also camped at nearby Rondaxe Lake, West Pond, Sisters' Lakes, Independence Creek and Fourth Lake.

It is not known whether the family had abandonded all use of Constable Point at Raquette Lake, as it became degraded; there is no further record of any large family parties at that spot. Wallace's 1872 Guide also reported:

> "Constable Point, long so popular as a camping place, has become too barren of trees to be any longer desireable for such."[6]

However, other groups of campers continued using Constable Point, some very carelessly. The worst destruction occurred in 1876, when a fire got out of control and "burned over WC's Point." Ned Crane, a conductor on the new Adirondack Railway, and his family had been camping there at the time, under the charge of guide John Coplin. The item was recorded only in Stevenson Constable's notebook, and there is no indication of how much damage was done.[7]

STEVENSON CONSTABLE'S BACHELOR TRIPS

Until now, Stevenson has been something of an enigma among the four brothers. Youngest of all, he never married. He appears to have lived somewhat in John's shadow, residing at Constable Hall and assisting with the business of running the estate. He is mentioned often and affectionately in letters and as a participant on many of the trips, but his own notebook is the only detailed information we have of his activities. From it we learn that he was as avid a sportsman as John, if not more so.

In 1877 and 1878, Stevenson spent long periods of time alone at Raquette Lake, except for his guide, Rueben Cary. Although he wrote in considerable detail about these trips, he did not mention the location of his camp, which probably means he was at Constable Point, despite the fire damage.

Family heirs long assumed that the notebook, like most other records in Constable Hall pertaining to the Adirondacks, had belonged to John Constable. However, the handwriting is different, and the records, which pertain mainly to Stevenson's trips, could only have been written by him. One is in diary form.

The book, bound in maroon leather, is slim and small enough to fit into a pocket—only 4½ by 6 inches. It was originally intended as an address book, but the only address it contains is that of William Constable III, at 52 West 35th Street, New York City. Dated notes cover entries from 1873 through 1878, with those from earlier years pertaining mostly to visits to New York, Philadelphia and Maryland, routine matters at Constable Hall, estate rental income, household accounts and various bills. Each page is frugally used, with computations (irrelevant to the written contents) occupying all the empty spaces. The writer is identified on several pages by his initials, "S.C."[8]

Reading the notebook is difficult because his handwriting is small, scrawled and sometimes illegible. Some writing is in purpled ink and some in pencil. In his old-fashioned script, many "s"s resemble modern "f"s. The bulk of the contents refer to long trips Stevenson made in the Adirondacks in 1877 and 1878, and to notes regarding distances between lakes, portages, hotels, camps, visitors, weather, equipment and supplies. Spelling is inconsistent—a common 19th century habit, even among the best-educated writers—for example, his

Daguerreotype of Stevenson Constable
This photo of Stevenson in his hunting jacket was probably taken in the 1850s.

guide's name is sometimes spelled "Carey" and other times "Cary." Beach's Lake is sometimes "Beeches."

In 1877, Stevenson made an extensive journey through the Adirondack waterways. His notes for this year are comprised mainly of lists —of clothing and equipment, of visitors, of lakes he visited and of routes and hotels. He does not seem to have possessed a published guidebook, but his own notes served the purpose adequately:

"1877 - Route to go to Raquette Lake:

Go to Saratoga and take Railway to North Creek, 55 miles.

Stage from North Creek to Blue Mountain Lake. Quite a good road, 30 miles. Takes 6 or 7 hours.

Good hotel at Blue Mountain Lake—Hollands —where Stage stops & Ordways below.

To go to Long Lake from North Creek, go to Minerva, 6 miles. From Minerva to Long Lake, 30 miles. Pretty good road! Stage leaves Wednesdays.

From Blue Mountain Lake to Raquette, say 12 miles, 2 short carries, 3 lakes, East Inlet six miles long.

From Blue Mountain Lake to Long Lake about 8 miles, 3 carries, say 4 miles, 3 ponds: Slim, Mud and South Ponds. Very pretty sheet of water.

From Fenton's to Stillwater Reservoir, 11 miles. Fearful road. Dunbar keeps Hotel.

To Albany Bridge Lake, 30 miles.

To Smith Lake, 7 miles, 3 carries. About 2 miles, Edwards keeps Hotel.

From South Lake to Little Mud Lake to Little Salmon to Big Salmon Lake, 20 miles in all.

Salmon Lake to Rock Pond, carry 2 miles to Little Tupper, short carry and then down inlet, 2½ miles.

From Big Salmon to Beaches Lake, carry 1½ miles to Raquette, 3¾ mile carry. Williams at Beaches Lake. Dr. Brandreth's man takes in strangers. Married D. Hoff's [sic; probably Hough's] daughter of Long Lake. Was very polite to me.

Kellogg keeps hotel at Long Lake.

John Coplin, guide at Long Lake.Was with Crane Family in 1876 when they burned over WC's Point. Mr. Crane Conductor on Adirondack Railroad.

Kenwell Hotel [at Raquette Lake], Pierce general guide of fishermen. Small cottage on bluff near Wood.

Forge Hotel, Jack Comstock. A. B. Lamberton Owner of Property, has cottage there.

On 4th Lake, Jack Sheppard Hotel. Crego has a shanty, Guide.

Lawrence of Utica has a handsome cottage."

In preparation for his trip, Stevenson scrawled lists of clothing, provisions and errands on several pages. His outfit was very similar to that recommended in Wallace's guide[9] except that the latter was more concerned with comfort—an inflatable pillow and camp cot were included among his necessities.

Stevenson's List of Supplies
His handwriting was difficult to decipher.

2 Woolen Shirts 2 under Shirts
2 pr. F. Drawers
3 Coll'd Shirts Collars.
Woolen Socks thin Socks
Handkerchiefs Cravats.
Felt Hat & Straw
Water proof Cap.
Extra pair Pants to sleep in—
Towells
Gurnsey Blanket.
[illegible] Specks Pencil
Night Shirt Match Safe & Matches
Studds Pipes & Tobacco.
Segars
Tape & thimble, &c
needles thread Button &c
Bottle Bay Rum.
give Jas Wife something
" allice Mrs Shaw Betty
Anna.
Checks get from [illegible]
Extra suspenders.
" Bagges from my trunk

for John's patches Bullet mould Stake & wedge
cap for rifle one screw
Rifle Balls & Cleaning things
Gun Powder horn Powder Caps & Wads
Shot Bag & Shot. Buck Shot.
Rods Reel Hooks line &c
Stake Ballard " & Balls
Drinking Cup Flask Fish Basket.
Knapsack. Blanket Gurnsey
India Coat India Rubbers.
Hunting Shoes Slippers heavy
Worm box
Knife Compass Spy Glass
Razor strap soap brush tooth B
C & Brush & Glass
Sheet Lead for Sinkers
Watch & Key patent
Bundle Matte paper.
Sponge for Boat &c
Bottle tar oil
Buggy Line
Hatchet
call on J A Perkins Dentist Albany
get some Beans 3 Hooks together
& some swivels" depth sizes

"*Supplies and Provisions*

[The following list has been slightly modified to eliminate duplication and insert punctuation and headings. Indecipherable items are indicated by __?__.]

2 woolen shirts — 2 undershirts
2 pr. French drawers
3 collared shirts and collars
Woolen socks — Thin socks
Handkerchiefs — Cravats
1 felt hat and straw
Waterproof cape
Extra pair Pants to sleep in
Nightshirt
Towels
Guernsey blanket
Mockasins [sic] — Specks — Pencils
Studs — Pipe and Tobacco, Segars
Tacks, thimbles, needles, thread, buttons, etc.
Cloth for clothes
Bottles of Bay Rum
Extra suspenders
Good suit of clothes
Baggs [sic] from my trunk
From John's: Bullets, mould, starter, smudge,
Caps for rifle, Core and __?__
Duffle bags and cleaning things
Gun, Powder horn, Powder, Caps, __?__
Shot Bag and Shot, Buck Shot, Fine Shot
Powder
Brads, Reel, Hooks, Line
Stake, Ballard & Balls
Drinking Cups, Flask, Fish Basket
Knapsack
India Coat, India Rubbers
Hunting Shoes, Slippers, heavy
Worm Box,
Knife and Compass, Fire Glass,
Razor strop, Soap, Brush, Toothbrush
Comb & Brush & Glass
Watch and Key __?__
Bundle of __?__ papers
Sponge for Boat
Bottle tan oil
Bug oil & Line
Hatchet
Canvas for tent for woods, say 12 x 10
Jack for floating
2 __?__ hooks, __?__ Flyer and Trot Line
Sinkers or lead ends
Fly rod and __?__, "fixed shank"

After listing his supplies, Stevenson noted repairs needed on some of his equipment, including his fly rod and rifles, and some other advance preparations:

"Get some Burrs, 3 Hooks together & some __?__, 3 different sizes
Send Cary Box of Drills

Wrote to Carey June 8th, letter sent 10th. Would be at Blue Mountain Lake say 27th of June, to meet me there with Boat and my Paddle and Knapsack. List of things to get and take to my camp at Raquette:

Paddle of mine.
40 [lbs.] flour, 10 pork, Sugar 10, Butter
4 potatos, maple sugar
Coffee, Baking powder
Cheese, Salt, Pepper
Pickles, Onions
Crackers and Bread

Me take from Blue Mountain to Camp:
__?__ __?__ and some large candles
Tack Nails, Lumber
Vinegar, Matches
Cheese, worms, teapot

S.C."

In 1877, Stevenson was sixty-one years old and apparently fit and strong—well able, alone, to carry his boat and pack on a portage. He frequently visited neighboring lakes and ponds, mainly for fishing. At the end of the summer, he listed every body of water he had been to that year:

Lakes Visited by Stevenson in 1877 & 1878 ▶

Stevenson ranged widely in 1877, fishing and hunting in all the lakes and ponds marked with an X. Those marked with an O indicate he stayed closer to Raquette Lake in 1878. These are plotted on Dr. Ely's Map of the New York Wilderness and the Adirondacks.

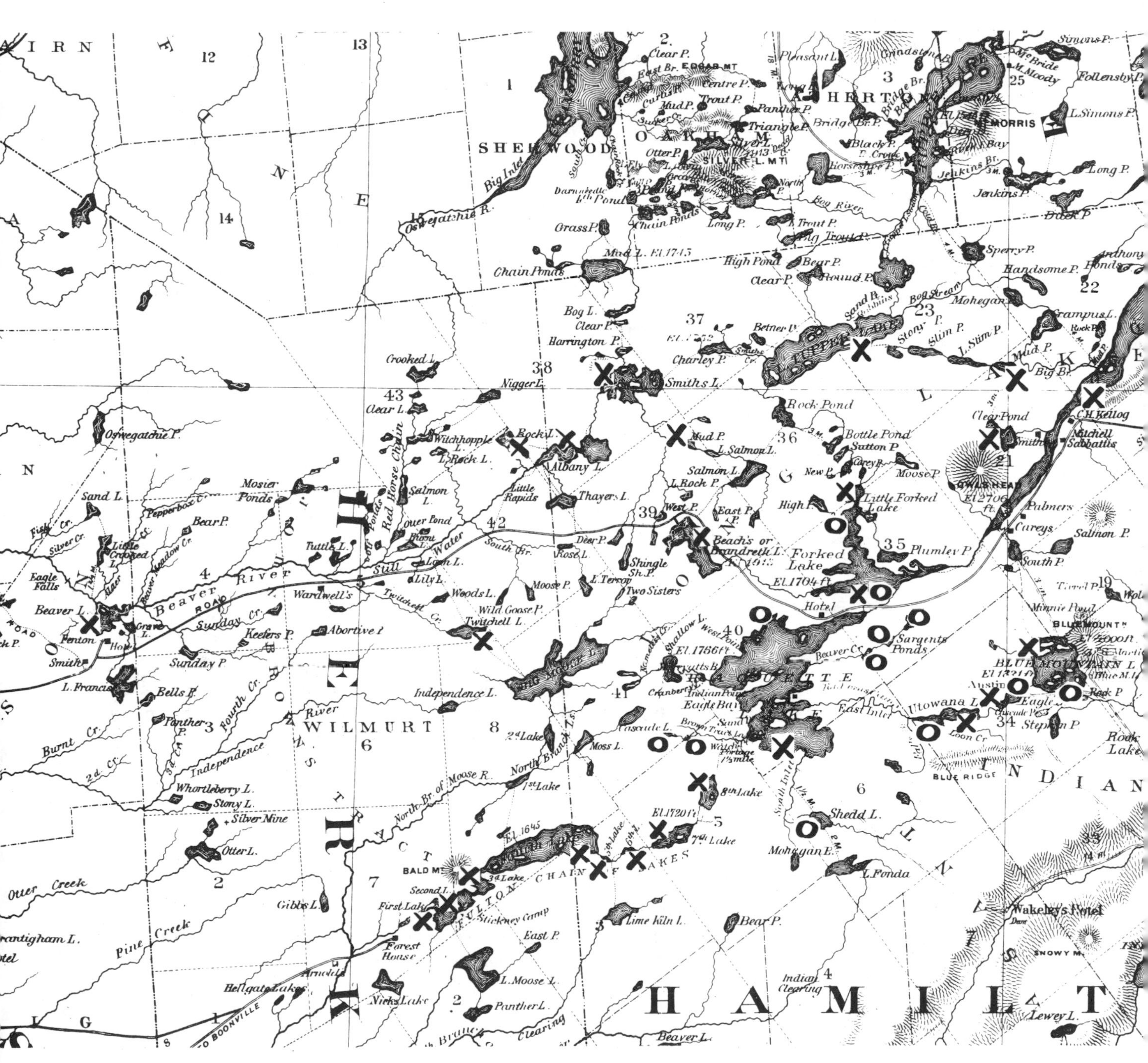

"S.C. Visited said Lakes in 1877,
R. Carey, Guide.

Beaver River Lake
Twitchell Creek Lake—Hotel Dunbar
Albany Bridge Lake [now Nehasane]
Smith's Lake—Hotel Edwards [now Lake Lila]
Mud Lake
Little Salmon
Big Salmon—Stay 2 weeks
Rock Pond
Little Tupper
Beaches Lake
West Pond
Raquette Lake
3 Blue Mountain Lakes! [The Eckford Chain includes Eagle and Utowana Lakes] Upper—Holland Hotel, Ordway Hotel
Big Forked Lake—Hotel Parker
Little Forked
Long Lake
Clear Pond
Mud Pond
Browns Tract Lakes,
8, 7, 6, 5, 4, 3, 2, 1 [Fulton Chain]
At Raquette Lake went to Shedd's Lake [now Sagamore] and Browns Tract Ponds"

1878 — SUMMER SOJOURN AT RAQUETTE LAKE

The following year Stevenson spent most of the summer at Raquette Lake visiting many of the same lakes as in the previous year, except the Fulton Chain, but this time he kept a terse diary. His account is difficult to follow in sequence because it starts near the back of the book, and proceeds forward, with no page numbering or punctuation.

Among Stevenson's lists is one of visitors who "called at my Camp Raquette." They included artist A.F. Tait and his wife and her sister; the guidebook writer E.R. Wallace; Reverend Tomilson of Hudson, New York; Daniel Wright of New York City; D.C. Hindsley of Essex County, "owner of a large tract on Raquette Lake" and the Frank Stott family who wanted to buy Constable Point! He noted:

"Stotts and Miss Julia, live up at N. River, Stottville, Columbia County. Wanted to purchase W.C.'s Point on sight and put up a cottage.

The Stotts had first visited Raquette Lake in 1875 and returned in subsequent summers, and they were seeking a suitable cottage site. In 1878, they settled on Bluff Point, on the northeasterly shore; there they built a camp consisting of a group of simple, one-story log cabins with fireplaces.[10] Nearly ten years later, William West Durant married their daughter Janet. Julia Stott, their other daughter, seems to have taken a particular interest in Stevenson, and it appears that he reciprocated.

Stevenson also listed the names of other summer camp owners around Raquette Lake, whose acquaintance he had made: Mr. and Mrs. John Boyd Thatcher (he later became the mayor of Albany), Mr. and Mrs. McMurray of Brooklyn, William Durant, and Chauncey Hathorne, who started a rustic cottage colony on Golden Beach in 1877.[11]

He also stopped, now and then, at Ike Kenwell's Raquette Lake House, a new hotel, not to be confused with a primitive earlier one by the same name, once operated by the Cary family near the lake's outlet. This one offered full hotel services, including a bar and dining room.

However, Stevenson was mostly alone except for his guide and he spent his time in solitary rounds of hunting and fishing. Although he may have missed the boisterous camaraderie of earlier family trips, his days were now punctuated with a large number of social calls, which he formally returned. This was a distinct change from the splendid isolation of camping in the 1840s and 1850s.

He ranged widely among the neighboring lakes and ponds, with a summary listing similar

Constable Point at Raquette Lake
Early photo by unknown photographer
(Courtesy of Edward Comstock Jr.)

Rueben Cary

Stevenson's guide at Raquette Lake during the 1870s. (Courtesy of The Adirondack Museum)

to that of 1877. Reproduced below are a selection from his notes which give a sample of his routine or which contain more personal or interesting matter. They have been abridged because his frequent references to trolling, fly-casting, hounding and floating become tediously repetitive:

Stevenson's Diary

[Again, illegible entries are indicated by __?__ and punctuation and paragraphing have been inserted. Dates are italicized to facilitate reading.]

"*1878* - Went up to Raquette Lake by way of the Adirondack RR to North Creek & by Stage 30 miles to Blue Mountain Lake. Boat to Raquette. Started 25th June. Left Woods for home 16th Sept./'78. Arrived 17th.

Blue Mountain Lakes (3) [3 lakes in Eckford Chain]
Raquette
Browns Tract Ponds (2)
Forked, Big and Little (2)

High Pond (1)
Plumley Pond (1)
Carey Pond, Sutton, Bottle (3)
Shallow Lake (1)
Shedd's " (1)
Sargent Ponds (3)

Left home Tuesday, *25th of June, 1878*. Anna came as far as Utica with me. Stayed in Albany. Left at 7:40 a.m. Reached Blue Mountain Lake at 9 p.m., *26th of June*.

June 27th - Evening, Carey arrived.

Friday/28th - Left for Raquette morning of 28th. Reached Raquette at 2 o'clock. Got a few fish for dinner.

Saturday/30th - Very hot. Carey gone to Beaches Lake. I spent day alone, not lonely. Temp. 93 degrees. Hooked a Bass fish. Evening caught 9.

Monday, 1st/July - Breakfasted at 5 a.m. and went Salmon fishing. Caught 3, lost 2 very large ones trolling. Came back at 10 a.m. Hotter and temperature 93 degrees in shade at 10 a.m. 97 degrees in afternoon. Caught a Bass, 2½ pounds.

Tuesday/2nd - Hot as ever. Caught 2 Salmon morning, lost 1 larger one. Fixing Camp all day. Too hot, bugs out. We peeled bark yesterday, __?__ pretty well used up.

Monday/8th - Very hot. Some little rain. Caught 1 Salmon Trout at Browns Tract Inlet. Caught 30 Trout. Hot.

Wednesday/11th - Warm day. Left Raquette at 12 a.m. for Browns Tract Pond. Caught some Salmon trout and took lunch at landing. Met Jerome Wood with 2 boys coming back from Pond. Reached Browns Tract Pond at 6 p.m. Had to wade and drag boat for a mile. Caught 7 fine black Bass, had a cup of tea & took a rest. Then went floating. Killed a fine buck. First venison - two deer we have seen. Mr. Benedict arrived at Raquette with 7 guides and 7 boats. [This was Farrand Benedict's son; Farrand had died in 1874.] Stopped at Kenwell's.

Friday/12th - Came back to Raquette. Fine day. Hurt my leg.

Saturday/13th - Did not sleep all night. In great pain. Bad ankle and leg. Stayed in camp all day. Could not walk. Went out in boat, evening.

Sunday/14th - Fine day. Am a cripple -

Monday/15th - Fine. Very warm. Blew hard. Caught some fine Bass & Salmon trout.

Tuesday/16th - Fished. Very warm. Went floating Bottle Lake. Saw one Deer in moonlight, floating near brook. Did not get a shot. Called upon Mr. Thatcher and spent an hour. Very hot. Caught 1 Salmon for dinner. Got to bed at 2 a.m.

Wednesday/17th - Pretty tired. Got up at 10 a.m. Warm night and warm morning. Slept in my drawers and bare feet. Hot last night.

Thursday/18th - VERY HOT. Caught 4 Salmon. Went floating in Little Forked. Fired at a Deer, only saw his eyes. Mr. and Mrs. Tait, A.F., painter, called upon me with her sister. Lives at Long Lake. Asked me to come see him.

Saturday/20th - Very warm. Got up at 4 and got ready to go to Browns Tract Ponds to hunt. Got as far as Inlet when we saw a fine buck coming to water and killed him and came back. Afternoon took a ham over to Mr. Thatcher and ran against Mr. Woodward and son and Guide Hy Salmon. Waller had told them where they could find us. Empty camp, and when we got back from fishing, found them at our camp and made them stay.

Sunday/21st - Very hard thunder showers last night and rain this morning. Some heavy showers, clear after. Mr. Woodward and son spent day with us.

Monday/22nd - Woodward and son left for Blue Mountain. A *cold* day and hard wind and rain all day. Afternoon blew great guns. Mr. W. arrived at 4 p.m. and intended to go to Salmon Lake but could not cross the Old Raquette. It was rough and no mistake - stayed with us - I did not get out of camp all day. Carey went to Long Lake to stay til Thursday. Amos C. Robinson [another guide] with me.

Tuesday/23rd - Fine day, warm. Got off at 6

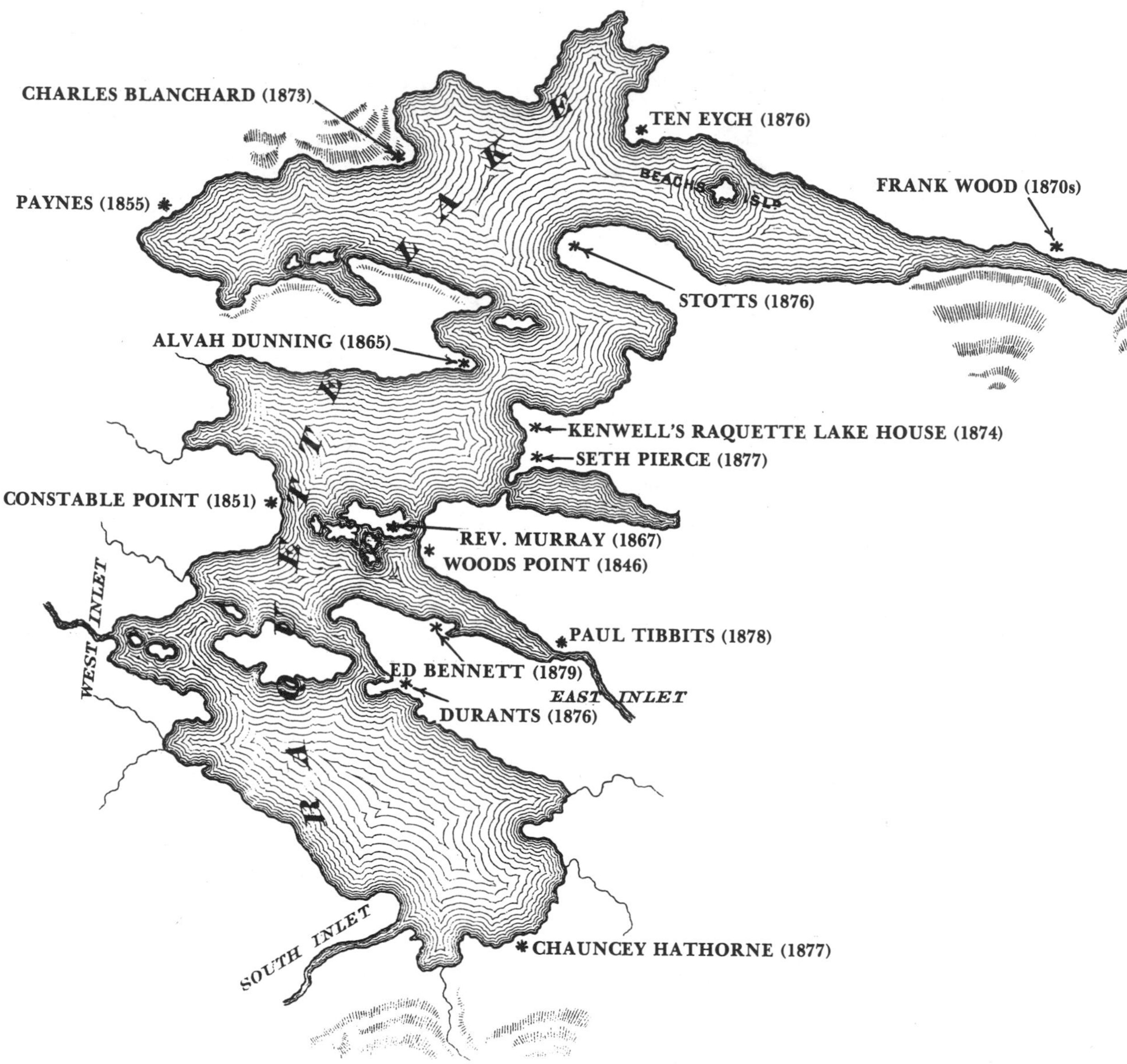

Camps and Hotels at Raquette Lake in the 1870s

Compare this with a similar map on page 62 which showed the settlers in the early 1850s. The transition from wilderness to populated lakeshores occurred within a 20 year span. Three resorts catered to visitors (Kenwell's Raquette Lake House, Ed Bennett's Hotel and Chauncey Hathorne's Forest Cottages). Settler families, such as the Woods and Paynes also took in paying guests. (For more details, see *Raquette Lake* by Ruth Timm.)

a.m. I went Salmon fishing, hooked 5 Salmon and lost them, also one very large one in afternoon. Went Bass fishing and caught a good strong one, large one, got birch bark for my dressing room. Fixed apron for fire place to prevent shanty from smoking. A perfect __?__.

Saturday/27th - Hard storm all night. Went fishing up East Inlet - caught 22 fine trout. Cleared off fine. Got a good dinner and went and put out a buoy and baited it.

Sunday/28th - Fine bright morning . . . Mr. Reynolds called here - went up to Browns Tract Ponds for a day - went floating and killed a fine, large Deer near Shanty on same beach and got back at 11 p.m.

Monday/29th - Next morning went trolling and caught some Bass - saw 2 fine Deer walk out on sand beach and went for the 2 bucks. Got within 30 Rods when they saw us. Fired at the largest and put a ball thru him. Followed him for some time and found where he had __?__. Went back for Dog at Camp and put him on - a pup, had never been after a Deer. He took the track. Soon we heard him, drove him into lake, and Shot him. Came back to Raquette in afternoon. Mr. Thatcher and party called. Rained all night.

Tuesday/30th - Rainy day and we could have killed the other Buck but would not. Fixing up things generally and putting venison away. We had a hard __?__ night at Ponds. Cold and no camp. At about 8 o'clock p.m., Pierce came to report that a man was shot at Browns Tract Pond. We left them there Monday afternoon, Sims and Johnson. Some 4 men. Carey had to go. Went up to bring him down. Poor Johnson was shot and killed at the landing - got back with him at 7 a.m.

Wednesday/31st - Storm day, __?__ and cool - called upon Mr. and Mrs. Reynolds Tuesday.

Thursday/1st day of August - Fine day, beautiful morning. Was up at 4 and went Salmon fishing. Carey went over about one mile from camp and cut a lot of hard wood, bringing back a boatload over. Went over to South Bay. Bass fishing afternoon. Stayed quite late, got a good soaking. Met Mr. Thatcher and party, asked us to dinner tomorrow.

Wednesday/7th - Rain and thunder, cleared off afternoon. Sun came out and warm.

Thursday/7th [sic] - Went to Browns Tract Ponds. Arrived about 7. Some dogs ran two deer in __?__. Got a splendid camp built when a heavy storm set in. Cleared off __?__. Went floating, no luck. Towards morning came one of the heaviest storms I ever saw. Thunder and lightning and rain in torrents. Lake rose 2½ feet.

Friday/8th - Went to Upper Lake. Caught some fine trout for dinner and came down outlet to Lower Lake. Floated, no luck. No others in, water too high. Some rain and thunder.

Saturday/9th - Put dogs out in afternoon. A Deer came in. I was alone. Had a good chase after him and killed him. One dog did not get back til 9 p.m.

Sunday/10th - Fine. Went fishing. Caught some Trout and black Bass, fixed up Camp. Had an old Bear within ten Rods of camp at night, eating up some of our deer. Tried to get a shot but he smelt us and put off.

Monday/11th - Fine. Came back to our headquarters at Raquette. Found all right. Fished a little in Evening. Called at Kenwells. Had out __?__ Miss Julia Stott. They arrived last Thursday, just before that fearful storm.

Tuesday/12th - Fine morning. I killed Rabbit last evening. Fishing. Called on the Stotts. Took them a piece of venison. Gave me some new potatoes, loaf of bread.

Saturday/16th - Helped kill a Deer. Called on Mr. Ward and gave them a Salmon trout. Rainy day.

Sunday/17th - One __?__ of the storm, thunder, lightning and very severe wind and hail. Hailstones 1¼ inch diam. Was to go to Browns Tract Ponds but didn't.

Wednesday/20th - Carried over to Upper Pond and floated. Rained hard but had a big time. No luck. Got a good soaking. I had to carry back in middle of night - pretty cold.

Thursday/22nd - Came back to Raquette. Fine warm day. Had a pleasant trip. Caught some fine Salmon trout at Catfish Bay - one Bass jumped into boat. Floating one-half hour __?__. I found Mr. Thatcher and family gone.

Saturday/24th - Good fishing. Caught 5. Cary went to Beeches Lake and spent day alone. Killed a Rabbit - and Cary brought home a Partridge. Paid for potatoes $1.25.

Monday/26th - fine day. Saw a Buck and had a chase and someone got the start and got the Buck. Old Mr. Carey got a very large Buck, driven in by some dog. Another very large and handsome. Spread at top 13 inches, in center 22 inches and heavy.

Tuesday/27th - Off for Forked Lake. Fine day, hot. Got to lake at 4 p.m. Had a good fish. Camped in front of Plumleys.

Saturday/31st - Hot. Very. Miss Stott came down from Raquette to spend day. Gave me a book.

Sunday/1st September - Were to go to Bottle Pond but it rained. We gave out and came back to Raquette afternoon.

Monday/2nd - All sorts of a day. Rain. We floated and fished up South Inlet. No fish. Heard one otter.

Tuesday/3rd - Rainy part of day. Warm. Called at Stotts. Got back at 1 a.m. No luck fishing.

Sunday/8th - Warm. Diff. Lakes, S.C.: Carey Pond, Sutton Pond, Bottle Pond, High Pond, Plumley Pond, Moose Pond, Shedd Lake, Shallow Lake - Party 2 men.

Tuesday/10th - Carey Pond.

Saturday/14th - Packed up. Hard wind all day and night. Old lake not safe to go on. Miss Julia Stott called.

Sunday/15th - Left for Blue Mountain Lake on my way home. Beautiful day. Hard frost at night.

Monday/16th - Left for home. Splendid day. Reached Albany at 8 o'clock.

Tuesday/17th - Reached Utica at 1 p.m. Got to Lyons Falls at 8 p.m."

Thus ended Stevenson's account, leaving two interesting questions. Had he developed a romantic interest in Julia Stott? (He remained a bachelor.) Secondly, did Mr. Stott make William Constable III a firm purchase offer for Constable Point? William did not sell the Point until 1884.[12]

There is no record extant of any Constable trips to Raquette Lake following Stevenson's in 1878, but an era was ending at Constable Point.

SUBSEQUENT HISTORY OF CONSTABLE POINT

The Point was sold on November 29, 1884 to Charles H. Bennett of Raquette Lake, who erected a hotel upon it. Known as "The Antlers," it was built in a rustic Adirondack style and immediately became popular. Wallace described it well in his guidebook:

> "Those seeking a sylvan retreat which supplies the primitive mode of enjoying a wild-wood life . . . and which with its environs, presents ideals of beauty and opportunities for sporting seldom excelled . . . will find a worthy subject of their search in this most favored spot. This 'Summer Camping Ground' has a lovely situation on Constable's Point . . . It consists of a picturesque grouping of wall-tents, open camps [leantos] and neat little cottages, affording the retirement and comforts of home life, all clustered around the main structure, a building well fitted with modern conveniences. This mode of entertainment is a pronounced success, and patrons of the establishment are enthusiastic over this new way of camping out . . . Capacity 80."[13]

Over the ensuing years, Bennett expanded and improved his hotel until it finally could accommodate 200 people. After his death in 1915, his sister operated it for five years and then the Cedar Island Corporation took it over and thereafter subdivided the property.

The Antlers' Boathouse on Constable Point
Circa early 1900s
(Courtesy of The Adirondack Museum)

Current view of Constable Point
Beach and picnic area on the sandy point where the Constables formerly camped. (1988 photo by V.E. Pilcher)

Current views of Constables' Spring
Top view faces the boxed-in spring. Bottom view faces the lake. (1988 photos by V. E. Pilcher)

The Raquette Lake Girls Camp was erected on part of the Point in 1922, and a large boathouse was built next to the Antlers boathouse to accommodate transportation to a boys camp across the lake on Wood's Point. The original hotel continued to operate under different managers for several decades, finally declining into a small motel.

In 1965, the Antlers Motel property was sold to the New York State University College at Cortland as an adjunct to their Outdoor Education Center at Camp Pine Knot (the former Durant family camp). The rest of the tract was redivided and sold in much smaller lots for family vacation cottages.[14]

THE SPRING AT CONSTABLE POINT

While engaged in writing this book I wondered whether the spring still existed at Constable Point. Although I had seen no trace of it on my first visit to the Point, my curiosity remained strong. I had been intrigued by "Adirondack" Murray's description of it plus that in the 1855 *Knickerbocker* article, repeated here from Chapter IV:

> "This is called Sand Point . . . and belongs to our Captain, who purchased it some years ago on account of its beauty of location and possessing a spring of most delicious water. It gushes out from beneath, or I might say from the very rock itself, and settles in a natural basin of white sand, fringed with moss, which serves as our refrigerator. . . ."

One fine day in the summer of 1988, my husband and I went hunting for the spring. I contacted historian Ruth Timm at Raquette Lake, who helpfully put me in touch with Joe Pierson of the Cortland College Outdoor Education Center. He made some inquiries of longtime residents and was able to point us in the right direction.

Walking north along the lakeshore from the Antlers (the former casino at the lakeside still bears that name because of the impressive spread of deer horns mounted over the doorway), we crossed several cottage lots and finally did find it—in a well-groomed backyard behind a pleasant cottage. Nobody was at home, so, like Murray's readers, we trespassed, for a closer look.

The spring has been boxed in but is lovingly maintained, still a little bower, now decorated with plantings of bright red geraniums—a contrast to the trees and moss of the Constable's days. We wondered whether the present owners ever cool a bottle of champagne in it, as the Constables had done, to celebrate a special event. We wished we could have plucked such a bottle from its depths, and saluted them appropriately, for maintaining this historic landmark.

Deer Harvest: "The Great Slaughter"
As the number of "sportsmen" increased, many deer were killed merely for sport, rather than as needed for meat, a practice opposed by such conservationists as Charles Fenton and John Constable. (Courtesy of The Adirondack Museum)

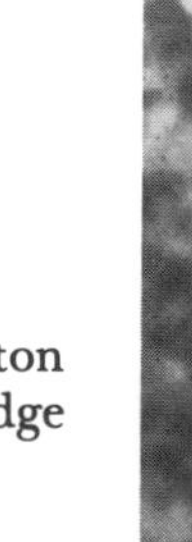

Charles Fenton
Second-generation proprietor of Fenton House at No. 4. (Courtesy of Judge George R. Davis of Lowville)

CHAPTER SEVEN

End of a Gracious Era: 1880s to the Present

By the 1880s the four Constable brothers were growing old. John had become much less active; in a letter written in December 1880 to Charles Fenton of No. 4 he disclosed:

> ". . . it is many years since I have been in the woods in winter, and many years since I have been east of your house . . ."[1]

Nevertheless, he retained his interest in "the woods," and in all matters pertaining to them.

It was in 1882 that he obtained a copy of the Stoddard map of the Adirondacks—the first accurate and detailed map of the region—and must have spent many happy hours poring over it, as he carefully noted the routes and highlights of some of his early expeditions.

He was also interested in the controversy then raging over laws restricting hunting and fishing; he had developed into an enlightened conservationist, as he had witnessed over his lifetime the bountiful supply of game dramatically dwindling.

GAME CONSERVATION

Although he no longer hunted, John's views were esteemed because of his reputation. He became involved in the struggle to place limits on deer hunting through the efforts of Charles Fenton of No. 4, who was very active in the game conservation movement. The battle concerned hunting seasons and use of hounds.

In 1877, a conservation law had finally been passed which banned hounding and limited deer hunting to just the fall months. However, these restrictions aroused such an outcry from hunting interests that, in 1879—only two years later—the Legislature reversed itself, and reverted to the former extended season (August 1st to January 1st). It also again permitted unrestricted use of hounds.[2]

Fenton opposed any hounding but recognized that political factors mitigated against acceptance of a total ban. Therefore, he proposed a compromise, i.e., amending the "dog clause" so that hounds could only be used in September, thereby avoiding "a great slaughter" as deer were much more apt to take to the water in October.[3] He sought John Constable's support for this position, and they exchanged letters in December 1880.

John responded cordially but cynically:

> ". . . As I have often told you, I have not the slightest hopes of honest, true sportsmen being able to check the destruction of deer . . . I have

observed a steady increase of the evil . . . The fate of the red deer and the red man is fixed . . . If you get up a petition to restrict the use of hounds to the last two weeks in September, I will sign it with pleasure . . ."[4]

SCHOLARLY STUDIES OF MAMMALS

In 1884, a book was published which attested to John's broad interest in animal studies and his acute powers of observation, as he had ranged through the Adirondacks in former years. Entitled *The Mammals of the Adirondack Region, Northeastern New York,*[5] it was the culmination of many years work. The author was Clinton Hart Merriam, an outstanding naturalist and a native of the Black River region, who had been John's friend and companion on some Adirondack trips. He was associated with the Smithsonian Institution.

Some of the material in Merriam's books had first been presented in a series of articles which appeared during the 1870s in *Forest and Stream*. In more scholarly form, most of it was delivered in lectures before the Linnean Society, and was then published in *The Transactions of the Linnean Society of New York* in 1882 and 1884.

Merriam often cited John Constable as an authority or as a source of unique information. These references are excerpted here; they give us a fascinating view of his keen interest in animal behavior:

Beaver: "Mr. John Constable has kindly presented me with the skull of a very large Beaver which was 'trapped by William Wood, in the fall of 1837, in a pond northwest of Indian Point on the Raquette.' Mr. Constable writes me that an old Indian, who had been unsuccesful in his attempts to capture this same Beaver, and who was about to leave this part of the Wilderness, told Wood where the animal was to be found. Wood carried his boat to the pond and paddled twice around it, searching carefully for signs without going ashore. At last he discovered fur upon the root of an old birch that projected into the water. Here he placed the trap, attached to a float, and on the second day found the Beaver in it."

Fisher: "In my Osteological Cabinet reposes the skull of a Fisher that measures five inches in length. It was presented to me by Mr. John Constable, who killed it between Stoney Lake and 'The Hollow,' near Independence River, during the early part of the winter of 1840. Mr. Constable tells me that it ascended a gigantic dead pine, the tip of which had broken off. The 'stub' of this tree was more than six feet through at the base, and upwards of an hundred and fifty feet in height. The Fisher climbed to the very top and lodged in a depression where the tip had broken off. He was shot but so lodged that he did not fall, and the tree had to be felled before he was secured. The pine was an unusually fine one—a straight pillar, tapering uniformly to the top, and so perpendicular and well-balanced that when the side choppings met it did not fall, and was with great difficulty overthrown. When it did finally tumble, and the cloud of snow that filled the air as it came crashing and thundering to the ground had cleared away, the Fisher was found to be dead. It proved to be in keeping with the tree it had climbed, for it was as large as an Otter, and by far the biggest Fisher that Mr. Constable, or the old hunter with him, had ever seen."

Marten and Hare: "Mr. John Constable has narrated to me a most interesting and vivid account of an affray that he once witnessed, in company with his brother, Mr. Stevenson Constable, between a Marten and a Great Northern Hare. The Marten, generally so meek and docile in appearance, assumed the savage mien and demeanor of a fierce tiger, as it attacked and slew the luckless hare—an animal of several times its own size and weight. And even after the poor hare was dead the Marten's fury did not abate, and he angrily jerked and twisted the lifeless body from side to side, as if to reek vengeance, for sins never committed, upon the defenceless body of his innocent victim. So intent was he upon this deed of carnage that he was utterly oblivious to the human spectators, who put an end to the scene by driving a bullet through his obdurate pate."

". . . Mr. Constable tells me that when the hunter discovers a Marten climbing about amidst the tree tops he has only to whistle, and the inquisitive animal will stop and peer down at him, affording an excellent shot."

Deer: "Mr. John Constable tells me that he once shot a Deer in the act of browsing among the lichens that clung to a fallen tree-top. The animal was standing on its hind-legs, with its fore-feet resting upon a huge limb, and was reaching up for the lichens."

Moose: "Early in March, 1851, Mr. John Constable and his brother Stevenson killed two Moose near the head of Independence Creek, in Herkimer County. They killed their last Moose in March, 1856, west of Charley's Pond, in Hamilton County. Mr. Constable writes me:

'I never recur to those hunts with any satisfaction, for much as I enjoyed at the time the tramp of more than 100 miles on snowshoes, the camping in the snow, the intense excitement of the search and pursuit, I must ever regret the part I have taken unwittingly in exterminating this noble animal from our forests. Were I younger, I would assist in reinstating them . . .'"

Porcupine: "When feeding upon lily-pads, along the borders of water-courses they sometimes utter extraordinary noises, and occasionally quarrels arise for the possession of some log which affords them easy access to the coveted plants. At Beaver Lake, in Lewis County, Mr. John Constable once witnessed an encounter during which one of the combatants was tumbled in the water. The animals did not attempt to bite, but growled and snarled and pushed."

YOUNG JAMES' 1883 ADIRONDACK TRIP

Although John was no longer able to go camping in his beloved Adirondacks, he could still enjoy such trips vicariously, through his sons' activities. In 1883, he wrote a long letter to James, his younger son, who was planning an extensive Adirondack trip, possibly with his brother Casimir, and had sought his father's advice and assistance. John wrote with enthusiasm, suggesting a choice of itineraries and arrangements for boats and guide, as well as a list of provisions and supplies:

"Wednesday, 27th June, 1883

My darling Son,

I have written to you of my journey up, and have now been in your cupboard in the hall. Find

- 39 paper cartridges or shells (new)
- 48 nickel shells, all caped [sic] and I have 100 of them, charged with powder. Shall I fire them in my gun and clean them nicely?
- Miss Shipman's straw hat, and a nice felt stiff skull hat of your own, with ventilation
- 2 English barred woolen shorts with collars and jackets
- 3 cans of powder caps
- 2 cans of __?__

Send me the key of your private closet in the woodshed.

I have a nice teapot which packs into a small camp kettle, with all your tea in a bag in the teapot and various towels to be packed around the teapot.

I have made a frying pan of one of the pressed plates. The handle screws on and takes off to pack. It deserves a patent. You want one Rod and reel and ought to have a fish basket, not too large; it is handy to carry lunch, fishing tackle, etc. Shall I give you a light axe with sheath on it?

I have a nice cardigan for you and Cas. I enclose a list to use when you come to pack."

"June 30th

I do not hear from Almerin Higby to whom I wrote to bring in our boats, so I think he must have gone for them and may be here any day . . ."

"1st of July

. . . Received letter from Almerin Higby this morning saying that 'Will go out today myself, and have the boats at your home by 2nd of July if I meet with no accident.' I am glad of this, as he is very ingenious and very careful.

I think a good trip would be to let me send Boat and Luggage to Arnolds [at Old Forge] & drive you both down, very easy to the Moose River, dine you there, and send you trotting out to Arnold's that morning to meet your boat. You could go that evening up to Alonzo Wood's [a hotel on Fourth Lake, run by one of Josiah Wood's sons] & next day . . . wend your way through the Chain of Lakes to the Raquette. Stop where you feel inclined. Turn up your boat and camp at night or visit some of the hotels. Investigate and visit old spots on the Raquette and cross over to Rock Pond and Little Tuppers. Up the River to Stoney Creek, then to Upper Saranac, Round Pond, Lower Saranac. Thence to its headwaters, and leave boat and pack and walk [to see] Sadie [his Uncle James' wife who was in a sanitarium near Saranac]. Could sell your boat about here probably. Thence by stage to Paul Smiths, Meacham's Lake to Malone. Good roads and good stage. Could stop at Paul's one day and take boat and visit the handsome cottages and camps on the Upper Saint Regis. In this case I could send one trunk around to meet you at Paul Smith's, or you could confine your trip to the Chain of Lakes, Raquette, Blue M., across from Raquette—Crooked and Forked Lake—Little Tuppers down to Big Tuppers, Up the River for Long Lake, thence up that lake and back to Arnold's, leaving your boat there in Mr. Barrett's or Paul Crego's care.

I send you a list of what I would take for such a trip. You can replenish your sugar, pork, etc. and buy bread in twenty places. Those things with a red cross are all arranged in your woodshed room in nice order. The celery seed is to flavor your soup occasionally. I have a nice padlock with two keys for your boat, and 2 light India Rubbers to sleep on at night and for when you have to get out in the rain. I will get what things I can together and weigh them. 2 blankets weigh nearly 9 pounds. I have a knapsack all ready—camp kettle and tea pot, 2½ pounds.

We commenced haying yesterday. I hope this weather will continue . . . We expect . . . Uncle William by Saturday . . . Also Uncle James. I long to see you my dear Boy. Mother hugs you.

Father"[6]

In 1988, I showed the foregoing letter to the late William K. Verner, an authority on early Adirondack history, and he was particularly interested in John's suggestion of selling a boat at the end of such a trip. He had never heard of that practice before and termed it "a novel but practical idea."

This letter is the last known written record of any major Adirondack expeditions by members of the Constable family.

John Constable died in 1887. His wife, Julia Pierrepont Constable, lived on at Constable Hall until her death in 1898.

CASIMIR'S LEGACY

Casimir, John's eldest son, inherited Constable Hall upon his father's death, only five years after he had married his first cousin, Jennie. They had no children. Primarily an intellectual, rather than a sportsman, Casimir expanded the already fine library at Constable Hall, adding many old and rare books, some first editions dating to the 15th century.

Casimir did not endear himself to the workmen on the estate. They found him to be a hard taskmaster, a perfectionist, exacting in his demands and impatient with any flaws. However, they acknowledged that he was a fair man: he would not allow nighttime work, lest they be short of energy in the mornings.

With the help of his brother James, an architect, Casimir began modernization of the Hall

John Pierrepont Constable Sr.
(1888-1926)
Engineer and Inventor
He inherited Constable Hall in 1923.

and introduced indoor plumbing. Renovations utilized a workshop which the brothers had established in an outbuilding years earlier; it included a massive workbench and custom-made lathe. Casimir also had a small forge. After Casimir died in 1905, Jennie lived on in the Hall until her own demise in 1923.

JOHN PIERREPONT CONSTABLE, SR.

Ownership of Constable Hall then passed to their nephew, John Pierrepont Constable (James' son). A graduate of the Massachusetts Institute of Technology, he was a brilliant naval and electrical engineer. After his graduation, he was employed by Thomas Alva Edison as chief engineer for several years and thereafter worked for the General Electric Company. His creative mind produced over 100 inventions, of which several were patented. He added modern improvements at Constable Hall, including an upstairs bathroom, a furnace, and a fire hose standpipe, which is credited with saving the Hall when a fire later broke out in a stovepipe and chimney.

Unfortunately, he lived only three years after inheriting the Hall. In 1926, when working with an electric company in Glens Falls, New York, he was killed in a trolley accident at the age of 38. His young wife was left to raise three small children by herself, and to cope with the end of the family fortune as a result of the Great Depression.

THE CURRENT JOHN CONSTABLE

Their son, John P. Constable Jr., was ten years old at the time of his father's death, living at the Hall and attending the Lowville Academy nearby. Life thereafter was difficult for him and his two sisters. Their mother took them to Europe to carry on a family tradition of foreign education. He attended French boarding schools for two years and was then sent to a preparatory school in New England. As a youth he seldom had time to spend at Constable Hall except during summer vacations; for years thereafter, he regretted having had so little opportunity to know people in the area around Constableville.

John received title to the Hall in 1936 when he was twenty-one years old. For this John (the fifth shown on the family tree in this book), the inheritance of Constable Hall has been more burden than pleasure. The estate was run down, encumbered with accumulated debts and all remnants of the family fortune had long been exhausted. He worked many years to pay off creditors, although he seldom was able to reside at the Hall. During those difficult years, he found it easier, on periodic visits home, to live in a small cottage on the estate grounds, which could be more easily maintained and heated.

During World War II, John served in the Air Force, enlisting as a private, and emerging as a captain. By this time he was married (to Marion Bisnett of Watertown, New York) and had started a family and a new career. Like his father and grandfather, he was interested in technical matters; he established a sales and service dealership in water pumps and other small machinery in Watertown.

THE RESTORATION OF CONSTABLE HALL

Postwar maintenance costs forced John to permanently relinquish Constable Hall as a family home in 1947. However, he was determined to preserve the mansion for its historic value and succeeded in doing so by refusing several commercial offers. Instead, he sold the estate in 1949 to benefactors Mr. and Mrs. Harry Lewis and her sister, Mrs. Grace Cornwall.

They restored it lovingly, and turned it over to the newly-founded Constable Hall Association—a non-profit, educational organization, operating under the jurisdiction of the New York State Education Department.

Constable Hall is listed on the National Register of Historic Places as a Historic House Museum. It displays the lifestyle of several generations and their varied possessions accumulated during the 18th and 19th centuries. Obtrusive 20th century additions, like the upstairs bathroom, have been removed.

Although some original furnishings from Constable Hall had been sold, most were replaced with items of equivalent age and value or appropriate replicas. Some old and valuable antiques and other family heirlooms still occupy the 16 gracious rooms. These include pieces of furniture by Chippendale, Sheraton and Duncan Phyfe, Sevre china once owned by Napoleon Bonaparte, a chair which belonged to Amerigo Vespucci, Marie Antoinette's satin sewing table, and fine weavings, glassware and china.

The main floor contains a central hall, dining room with pantry, drawing room, game room and library. The oldest family treasures are on display in the original, fire-proof land office of the west wing, where the first American John Constable—immigrant during the French and Indian War—is remembered by his surgical instruments and Commission in the British Army. Documents related to William Constable I's land speculations are also on display, as well as an old safe and locking mail pouch.

The gun collection is stored in the game room; it includes some old and rare rifles, shotguns and pistols, most of which were owned by John Constable III. Some of his hunting trophies decorate the main hall.

Upstairs, the second floor is composed of four bedrooms, which still contain some original furnishings. In the basement are the kitchen, cold cellars and Indian room, which now houses a gift shop.

Outside in the back are the workshop and former carriage house and servant quarters, now used for storage and exhibits. The formal garden of one and a half acres is notable for retaining its design of the Georgian/American Baroque period, and current flowers probably derive from the original 1820 plantings of roses, oriental poppies, lemon lilies and southernwood. At the center is a sundial designed and constructed by James Constable in 1872. A blackthorn hedge surrounds the garden.

The Drawing Room at Constable Hall

The furnishings, largely early 19th century, also include more modern furniture in an eclectic and comfortable arrangement.

The Library at Constable Hall

The Master Bedroom has a Chippendale canopied four poster bed. It is believed to be one of only six made in America. At its foot stands an intricately-carved bedding chest, made in Tuscany in the 14th century. The crib, used until 1966, nestled many generations of Constable babies.

The Dining Room contains many valuable heirlooms. The antique grandfather clock was made in Scotland in 1710, and is still running. The sideboard and cellarette were created by Duncan Phyfe. A Sevre tea service is marked "Chateau de Tuilleries" and some china is embellished with Napoleon Bonaparte's monogram. There is also a Wedgewood teapot and William I's china dinner service from Nanking.

Constable Hall is open for visitors several days weekly from late May to mid-October; it also hosts an annual Antique and Crafts Show, historical lecture series, candlelight concerts, crafts classes and special exhibits.

THE PISTOL COLLECTION

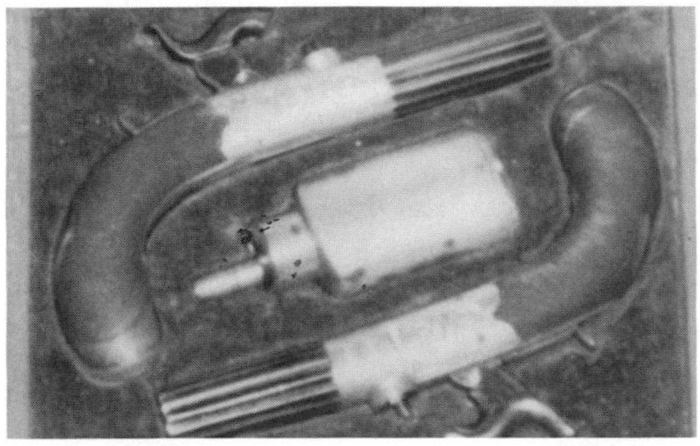

Cased pair of silver-mounted percussion screw-barrel pocket pistols were made by J. Meredith in England, probably mid-19th century. Such guns were usually carried for self-defense, rather than duelling.

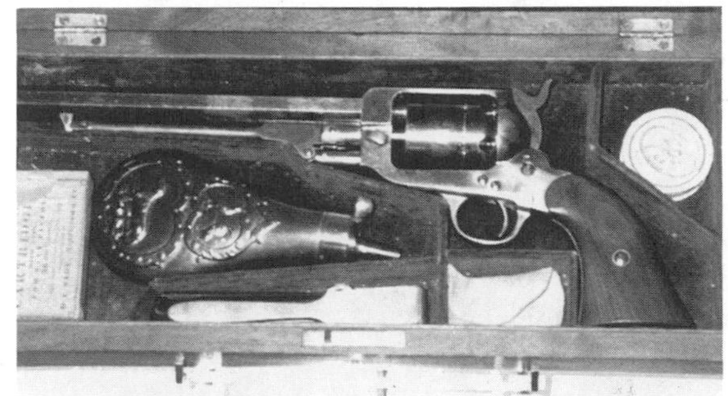

Whitney Navy Revolver, .36 caliber, dates from about 1860. It was given to John Constable by his cousin David (son of John's Uncle John, William Jr.'s brother), who was then in military service. It had been presented to David by the inventor, who deemed it superior to the Colt revolver, then in common usage. The gun, with case and accessories, is in unusually good condition.

Pair of smooth-bore, muzzle-loading pistols were made by Van Wart and Son in London. Small silver ovals on back of stocks are engraved "J.C." on one and "1835" on the other. Although duelling size and style, these probably were used as saddle pistols. They are among the oldest guns in the collection.

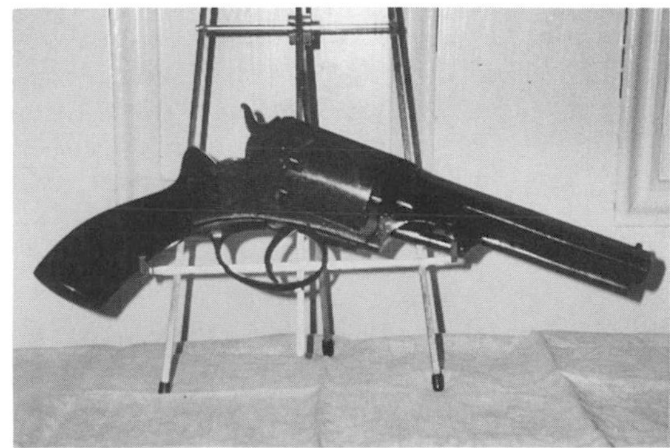

Adams Percussion Revolver was imported from England, probably during the Civil War. It too was useful as a saddle gun.

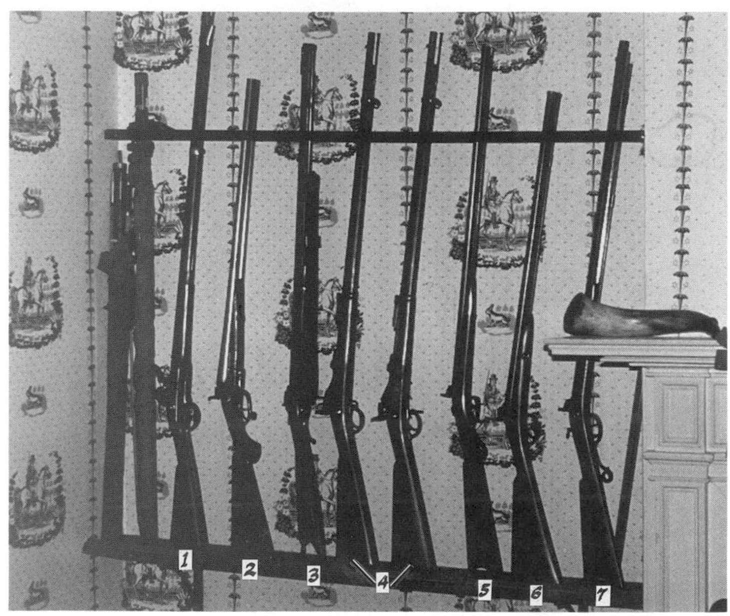

The Gun Collection at Constable Hall is stored in the Game Room, where a special rack holds seven long-barreled models. Most of them belonged to John Constable, gentleman sportsman of the third generation. (Photo by V. E. Pilcher)

1. **U.S. Flintlock Musket, Model 1795, Type III** is the oldest gun in the collection. Made in Springfield, Massachusetts in 1813, it was a regulation military arm commonly issued to militia members. It may have been used by William Jr. and his sons for hunting game. This gun became obsolete before the Civil War and was stored for many decades in the Carriage House behind Constable Hall, until rescued from oblivion by the current John Constable.

2. **Double-barreled, 10 gauge, breech-loading shotgun** is a fancy, rare, heavily-ornamented piece, used for shooting fowl and small game. Manufactured by Stephen Middleton in England, its ornate Damascus barrels are engraved in a stylish pattern typical of the 1860s or 1870s. The name "S. E. Bugbee" is engraved upon the hammer, on the right side of the plate.

3. **Swiss Military-Style Rifle**, a .50 caliber muzzle-loader, dates from the middle of the 19th century and was probably acquired by John when living in Switzerland in 1857 and '58. It was useful for target practice (a popular Swiss sport in which John probably participated) but not for hunting.

4. **Two U.S. Army Rifles, Model 1884, .45-70** caliber, are of the type called "trap door Springfields" because the breechblock hinged up and forward, for loading. The Army used such rifles through the Spanish American War and after World War I sold them off as military surplus. Although deemed heavy and clumsy today, they may have been useful for local hunting.

5. **James and Ferriss Double-Barreled Hunting Rifle** is a muzzle-loader, made in Utica between 1851 and 1854. Normally the gun was special-ordered, and was largely hand-made by skilled craftsmen, with weight and balance tailored to the specifications of its buyer.

6. **Double-barreled shotgun** was an early muzzle-loader, particularly useful for shooting partridges, doves and small game.

7. **Cast Steel Muzzle-Loading Rifle** is one of the oldest pieces. It was specially built for John Constable, probably by Hiram Felshaw of Constableville. Its history is something of a mystery, as a brass plate is now affixed to its stock which may bear inaccurate information. It states: "The old cast steel rifle made in Constableville for John Constable, 1835." However, cast steel rifle barrels were probably not made before the early 1840s. It is possible that the plate was attached many years later, when the original date of manufacture had been forgotten or was unknown. In any case, it has a fine stock made of curly maple, and a lock bearing J. Dana's name (Dana was a Utica hardware dealer who imported gunlocks from Birmingham, England). This gun probably accompanied John on many of his Adirondack hunting trips.

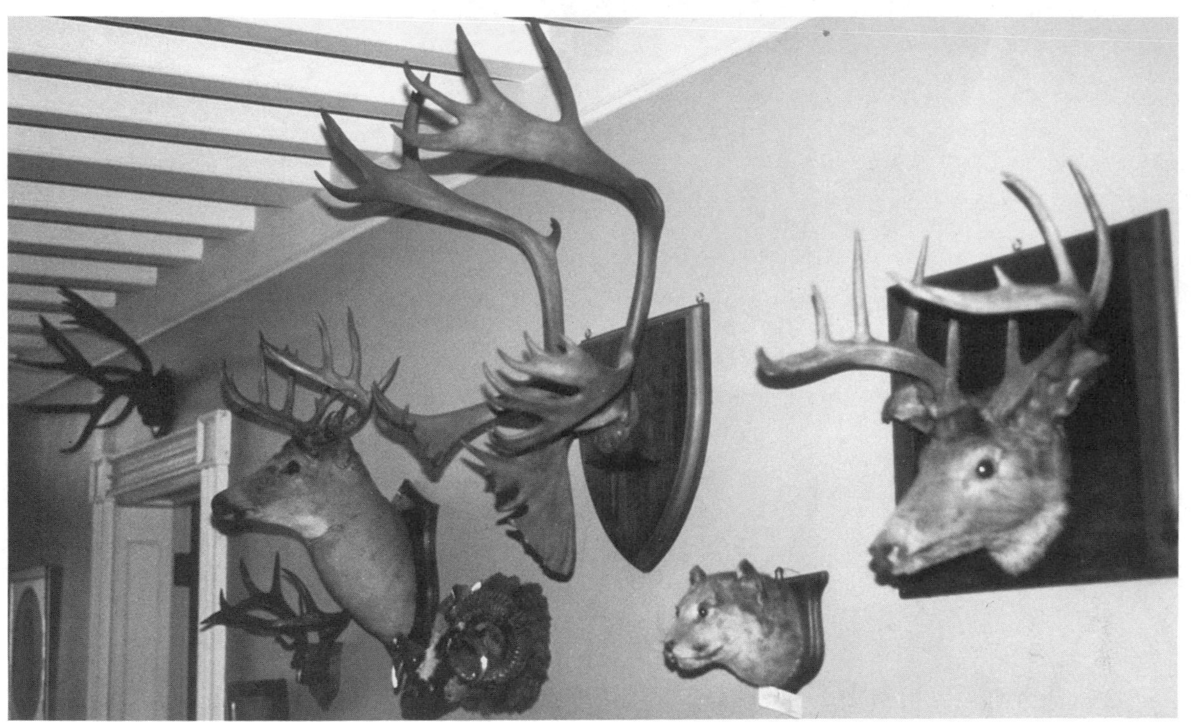

Some of John Constable's hunting trophies decorate the main hall. (Photo by V.E. Pilcher)

The "Registered Flyer" was a 19th century target practice device. The whirling target—a metal wing on a spool—resembled a bird. It was launched into the air by holding the handle, while pulling the string which was wound around the wheel. Like modern trapshooting, practice shooting with a shotgun enabled a hunter to perfect his aim and timing. The device probably dates from the latter quarter of the 19th century and it still works today, although it is in fragile condition. (Photo by V.E. Pilcher)

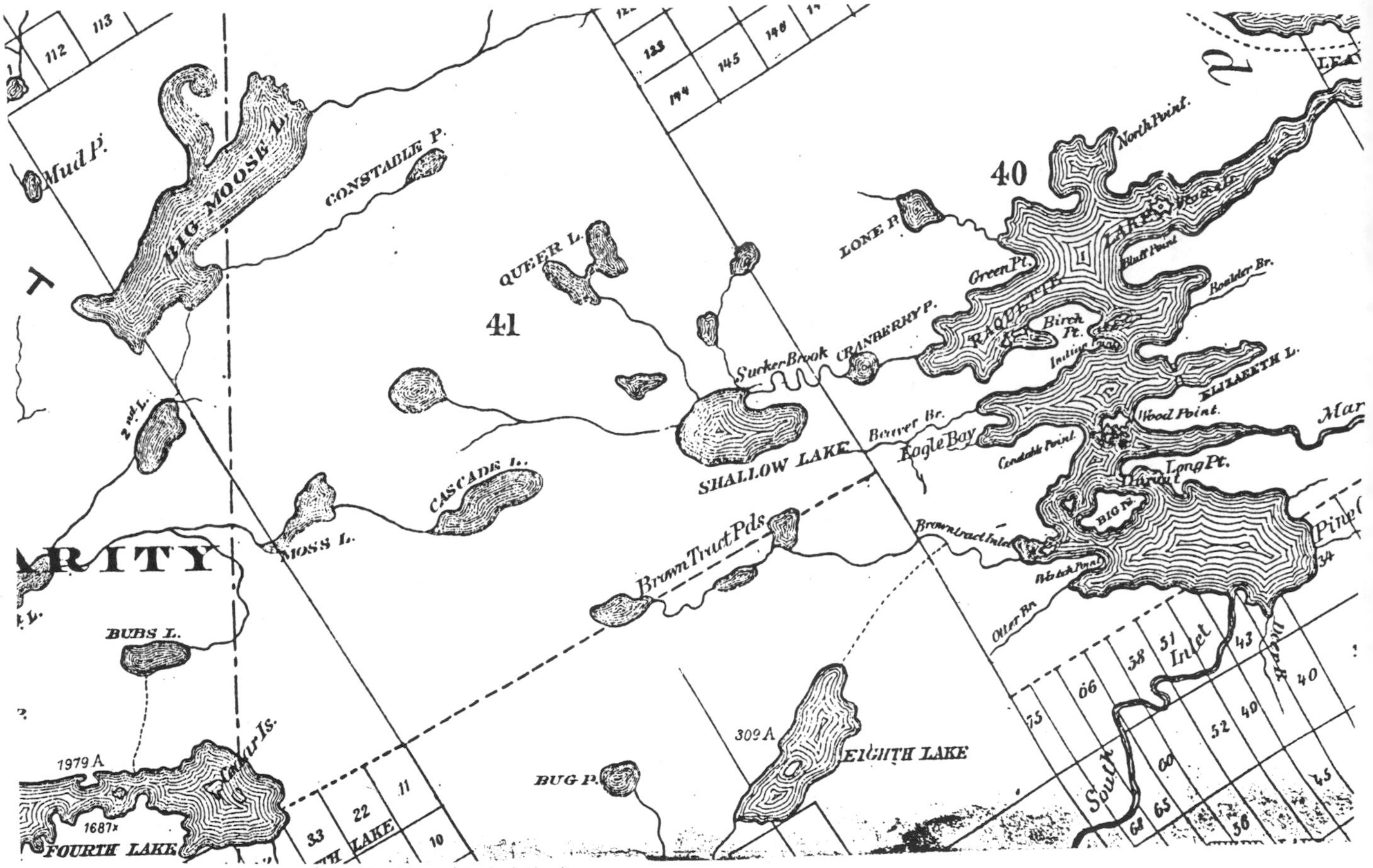

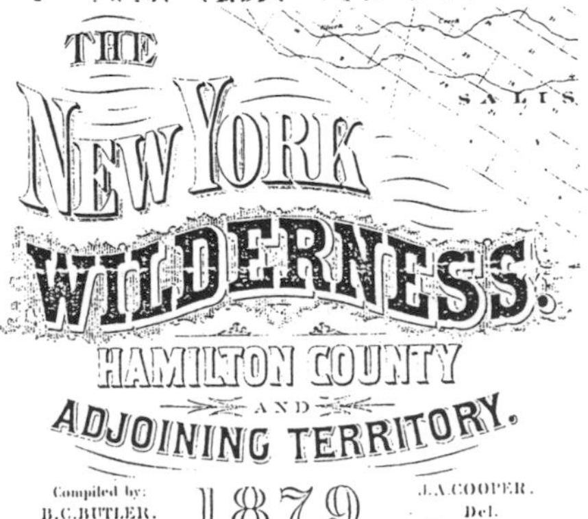

The earliest map showing Constable Pond and Constable Creek dates from 1879. It is B.C. Butler's Map of the New York Wilderness. (Courtesy of The Adirondack Museum)

John Pierrepont Constable Jr.
Visiting at Big Moose Lake in 1989.
(Photo by V.E. Pilcher)

CONTEMPORARY HISTORY

John P. Jr. is now a hale and hearty man in his mid-seventies, retired but very active; he and his wife still reside in Watertown. They are proud of many family photos and mementos which adorn their home, including a chair once owned by Marie Antoinette. Family papers and photos which he inherited are carefully kept in good order.

Since the inception of the Constable Hall Association, John has worked in various capacities, most importantly as president and fund-raiser. He has supervised restoration and repairs and preserved family treasures and estate records. He still expends many hours weekly working on funding proposals; recent grants have paid for roof and plumbing repairs and part-time curator services.

John's four children, Jane, Martha, Mary and John P. III, all share his interest in family history. Martha has written a booklet dealing with the history and treasures of Constable Hall (from which much information in this chapter is derived), and Mary presides over its gift shop.

These current generations of Constables only visit the Adirondacks occasionally, although they do enjoy outdoor activities. John owns a waterfront camp on Lake Ontario at Sackett's Harbor and a small hunting camp on the Tug Hill Plateau, above Constableville—in New York State's Lesser Wilderness. Like his great uncle of the same name, he too relishes a winter tramp through the snow, the excitement of hunting deer and the rigors of winter camping.

In the summer of 1989, John and I made a little bit of history together. He visited me and my husband at our cabin on Big Moose Lake—at the opposite end of the lake from where his great-grandfather and great-uncles once had a campsite.

We had the extreme pleasure of showing him a part of the Adirondacks named after his family. Constable Creek flows into the south bay of Big Moose Lake, and Constable Pond is located some two miles upstream. He had not known of their existence until I'd shown him a map of this area.

Despite extensive research, I have not been able to determine how or when these waters were named. The earliest map I have uncovered which designates Constable Pond is an 1879 Hamilton County Map compiled by B.C. Butler. Although it errs in regard to the shape of Big Moose Lake and the location of the county line which bisects it, it does correctly indicate the creek and pond. Stoddard's 1880 and later maps are more accurate.

Constable Pond
(Photo by V. E. Pilcher)

We took John for a short walk on the state hiking trail which runs along Constable Creek toward West Mountain on Raquette Lake, 12 miles distant. Regrettably, limited time precluded our walking the full two miles to Constable Pond—a small, narrow lake which has doubled its length during this century because of dam-building by its resident beavers. Now nearly a mile long, it is ringed by tamarack swamps and fed by outlets from Pigeon Lake and Chub Pond. All of this area is state-owned land.

John signed the trail register, writing in a clear hand: "John Constable of Constableville." We regretted that such registers had not existed in the last century, which might have recorded the visits of his great-grandfather, great uncles and perhaps other members of the family.

Although no one knows which Constable the pond and stream were named for, we do know that William, John, James and Stevenson traversed this area frequently during the mid 19th century on their sporting trips, followed by their sons as they became old enough for camping. It is probable that they, their friends or guides named the waters of this little scenic valley after one or all of the four brothers.

Now part of the Pigeon Lake Wilderness Area, Constable Pond and Constable Creek remain as wild and beautiful as they were in the 1800s. Today they constitute a fitting memorial to members of the family who ranged so often and so widely through the central Adirondacks.

Constable Creek
(Photo by V.E. Pilcher)

Notes

Chapter I: The Early Constables: Founders and Fortunes

Biographical information on the Constable Family derives mainly from the following sources:

Abbott Low Moffat, "The Pierreponts, 1806-1962. The American Forbears and the Descendants of Hezekiah Beers Pierpont and Anna Maria Constable." (Typescript, Washington, D.C., 1962) A copy is owned by John P. Constable Jr. Particular items noted from pp. 16-19, 29, 33.

Anna Maria Constable Pierrepont's "Recollections" which were recorded informally by family members when she was 74 years old. These are several handwritten pages among John P. Constable Jr.'s family papers.

William A. Davis, "William Constable, New York Merchant and Land Speculator." Ph.D. Thesis, Harvard University, 1955.

Gretchen Sullivan Sorin, "Constable Hall: An Historic Furnishing Plan," (1984). Typescript at Constable Hall.

Letters & papers currently in the private possession of John P. Constable Jr. of Watertown, New York.

Constable-Pierrepont Family Papers, Collection at New York City Public Library. [The Constable Family roots in Schenectady have long been obscure, partially due to a mistake upon the acquisition sheet of the Constable Papers in the New York Public Library, on which *Syracuse* was mistakenly listed as their home.]

Pertinent records at the Schenectady County Historical Society include:

The Harriet Paige "Diaries," 2 Vol. Typescript copy from original.

Willis T. Hanson, *History of St. George's Church in the City of Schenectady* (Schenectady, N.Y., 1919.) Historical records based upon this book include family name worksheets by Howard A. McConville and "List of Schenectady Slave Holders" abstracted by Elsa Church.

Court Martial Proceedings of Thomas B. Clinch, Dec. 5, 1805. (The name of James Constable is included in the Company List.)

Standard local histories by Jonathan Pearson, Joel Monroe and Howell and Munsell.

"Street Book" scrapbooks by Jonathan Pearson.

Information re Sir William Johnson and Dr. Constable is derived from the following:

William Johnson, *Collected Papers of Sir William Johnson*, 13 vol. ed. by James Sullivan (Albany, University of the State of New York, 1921-1962) Vol. 13, pp. 238, 409.

William L. Stone, *Reminiscences of Saratoga and Ballston* (New York: R. Worthington, 1880) pp. 6-11.

Endnotes

Chapter I: The Early Constables: Founders and Fortunes

1 Ewerettta was also the name of their first daughter, who was born in 1750 and died in infancy. This unusual name was derived from their maternal grandmother's family name "Ewer." Ewerettta is pronounced with a *v* sound as in *Eve*.

2 The year of James' birth varies in different sources. 1769 is inscribed on his tombstone, but 1768 is indicated as a baptismal date in the records of St. George's Church in Schenectady. According to family biographer Moffat, James was 12 years younger than William ("The Pierreponts," p. 18), which would indicate a birth in 1764, but on the preceding page Moffat stated James was 16 years old in 1774, which would mean he was born in 1758. Compounding the confusion, James' niece, Anna Constable Pierrepont, stated in her "Recollections" that James was born in 1763.

3 Franklin B. Hough, *History of Lewis County*, 2nd ed. (Syracuse: D. Mason and Co., 1883) p. 564.

4 Edward Dean Sullivan, *Benedict Arnold—Military Racketeer*, (New York: Vanguard Press, 1932) pp. 244, 245.

5 Hough, *Lewis County*, p. 565.

6 See Edith Pilcher, *Castorland* (Harrison, N.Y.: Harbor Hill Books, 1985).

7 The map is in Box #144 among the Constable Papers at the New York Public Library.

8 Letter owned by John P. Constable Jr.

9 Letter from James Constable in New York City to James Forsyth in London, Jan. 20, 1804. Box #17, Constable Papers, New York Public Library.

10 Ibid.

11 Moffat, "The Pierreponts", p. 19.

12 The children were named John, Gilbert Livingston, David, Mary and William Bell.

13 Letter from James Constable to James Forsyth, April 28, 1807.

14 Diary of John Brown Francis, Sept. 15, 1816. (Notes are courtesy of Henry A. L. Brown, author of *John Brown's Tract, Lost Adirondack Empire*.)

15 Letter from Daniel McCormick to William Constable Jr., Oct. 22, 1812.

16 These sentiments were recollected in 1882 by sons William and John and were recorded, with notation, by grandson Casimir.

17 Diary of John Brown Francis, Sept. 15, 1816.

Chapter II: Early Adirondack Explorations (1830s and 1840s)

1 Edward McVickar and William Constable Breed, *Memoranda relating to the McVickar family in America* (New York: 1906)

[An interesting sidelight on family relationships is revealed in a minor controversy over a Christmas visit by one of the Constables' prominent relatives, Clement Clarke Moore, author of the famous poem "A Visit from St. Nicholas," also known as "The Night Before Christmas."

Moore was Professor of Oriental and Greek Literature at the General Theological Seminary in New York City. He was related on both sides of the family, Constables and McVickars.

Members of the Constable family have long believed the poem was composed at Constable Hall on Christmas Eve in 1822, when Moore was supposed to have visited in order to comfort his newly-widowed cousin Eliza and her five children. The interior window shutters, described in the poem, are like those at Constable Hall, as is the fireplace. His "right jolly old elf" is said to have been patterned on Pieter, an elderly Dutch caretaker at the estate. This story was described and illustrated in *Adirondack Life* in December 1988 by Margot Badran, entitled ". . . and all through the house . . ."

However charming, the story is contradicted by evidence from other sources, as well as the fact that in those days the Constables did not habitually spend winters at the Hall. I am indebted to Casimir de Rham of Cambridge, Massachusetts for sending me clippings which give an entirely different version of events. (He is a namesake and distant relative of the youth who accompanied John and Stevenson Constable on their 1836 trip through the Adirondacks.)

Moore was living in the Chelsea section of New York at the time the poem was composed, and one source claims that his Dutch handyman and driver, also named Pieter, provided a model for his vision of Santa Claus, as they drove about on Christmas Eve, delivering family gifts. In this version, the poem was composed for Moore's own children, eagerly awaiting their father's return at home. (Edmund A. Prentice, *Buzz* [Columbia University Alumni Periodical], Dec. 1953, pp. 3, 4.)

A related article concerning the poem's creation, written by Raymond Schuessler and entitled "Clement Moore and 'The Night Before Christmas'" appeared recently in *Heritage* (Nov./Dec., 1990), a periodical of The New York Historical Association. It agrees with the foregoing and amplifies the derivation of Santa Claus from the Dutch Sinterklaus.

All sources agree that the poem was first published anonymously at Christmas, 1823 in the *Troy Sentinel*, submitted to the paper by another cousin of Moore who resided in Troy. Years later it was acknowledged by its author, and published in collections of Moore's poetry.

One of those volumes, with an affectionate inscription by the author, has been enjoyed and cherished by generations of Constable children.]

2 Letter from John Constable in Switzerland to his Mother at Constable Hall, June 15, 1857: ". . . Perhaps James could help keep the house and attend to affairs if the climate is not too much for him . . ."

3 Paul G. Bourcier, *History in the Mapping* (Blue Mountain Lake, N.Y.: The Adirondack Museum, 1986) p. 61.

4 Alfred L. Donaldson, *A History of the Adirondacks*, 2 Vol. (New York: Century Co., 1921; reprint ed. Harrison, N.Y.: Harbor Hill Books, 1977), Vol. I, pp. 42, 43.

Harold Hochschild, *Township 34* (New York: 1952), p. 250.

Ruth Timm, *Raquette Lake* (Utica, N.Y.: North Country Books, 1989), p. 4.

5 Joseph F. Grady, *The Adirondacks, Fulton Chain—Big Moose Region* (Old Forge, N.Y.: North Country Books, 1953), p. 77.

6 Ibid. p. 76 and Jeptha R. Simms, *Trappers of New York* (Albany: J. Munsell, 1871; reprint ed. Harrison, N.Y.: Harbor Hill Books, 1980), p. 208.

7 Farrand N. Benedict [attributed], "The Wilds of Northern New York," *Putnam Magazine* (Sept. 1854), pp. 263-270.

8 New York State: *First Annual Report of the Commissioners of Fisheries, Game and Forests* (Albany: Wynkoop Hallenbeck Crawford Co., 1896), p. 111.

9 Kenneth Durant, *Guide-Boat Days and Ways* (Blue Mountain Lake, N.Y.: The Adirondack Museum, 1963), p. 17.

10 Kenneth and Helen Durant, *The Adirondack Guide-boat* (Blue Mountain Lake, N.Y.: The Adirondack Museum, 1980), p. 14.

11 Information on Higby the Hunter is derived from:

Clinton D. Higby, Compiler, *Edward Higby and his Descendants* (Boston: T. R. Marvin and Son, 1927), p. 275.

Hough, *Lewis County*, pp. 505, 506, 544.

Census Records of Lewis County to 1850, Towns of Turin and Watson.

E. R. Wallace, *Descriptive Guide to the Adirondacks and Handbook of Travel*, 5th ed. (New York: Forest and Stream Publishing Co., 1876), p. 261.

Almeron Higby, Diary. May 12, 1876. In possession of Charles Bunke, Watson Town Historian.

Hochschild, *Township 34*, p. 165.

W. Hudson Stephens, *Historical Notes on the Settlement at No. 4, Brown's Tract, in Watson, Lewis County, N.Y.* (Utica, N.Y.: Roberts, 1864), p. 9.

12 Jervis McEntee, Diary (typescript) at Adirondack Museum Library, p. 16.

13 Stephens, *Historical Notes . . .*, p. 6.

14 Information on Wood and Beach is derived from:

Grady, *The Adirondacks*, p. 77.

Simms, *Trappers of New York*, p. 209.

Ted Aber and Stella King, *The History of Hamilton County* (Lake Pleasant, N.Y.: Great Wilderness Books, 1965), pp. 750, 751, 786-788.

Timm, *Raquette Lake*, pp. 12, 13.

Ebenezer Emmons, "Fifth Annual Report of the Survey of the Second Geological District," *Document* #150 of the Assembly of the State of New York, 1841, p. 122.

Jervis McEntee, "The Lakes of the Wilderness," (edited, unsigned version of his diary) *The Great Republic Monthly* (April 1859), p. 346.

William James Stillman, "Sketchings," *The Crayon* (Nov. 28, 1855), p. 344.

Joel T. Headley, *The Adirondack or Life in the Woods* (New York: Baker and Scribner, 1849; reprint ed. Harrison, N.Y.: Harbor Hill Books, 1982), pp. 226, 231, 232.

Hochschild, *Township 34*, p. 155, 170H (Addendum to Chapter 13).

Chapter III: First Ladies Expedition to the Woods

1 Donaldson, *History of the Adirondacks*, Vol. I, p. 125.

2 Hochschild, *Township 34*, p. 165.

3 By 1855 William Constable III owned 100 acres on Constable Point, according to the 1855 trip account mentioned in Chapter IV.

4 McEntee, Diary typescript at The Adirondack Museum Library, p. 51.

5 McEntee, "The Lakes of the Wilderness," p. 347.

6 Hochschild, *Township 34*, p. 166.

7 I am indebted to Professor Warder H. Cadbury for elucidating this puzzle for me and directing me to the above references.

8 Donaldson, *History of the Adirondacks*, Vol. I, pp. 132, 133.
Also Nathaniel Sylvester, *Historical Sketches of Northern New York and the Adirondack Wilderness* (Troy, N.Y.: William H. Young, 1877; reprint ed.: Harrison, N.Y.: Harbor Hill Books, 1973), p. 190.

9 McEntee, Diary, p. 1.

10 Donaldson, *History of the Adirondacks*, Vol. I, p. 132.

11 Wallace, *Descriptive Guide to the Adirondacks*, 5th ed. , p. 27.

12 *Journal and Republican*, Lowville N.Y. May 27, 1965. Courtesy of Faye K. Brown of Syracuse, a summer resident of No. 4, who allowed me to copy some photos and news clippings concerning the Fenton House.

13 McEntee, "Lakes of the Wilderness," p. 337.

Chapter IV: Adventures in the 1850s

1 Abner Leavenworth Diary, entry for August 22, 1851, pp. 72 and 73. Microfilm at The Adirondack Museum Library. I am indebted to Warder Cadbury for informing me of this notation.

2 William R. Marleau, *Big Moose Station* (Big Moose, N.Y.: Marleau Family Press, 1986), p. 12.

3 The date of this expedition, 1855, was deduced by Kenneth Durant and elucidated in a letter to Warder Cadbury, dated September 19, 1963.

4 Higby, *Higby Descendants*, p. 275.

5 Wallace, *Descriptive Guide to the Adirondacks*, p. 261.

6 McEntee, "Lakes of the Wilderness," p. 337.

7 McEntee, Diary, p. 3.

8 McEntee, "Lakes of the Wilderness," p. 338.

9 Sylvestor, *Historical Sketches*, pp. 192-195.

10 Stephens, *Settlement at No. 4*, pp. 23 and 24.

11 These letters are among family papers owned by John P. Constable Jr. of Watertown.

12 "Alph," "Games and Game Places in the Adirondack Regions," *Spirit of the Times*, April 17, 1858, p. 99.

13 Augustus Low later became owner of a forest empire of his own (some 40,000 acres of lakes and forests in the Bog River area of the Adirondacks,* just north of William Seward Webb's Nehasane estate). Low's Lake is named after him.

* Paul Jamieson, *Adirondack Canoe Waters, North Flow* (Glens Falls: Adirondack Mountain Club, Inc., 1975) pp. 106-108.

See also F. Mark Clark, "The Low Dynasty," *St. Lawrence County Historical Association Quarterly*, January 1974, pp. 9-15.

14 William G. Low, *Some Recollections for his Children and Grandchildren* (New York: G.P. Putnam Sons, 1909), pp. 69, 70.

Chapter V: The 1860s: Passing Campers and a New Generation

1 Albert Bigelow, "Adirondacks of 1858 and 1859," *Forest and Stream* (Oct. 5, 1912), pp. 423, 424.

2 Warder H. Cadbury, *Arthur Fitzwilliam Tait, Artist in the Adirondacks* (Newark: University of Delaware Press, 1988), p. 63.

3 Ibid., p. 67.

4 Clinton Hart Merriam, *The Mammals of the Adirondack Region, Northeastern New York* (New York: L.S. Foster, 1884; reprint ed.: New York: Arno Press, 1974), pp. 140, 141.

5 Warder H. Cadbury, Introduction to reprint ed. of *Adventures in the Wilderness* by W.H.H. Murray (Syracuse, N.Y.: The Adirondack Museum/Syracuse University Press, 1970), p. 32.

6 The first edition of E.R. Wallace's *Descriptive Guide to the Adirondacks* was combined with H. Perry Smith, *The Modern Babes in The Wood or Summerings in the Wilderness*, (Hartford, Conn. and Syracuse, N.Y.: W. Gill, 1872). The reference is on pp. 185, 186.

7 I am indebted to Warder Cadbury for this reference.

8 Stephens, *History of No. 4*, pp. 11 and 12.

9 Letter among family papers of John P. Constable Jr.

10 Hochschild, *Township 34*, p. 454, quoting Phelps' testimony at Ladew Case hearing in 1915.

11 Timm, *Raquette Lake*, p. 246.

12 Letter among family papers of John P. Constable Jr.

13 Cadbury, Introduction to reprint ed. of *Adventures in the Wilderness*, p. 49.

14 Murray, W.H.H., *Adventures in the Wilderness* (Boston: Fields, Osgood and Co., 1869), p. 53.

Chapter VI: The 1870s: Time of Rapid Changes

1 Cadbury, Introduction to reprint ed. of W.H. Murray's *Adventures in the Wilderness*, p. 52.

2 Casimir's envelope is among family papers owned by John P. Constable Jr.

3 Grady, *The Adirondacks*, p. 162.

4 Forge House Hotel Register is at The Adirondack Museum Library.

5 Wallace, *Descriptive Guide to the Adirondacks* (First ed., 1872), p. 256. In subsequent editions until 1887, the paragraph appeared on page 20.

6 Ibid., p. 403.

7 Stevenson Constable's notebook, p. 20.

8 Ibid., pp. 8, 9, 17, 21.

9 Wallace, *Descriptive Guide to the Adirondacks* (5th ed., 1876), pp. 238-244.

10 Timm, *Raquette Lake*, p. 171.

11 Ibid., pp. 62, 63.

12 Cadbury, *Tait, Artist in the Adirondacks*, p. 72.

13 Wallace, *Guide to the Adirondacks*, 1894 ed., pp. 432, 433.

14 Timm, *Raquette Lake*, pp. 58-60.

Chapter VII: End of a Gracious Era (1880s to present)

1 Letter from John Constable to Charles Fenton, Dec. 26, 1880. Now in possession of John P. Con-stable Jr.

2 Marvin W. Kranz, "A History of the Conservation Movement in New York State, 1865-1903," unpublished Ph.D. thesis for Syracuse University, 1961. Copy at The Adirondack Museum Library.

3 Letter from Charles Fenton to John Constable, Dec. 14, 1880; in possession of John P. Constable Jr.

4 Letter from John Constable to Charles Fenton, Dec. 26, 1880.

5 Merriam, *The Mammals of the Adirondack Region*, pp. 51-53, 132, 139, 254, 303.

6 The letter is in the possession of John P. Constable Jr.

Bibliography

ORIGINAL SOURCES (Unpublished)

Census Records to 1850 for Turin and Watson Towns, Lewis County, New York.

Church, Elsa. "List of Schenectady Slave Owners, 1767-88." Extract from Record by Mary Stevens of "Annual Register of Births" from Willis T. Hanson's *History of St. George's Church in the City of Schenectady, N.Y.*, Vol. 2. By author, 1919. Slave Owners List at Schenectady County Historical Society.

Constable Family Papers. Letters, notes, estate papers and maps by and about several generations (John, William I, William II, William III, Jane Kerin C., Ann, Anna Maria, John, Casimir and his brother James) in possession of John P. Constable Jr. of Watertown, New York.

Constable-Pierrepont Family Papers, Collection at New York Public Library. Letters, maps, deeds, business records, diaries. 44 boxes, 80 vol.

Constable, James. Diary [of Adirondack Trips, 1803-1806]. Constable Papers, New York City Public Library.

Constable, Stevenson. Notebook. Dated entries from 1873-78. Major part devoted to diary-like notes during long Adirondack camping trips in 1877 and 1878. Among Constable Family Papers of John P. Constable Jr., Watertown, New York.

Court Transcript: People of the State of New York Against Jennie H. Ladew and Joseph H. Ladew, County of Hamilton. Supreme Court, Appellate Division, 1920.

Davis, William A. "William Constable, New York Merchant and Land Speculator." Ph. D. thesis, Harvard University, 1955.

Higby, Almeron. Diary for 1876. In possession of Charles Bunke, Watson Town Historian.

Kranz, Marvin W. "Pioneering in Conservation: A History of the Conservation Movement in New York State, 1865-1903." Ph.D. thesis, Syracuse University, 1961. Manuscript at The Adirondack Museum, Blue Mountain Lake, New York.

Leavenworth, Abner. Diary entry for Aug. 22, 1851, on microfilm at The Adirondack Museum Library, pp. 72, 73.

McConville, Howard A. Worksheets summarizing by family name the "Annual Register of Births" from Hanson's History of St. George's Church, Schenectady, New York.

McEntee, Jervis. Diary [of Adirondack Trip] Summer, 1851. Manuscript and typescript at The Adirondack Museum Library, Blue Mountain Lake. See published version under Secondary Sources.

Moffat, Abbot Low. "The Pierreponts, 1806-1962, The American Forbears and the Descendants of Hezekiah Beers Pierpont and Anna Maria Constable." Washington, D.C., typescript, 1962. Copy among family papers of John P. Constable Jr., Watertown, New York.

Paige, Harriet. Diaries. Typescript, 2 Vol. at Schenectady County Historical Society.

Pearson, Jonathan. "Union Street" and "Washington Avenue" Steet Books. Scrapbooks at the Schenectady County Historical Society.

Pierrepont, Anna Maria Constable. Informal recollections recorded by family members in 1857 when she was 74 years old. Handwritten pages among family papers owned by John P. Constable Jr., Watertown, New York.

Records and deeds in the Schenectady County Historical Society and in the City of Schenectady Archival Files.

Sorin, Gretchen Sullivan. Typescript: "Constable Hall, An Historic Furnishing Plan." 1984. Copy in files at Constable Hall.

SECONDARY SOURCES

Aber, Ted and King, Stella. *History of Hamilton County*. Lake Pleasant, New York: Great Wilderness Books, 1965.

"Alph" (pseudonym). "Games and Game Places in the Adirondack Region," *Spirit of the Times*, April 17, 1858. p. 99.

Badran, Margot. ". . . and all through the house . . ." *Adirondack Life*, Dec. 1988, pp. 64-67.

Beetle, David. *Up Old Forge Way and West Canada Creek*, Lakemont and Old Forge, N.Y.: North Country Books, 1972.

Benedict, Farrand N. (attributed). "The Wilds of Northern New York." *Putnam Magazine* (Sept. 1854). pp. 263-70.

Bigelow, Albert. "The Adirondacks of 1858 and 1859." *Forest and Stream* (Oct. 5, 1912). pp. 423, 424.

Bourcier, Paul. *History in the Mapping, Four Centuries of Adirondack Cartography*. Blue Mountain Lake, N.Y.: The Adirondack Museum, 1986.

Brinley, Francis. *Life of William T. Porter*. New York: D. Appleton, and Co., 1860. Reprint by Arno Press, 1970.

Brown, Henry and Walton, Richard. *John Brown's Tract: Lost Adirondack Empire*. Canaan, N.H.: Phoenix Publishing, for the Rhode Island Historical Society. 1988.

Cadbury, Warder H. *Arthur Fitzwilliam Tait, Artist in the Adirondacks*. Newark: The American Art Journal/University of Delaware Press, 1986.

______. Introduction to reprint ed. of William H.H. Murray's *Adventures in the Wilderness*. Blue Mountain Lake, N.Y.: The Adirondack Museum/Syracuse University Press, 1970.

______. "Men to Match My Mountains . . ." *A Century Wild*. Neil S. Burdick, Ed. Saranac Lake: Chauncey Press, 1985.

Carson, Russell M.L. *Peaks and People of the Adirondacks*. Reprint ed. Glens Falls, N.Y.: Adirondack Mountain Club, 1972.

Donaldson, Alfred L. *A History of the Adirondacks*, 2 Vol. New York: The Century Co., 1921; reprint ed.: Harrison, N.Y.: Harbor Hill Books, 1977.

Durant, Kenneth. *Guide-Boat Days and Ways*. Blue Mountain Lake, N.Y.: The Adirondack Museum, 1963.

______ and Helen. *The Adirondack Guide-Boat*. Blue Mountain Lake: The Adirondack Museum, 1980.

Ellis, David et al. *A History of New York State*. Ithaca, N.Y.: Cornell University Press, Revised ed., 1967.

Frese, Joseph R. and Judd, Jacob, ed. *Business Enterprise in Early New York*. Tarrytown, N.Y.: Sleepy Hollow Press, 1979.

Grady, Joseph F. *The Adirondacks, Fulton Chain - Big Moose Region, The Story of a Wilderness*. Old Forge, N.Y.: North Country Books, 1933.

Hammond, S.H. *Wild Northern Scenes or Sporting Adventures with the Rifle and the Rod*. New York: Derby and Jackson, 1857; reprint ed. Harrison, N.Y.: Harbor Hill Books, 1979.

Hanson, Willis T. Jr. *A History of St. George's Church in the City of Schenectady, N.Y.* 2 Vol.: By Author, 1919.

Headley, Joel T. *The Adirondack, or Life in the Woods*. New York: Scribner, Armstrong and Co., 1849; reprint ed., Harrison, N.Y.: Harbor Hill Books, 1982 with Introduction by Philip G. Terrie.

Higby, Clinton D., ed. *Edward Higby and His Descendants*. Boston: T.R. Marvin and Son, 1927.

"Historic Constable Farm Sold, But Hall will Stay in Family." *Watertown Daily Times*. June 14, 1945.

Hochschild, Harold. *Township 34*. New York: By the author, 1952.

Hough, Franklin B. *History of Lewis County, N.Y.*, 2nd ed. Syracuse, N.Y.: D. Mason and Co., 1883.

Howell and Munsell. *History of the County of Schenectady, N.Y., 1662-1886*. New York: W.W. Munsell and Co., 1886.

Jamieson, Paul. *Adirondack Canoe Waters, North Flow*. Glens Falls, N.Y.: Adirondack Mountain Club, Inc., 1975.

Johnson, William. *Papers of Sir William Johnson*, 13 Vol. Ed. by James Sullivan. Albany: University of the State of New York, 1921-1962.

Lane, David F. "Stately Old Constable Hall is Put on the Market." *Watertown Daily Times*, June 22, 1946.

______. "North Country Mansions." *New York History*, July, 1943, pp. 392-401.

Low, William G. *Some Recollections for his Children and Grandchildren*. New York City: G.P. Putnam and Sons, 1909.

Marleau, William R. *Big Moose Station*. Eagle Bay, N.Y.: Marleau Family Press, 1986.

McEntee, Jervis. "The Lakes of the Wilderness." *The Great Republic Monthly* (April 1859), pp. 335-350.

McVickar, Edward and William Constable Breed. Memoranda relating to the McVickar Family in America. New York: By the authors, 1906.

Merriam, Clinton Hart. *The Mammals of the Adirondack Region, Northeastern New York*. New York: L.S. Foster, 1884; reprint ed., New York: Arno Press, 1974.

Monroe, Joel. *Schenectady Ancient and Modern*. By the author, 1914.

Murray, Hon. Amelia Martha. *Letters from the United States, Cuba and Canada*. New York: Putnam, 1856.

Murray, Martha Constable. *Constable Hall* (Pamphlet for visitors), 1986.

Murray, William H.H. *Adventures in the Wilderness* or *Camp-Life in the Adirondacks*. Boston: Fields, Osgood and Co., 1869; reprint ed., Blue Mountain Lake, N.Y.: The Adirondack Museum/Syracuse University Press, 1970.

New York State. *First Annual Report of the Commissioners of Fisheries, Game and Forests*. Albany: Wynkoop, Hallenbeck Crawford Co., 1886.

New York State. Documents of the Assembly, #150, 1841. Report of Ebenezer Emmons, M.D., of the Survey of the Second Geological District, Vol. V. Albany: Thurlow Weed, 1841.

Pearson, Jonathan. *First Settlers of the Patent and City of Schenectady, 1662-1800.* Albany: J. Munsell, 1873.

______. *A History of the Schenectady Patent.* Albany: Joel Munsell and Sons, 1883.

Pilcher, Edith. *Castorland, French Refugees in the Western Adirondacks.* Harrison, N.Y.: Harbor Hill Books, 1985.

Pound, Arthur. *Johnson of the Mohawks.* New York: Macmillan Co., 1930.

Prentice, Edmond A. "Clement Clark Moore." *Buzz* (Columbia University, Dec. 1953) pp. 3, 4.

Racket, Bob, (pseudonym). "To the Editor." *The Spirit of the Times* (Jan. 30, 1844), pp. 582-583.

______. "A Month at the Racket." *The Knickerbocker*, Vol. XLVIII, Sept., Oct. and Nov., 1856.

Roberts, George S. *Old Schenectady.* Schenectady, N.Y.: Robson & Adee, 1904.

Sakolski, A.M. *The Great American Land Bubble.* New York City: Harper & Bros., 1932.

Schenectady Directory and City Register for 1841-2. Schenectady: Rigg, 1841; reprint ed. Schenectady: John P. Papp, Historical Publications, 1979.

Simms, Jeptha. *Trappers of New York.* Albany: J. Munsell, 1871; reprint ed.: Harrison, N.Y.: Harbor Hill Books, 1980.

Smith, H. Perry. *The Modern Babes in the Wood or Summerings in the Wilderness.* Published with Wallace's first *Descriptive Guide to the Adirondacks.* Hartford, Conn. and Syracuse, N.Y.: W. Gill, 1872.

Staffa, Susan Jones. *Colonial Schenectady in Maps.* By the author, 1985.

Stephens, W. Hudson. *Historical Notes on the Settlement at No. 4, Brown's Tract, in Watson, Lewis County, N.Y.* Utica: Roberts, 1864.

Stillman, William James, ed. "Sketchings." *The Crayon.* Journal Devoted to the Graphic Arts and Literature Related to Them. (Nov. 28, 1855) pp. 344-345.

Stoddard, Seneca Ray. *The Adirondacks Illustrated.* Albany: Weed, Parsons & Co., 1874; reprint ed.: Glens Falls: Chapman Historical Museum, 1983.

______. *Old Times in the Adirondacks.* Saranac Lake: Adirondack Yesteryears, Inc., 1971.

Stone, William L. *Reminiscences of Saratoga and Ballston.* New York: R. Worthington, 1880.

Sullivan, Edward Dean. *Benedict Arnold—Military Racketeer.* New York: Vanguard Press, 1932.

Sylvestor, Nathaniel. *Historical Sketches of Northern New York and the Adirondack Wilderness.* Troy, N.Y.: William H. Young, 1877; reprint ed.: Harrison, N.Y.: Harbor Hill Books, 1973.

Timm, Ruth. *Raquette Lake, A Time to Remember.* Utica, N.Y.: North Country Books, 1989.

Todd, John. *Long Lake.* Pittsfield, Mass.: E.P. Little, 1845; reprint ed.: Harrison, N.Y., Harbor Hill Books, 1983.

Traxel, Mary E. *A History of Constableville.* Constableville, New York: 1977.

Veeder, Millicent Winton. *Door to the Mohawk Valley.* Albany: Cromwell Printery, 1947.

Wallace, E.R. *Descriptive Guide to the Adirondacks,* First ed. published with Smith's *Babes in the Woods.*) Hartford, Conn. and Syracuse, N.Y.: W. Gill, 1872.

______. *Descriptive Guide to the Adirondacks, Handbook of Travel*, 5th ed. New York: Forest and Stream Publishing Co., 1876.

______. *Descriptive Guide to the Adirondacks, (Land of the Thousand Lakes)*. Syracuse, N.Y.: By the author, 1894.

Whipple, Gurth. *Fifty Years of Conservation in New York State, 1885-1935.* Conservation Department and New York State College of Forestry, 1935.

Wilcox, Altsie. *Port Leyden and Vicinity*. Port Leyden, N.Y.: Boonville Graphics, 1971.

Williams, Emily B. and Buckley, Edwin. *Tribute to a Country Church - History of St. Paul's, Constableville, N.Y.*, 1985.

Index

Adirondack League Club, 70
Adirondack Museum, 50
Adirondack Railroad, 107, 108, 118
Adventures in the Wilderness, 105-107
ALBANY LAKE, *see* Nehasane Lake
ALBANY MOUNTAIN, 72, 87
Albany Road, *see* Old Military Road
Alger, John, 18
Antler's Hotel, 122-125
ANTLERS POINT, *see* Constable Point
Antoinette, Marie, 26, 132, 139
Antwerp Co., 15
Arnold, Benedict, 8, 9, 35, 40
Arnold's Inn, 37, 40, 41, 130
Arnold, Otis, 37, 40, 41, 109
AUSABLE FALLS, 35
Austin, William, 60

BALD MOUNTAIN, 42
Bard Family, 29
Barrett, Mr., 130
Bass, 119-122
Beach, Matthew, 42, 44, 49-54, 60, 62
BEACHES LAKE, *see* Brandreth Lake
Bears, 83, 88, 96, 100
Beavers, 128
BEAVER LAKE, 64-66, 116, 129
BEAVER RIVER, 32, 37, 39, 50, 51, 58, 89
Beetle, David H., 110
Benedict, Farrand N., 35, 37, 52, 58, 69
Benedict, (Farrand's son), 119
Bennett, Charles H., 122
Bigelow, Albert, 93
BIG MOOSE LAKE, 37, 68-70, 110, 111, 139
BIG MOOSE REGION, 68-70, 111
BIG SALMON LAKE, *see* Salmon Lake
Bisby Club, 70
BLACK RIVER, 14, 15, 25, 32, 50, 58, 66, 67, 71, 128
BLOOMINGDALE, 10
BLUE MOUNTAIN, 51, 64, 81-83, 93, 97
BLUE MOUNTAIN LAKE, 32, 37, 38, 50, 108, 112-122
BOG FALLS, 37
BOONVILLE, 23, 35, 97, 109
BOTTLE POND, 119, 122, 130
Brandreth, Dr. Benjamin, 72, 87, 112
BRANDRETH LAKE, 32, 37, 53, 58, 72, 73, 87, 112, 116, 119
Brook Trout, 45, 49
Brown, John, 35
BROWN'S TRACT, *see* John Brown Tract
BROWN'S TRACT INLET, 80, 119
BROWN'S TRACT PONDS, 116, 118, 119
BROWNVILLE, 18
Bucknor Family, 29
Bunke, Charles, 50
Burt, C.H., 52
Butler, B.C., 138, 139

Cadbury, Warder H., 35, 39, 95
Cain, Jimmy, *see* O'Kane, James
CARTHAGE, 67
Cary's Hotel, *see* Raquette Lake House
Cary, Nelson, 104
CARY POND, 112, 119
Cary, Rueben, 104, 111-119, 122
Cary, William, 60, 122
CASTORLAND, 13, 15
Catamount Road, *see* Old Military Road
CHARLEY'S POND, 129
Charming Nancy, 8
Chase, David, 32, 35, 36
Chassanis, Pierre, 13
CHUB POND, 141
CLEAR POND, 116
Clinton, Gov. George, 9, 13
Cock of the Woods, 49
Coe, Eric, 63
Colden, Gov. Cadwallader, 2, 5
Colvin, Verplanck, 35, 70, 107
Compagnie de New York, *see* Castorland
Compass, 37, 38
Comstock, Edward Jr., 39
Comstock, Jack, 112
Constable, *see also* Family Tree (Frontis)
Constable, Ann White (wife of Wm. I), 10, 13, 16-19
Constable, Anna (sister of Wm. III), 28-32, 57-60, 63, 71, 98, 119
Constable, Anna Maria (dau. of Wm. I, wife of H.B. Pierpont), 10, 13, 15, 16, 18, 19, 20, 22, 23, 26, 55
Constable, Emily (dau. of Wm. I, wife of Dr. Samuel Moore), 10, 13, 20
Constable, Casimir (son of John III), 22, 55, 90, 91, 98, 101-104, 108, 109, 129-131
Constable, Eweretta (dau. of Dr. John, sister of Wm. I, wife of James Phyn), 3, 5, 6, 8, 13
Constable, Eweretta (dau. of Wm. I, wife of James McVickar), 10, 20, 26, 97
Constable, Fannie Barclay (wife of Wm. IV), 102
Constable, Harriet (dau. of Dr. John, sister of Wm. I), 5, 13

Constable, Harriet, (dau. of Wm. I, wife of James Duane), 10, 13, 20
Constable, James (son of Dr. John, bro. of Wm. I), 5, 6, 8, 11, 13-18, 21, 22, 144
Constable, James II (bro. of Wm. III), 28-30, 57-59, 71, 104, 110, 130, 141
Constable, James III (son of John III, bro. of Casimir), 55, 90, 91, 96, 98, 104, 110, 129-132
Constable, Jane Kerin (wife of Dr. John), 3, 6, 7, 16, 17, 20
Constable, Jane ("Jennie," dau. of Wm. III, wife of Casimir), 71, 74, 76, 82, 83, 101, 104, 130, 131
Constable, Jane (dau. of Wm. P. Constable Jr.), 139
Constable, John (Doctor), 2-9, 16, 17, 132
Constable, John (English painter), 3
Constable, John (son of Wm. I), 6, 10, 17, 20
Constable, John III (son of Wm., Jr., bro. of Wm. III), 28-46, 55, 57-59, 70-88, 90, 98-101, 111, 127-130, 141
Constable, John Pierrepont (son of James III), 131
Constable, John P., Jr. (son of Jn. Pierrepont Constable), 131, 132, 139, 141
Constable, John P. III (son of John P., Jr.), 139
Constable, Julia E. Pierrepont (dau. of Anna Maria Constable & H. B. Pierpont, wife of John III), 30, 55, 70, 98
Constable, Martha, 139
Constable, Mary Eliza (wife of Wm. Jr.), 20-30
Constable, Mary, 139
Constable, Matilda (dau. of Wm. I), 10, 20, 26
Constable, Stevenson I (bro. of Wm. III), 28-30, 37-48, 58, 59, 70, 71, 84, 85, 90, 95, 97, 98, 100, 104, 111-122, 128, 129, 141
Constable, Stevenson II (son of James, nephew of Stevenson I), 97
Constable, William I (son of Dr. John), 3, 6-16, 20, 22, 25, 26, 132
Constable, William Jr., 10, 16-18, 20-27
Constable, William III, 28-32, 35, 36, 56-64, 69, 70, 74-87, 90, 97, 101, 104, 111, 122, 141
Constable, William IV, (son of Wm. III), 58, 59, 70, 74-83, 101-104
Constable & Co., 11
CONSTABLE CREEK, 138-141
Constable Hall, 20-27, 29, 30, 58, 59, 97, 111, 130-138
Constable Hall Assn., 132, 139
CONSTABLE POINT (formerly Sand Point, later Antlers Point), 30, 32, 58, 60-64, 69, 73-88, 90-106, 111, 112, 116, 119, 122, 123
CONSTABLE POND, 138-141
CONSTABLEVILLE, 17, 22, 23, 26, 40, 43, 57, 64, 71, 88, 108, 110, 131, 139, 141
Coplin, John, 111, 112
Cornwall, Grace, 132
Cortland College Outdoor Recreation Center, 125
Crane, Ned, 111
Crego, Paul, 112, 130
CROOKED LAKE, 130
CROWN POINT, 67
Currier & Ives, 94, 95

Davis, Theodore R., 75
Dean, Fannie, 50
Deane, Silas, 9
Deer, 37, 42, 45-47, 49, 53, 74-80, 82, 83, 88, 93, 95, 99-101, 119, 121, 122, 125-127
DeRham, Casimir, 37, 38
Donaldson, Alfred L., 32, 57, 64
Duane, James, 20, 29
Dunbar's Hotel, 112, 116
Duer, Wm., 9
Dunning, Alvah, 53
Durant, Kenneth, 39, 49, 50
Durant, Thomas C., 108
Durant, Wm. West, 108, 116

Eagles, 37, 93
EAGLE LAKE, 108, 116
EAST INLET (Marion River), 74, 76, 80, 83, 84, 95, 108
ECKFORD CHAIN OF LAKES, 108, 116, 118
Edwards, A. P., 32, 35, 36, 51, 62
Edwards' Hotel, 112, 116
EIGHTH LAKE, 42, 49, 116
ELIZABETHTOWN, 35, 53
Ellice, Alexander, 8
Ellis, 63
ELLISBURGH, 17
Ely, Dr. W. W.'s Map, sections on 43, 61, 115, endpapers
Emmons, Ebenezer, 35, 51, 54
ESSEX COUNTY, 116
Evans, Peter, 60, 63

Fenton House, 32, 58, 60, 64-66, 72, 87, 88, 101, 112
Fenton, Charles, 65, 66, 126, 127
Fenton, Orrin, 58, 60, 64-66, 88
FIFTH LAKE, 116
FIRST LAKE, 35, 40-42, 49, 97, 109, 116
Fisher, 128
Fish Hawk, 93
Fishing, *see* Bass, Fly-fishing, Trout
Floating, 45, 46, 74-76, 82, 95, 119
Fly-fishing, 41, 45-48, 71, 80
Force, John C., 95
Forest & Stream, 93, 128
Forge House, 109, 110, 112
FORKED LAKE, 116, 118, 119, 122, 130
Forsyth, James, 22
Foster, Nat, 51

FOURTH LAKE, 32, 35, 37, 41, 42, 49, 111, 116, 130
Francis, John Brown, 23
FRANKLIN COUNTY, 26, 30
FULTON CHAIN OF LAKES, 35, 42, 49, 50, 58, 70, 88, 97, 109, 116, 130

Gignoux, Regis Francois, 66
Goodale (driver), 88
Grouse, 49
Guides, *see* Beech, Matthew
Cary, Nelson
Cary, Rueben
Cary, William
Chase, David
Coplin, John
Dunning, Alvah
Crego, Paul
Foster, Nat
Higby, Almeron
Higby the Hunter
Johnson, Willard
Johnson, ____
Kenwell, Ike
Pierce, Seth
Puffer, Asa
Salmon, Hy
Sims, ____
Robinson, Amos C.
Spofford, Amos
Wood, Alonzo
Wood, Josiah
Wood, William
Guns, 25, 30, 132, 135-137

Hamilton, Alexander, 13
HAMILTON COUNTY, 30, 39, 40, 66, 71, 129, 139
Hare, 128, 129
Harris, J. L., 32, 38
Hathorne, Chauncey, 116
Headley, Rev. Joel, 35, 51, 53
HERKIMER COUNTY, 30, 39, 40, 129
Herreshoff, Charles F., 35
HERRESHOFF'S MANOR, 32, 35, 37, 49, 109
Higby, Almeron, 51, 88, 129, 130
Higby the Hunter (Wm. R.), 28, 40-51, 58, 70, 73-76, 80, 82, 84-88, 95, 98
Higby, Wm. Wey, 50
HIGHMARKET, 21
HIGH POND, 119, 122
Hill, John William, 52
Hindsley, D. C., 116
Hochschild, Harold, 32, 57, 64
Hoff, D. (Hough?), 112
Holland's Hotel, 112, 116
Homer, Winslow, 99
Hotels & Inns, *see* Arnold's
Dunbar's
Edwards'
Fenton House
Forge House
Hathorne
Holland's
Kellogg's
Lawrence's
Ordway's
Parker's
Raquette Lake House I
Raquette Lake House II
Seargeant's
Sheppard's
Smith's, (Paul)
Wood's (Alonzo)
Hough, Amos, 54
Hough, Franklin B., 7
Hounding, 46, 76, 78, 79, 127, 128
Hudson River School of Art, 50

INDEPENDENCE RIVER, 51, 69, 111, 128, 129
Ingraham, Nathaniel, 15
INDIAN LAKE, 71
INDIAN RIVER, 71
Indians, 5-8, 23-25, 35, 45, 51, 71, 76, 128
Insects, 41, 45, 74, 80, 119

JAY, 35
Jay Family, 29
JOHN BROWN TRACT, 23, 30, 35, 41, 66, 104
Johnson, ____, 121
Johnson, Sir John, 32
Johnson, Willard, 32, 35, 36
Johnson, Sir William, 5-7
JOHNSON HALL, 5-7
JOHNSTOWN, 6
JOY TRACT, 51

Kane, Alida Van Rensselaer (wife of John II), 20
Kane, Jimmy, *see* O'Kane, James
KEENE, 35
Kellogg's Hotel, 112
Kenwell's Hotel, *see* Raquette Lake House II
Killoquah Steamer, 108
The Knickerbocker, 70, 88, 125

Lafayette, Marquis de, 9, 10, 13, 19
LAKE CHAMPLAIN, 30, 35, 67, 139
LAKE LILA, 32, 37, 51, 89, 96, 97, 112, 116
LAKE ONTARIO, 15, 67, 139
LAKE PLEASANT, 71
Lamberton, A. B., 112
Land Speculation & Development, 3, 11-18, 20-23, 26, 27, 98
Lawrence, Abner, 109
Lawrence Family (NYC), 29

Lawrence (Utica), 112
LAWRENCE HOTEL, 97, 101, 104, 109
Leavenworth, Abner, 69
Lent, Cornelia, 57, 59
LeRay, James (de Chaumont), 13, 15
Levick, Dr. James L., 101-104, 108
LEWIS COUNTY, 21, 26, 30, 35, 129
Lewis, Mr. & Mrs. Harry, 132
LITTLE MUD LAKE, 112
LITTLE SALMON LAKE, 112, 116
LITTLE TUPPER LAKE, 32, 112, 116, 130
Livingston, John & Robert, 8
Livingston, Susan (wife of John II), 20, 29
LONG LAKE, 32, 37, 39, 130
LONG LAKE (Town of), 52, 54, 60, 71, 112, 116, 119
Loons, 73
LOWVILLE, 18, 39, 50, 58
Low, Augustus, 91
Low, William G., 91
Lyon, Caleb, 35
LYONS FALLS, 30, 35, 122

Macomb, Alexander, 11-14
Macomb Purchase, 7, 10-18, 20, 21, 23, 26
Major, Andrew, 58, 59
Major, Jane, 57, 59
Major, Mary, 57, 59
MALONE, 18, 130
Mammals of the Adirondack Region, 128, 129
Marten, 128, 129
MARTINSBURGH, 21
McCormick, Daniel, 13, 21, 22
McEntee, Jervis, 47, 50, 51, 54, 57, 64, 67, 69, 81, 88, 89
McMurray, Mr. & Mrs. (B'klyn), 11
McVickar, Annie, 57, 59
McVickar, Archibald, 30
McVickar, Edward, 20, 26, 29
McVickar, James, 20, 23, 26, 29, 97
McVickar, John, 16, 20
McVickar, Mary Eliza, *see* Mary Eliza McVickar Constable
McVickar, Matilda, 57, 59
McVickar, William Constable, 97
MARION RIVER, *see* East Inlet
MEACHAM'S LAKE, 130
Merriam, Clinton Hart, 30, 101, 128, 129
Merritt's Book & Map, 32, 33, 103
MINERVA, 112
Mink, 49
Mohawk and St. Lawrence Railroad, 30
MOHAWK RIVER, 7, 25
MONTGOMERY COUNTY, 30
MONTREAL, 3, 5, 8, 32
Moore, Samuel (Doctor), 20, 29
Moose, 30, 32, 37, 42, 47-49, 53, 68-70, 84, 85, 95, 129
MOOSE POND, 122
MOOSE RIVER, 35, 39, 50, 71, 97
Moose River Road, 23, 35, 97, 101, 104, 109, 130
Moran, Thomas, 79
Morris, Gouverneur, 9, 11, 13, 15
Morris, Robert, 9, 11
MORT LAKE, *see* Tupper Lake
MOUNT EMMONS, *see* Blue Mountain
MUD LAKE, 116
MUD POND, 37, 112, 116
Murray, Lady Amelia, 57
Murray, Wm. H.H. ("Adirondack"), 95, 96, 105-107, 125

Neckar, Jacques, 15
NEHASANE LAKE (formerly Albany Lake, Albany Bridge Lake), 32, 37, 50, 51, 89, 112, 116
Newcome, Andrew, 85
NORTH ELBA, 35
NORTH CREEK, 107, 108, 112, 118
NO. 4, 32, 58-67, 97

OGDENSBURG, 30
OLD FORGE, 23, 32, 35, 37, 40, 51, 70, 109
Old Military Road, 58, 67, 101
O'Kane, James, 72, 88-90
ONEIDA COUNTY, 30
Ordway's Hotel, 112, 116
Osprey, *see* Fish Hawk
Otter, 122

Parish, David, 15
Parker, Cora Fenton, 67
Parker's Hotel, 116
Partridges, 41, 80, 88, 122
Peabody, James H., 110
Phelps, Charlie, 101
PHILIPSE MANOR, 10
Phyn, James, 6, 8
Phyn & Ellice Trading Co., 6, 8
Pierce, Seth, 112
Pierpont, Hezekiah Beers, 15-19, 20, 23, 26, 29, 55
Pierrepont, Anna, *see* Anna Maria Constable
Pierrepont, Harry, 91
Pierrepont, Henry, 26
Pierrepont, Julia E., *see* Julia E. P. Constable
Pierrepont, Wm. Constable, 26, 33
Pierrepont, William Delaney, 91
Pierson, Joe, 125
PIGEON LAKE, 141
Pigeon Lake Wilderness Area, 141
Pigeons, 41, 49, 88
PISECO LAKE, 71
PLATTSBURGH, 32
PLUMLEY POND, 119, 122
Plumley's Hotel, 30, 122

Porcupine, 129
Prentice, Levi Wells, 97
Puffer, Asa, 70, 73, 74, 76, 80, 81, 83, 87-89, 98-100, 104
Puffer, Eliza, 51, 88
Puffer, Thomas, 88

QUEBEC, 3
Queen Victoria, 57

Rabbits, 80, 89, 121, 122. *Also see* Hare
Racket, Bob, 39, 49, 51, 70, 73
Ralph, M.D., 32, 34
RAQUETTE FALLS, 37
RAQUETTE LAKE, 32, 35-37, 40, 42-64, 67-87, 91-106, 108-125, 130, 141
Raquette Lake Girls' Camp, 125
RAQUETTE LAKE HOUSE (I - Cary's), 91, 104, 105
RAQUETTE LAKE HOUSE (II - Kenwell's), 112, 116, 119, 121
RAQUETTE RIVER, 32, 39, 49, 71
Raven, 37
Richards Sarah, 57, 59, 60
Roads, 65, 66. *Also see*
  Moose River Road
  Old Military Road
Robinson Amos C., 119
ROCK POND, 37, 112, 116, 130
RONDAXE LAKE, 37, 111
Rubergall, 37

SACANDAGA RIVER, 71
SACKETT'S HARBOR, 67, 139
Salmon, Hy, 119
SALMON LAKE, 37, 112, 116, 119
St. George's Episcopal Church, 5, 18
St. Paul's Episcopal Church (NYC), 6, 15, 16
St. Paul's Episcopal Church (Constableville), 27
ST. LAWRENCE COUNTY, 26, 30
ST. LAWRENCE RIVER, 12, 71
ST. REGIS RIVER, 71
SAND PONT, *see* Constable Point
Saratoga & Sackett's Harbor Railroad, 36
SARATOGA, 5, 108, 112
SARANAC LAKES, 32, 53, 130
Sargent Ponds, 119
Sauthier's Map, 14, 15
SCHENECTADY, 4-9, 17, 18, 20-22
Seagrave, James, 9
Seargeant's, 30
SECOND LAKE, 40, 42, 116
SEVENTH LAKE, 42, 49, 116
Seymour, Gov. Horatio, 57
Shaler, Nathaniel, 17, 21, 22, 27, 50
SHALERVILLE, 17, 22, 50. *See also* Constableville
SHALLOW LAKE, 119, 122
SHEDD'S LAKE (now Sagamore), 119. 122
Sheppard's (Jack) Hotel, 112
SHERMAN'S LAKE, *see* Big Moose Lake
Sherman, Gen. Richard U., 70
Sims, ____, 121
SISTERS' LAKES, 111
SIXTH LAKE, 41, 42, 49, 116
SLIM POND, 112
Smillie, James D., 86
Smith, H. Perry, 96
Smith's Hotel (Paul), 130
SMITH'S LAKE, *see* Lake Lila
Society of the Friendly Sons of St. Patrick, 10
SOUTH POND, 112
Speckled Trout, *see* Trout
Sperry, Sanford, 109
Spirit of the Times, 39, 40, 55, 70
Spofford, Amos, 74
Spring at Constable Point, 73, 80, 106, 124, 125
Staffa, Susan Jane, 4
Stephens, W. Hudson, 89, 97
Stillman, William J., 51, 52, 54
STILLWATER, 60, 72, 87, 89
STILLWATER RESERVOIR, 112
Stoddard's Map, 32, 34, 37, 68, 110, 127, 139
Stoddard, S.R., 77
STONEY CREEK, 32, 130
STONEY LAKE, 128
Stott, Frank, 116, 121
Stott, Julia, 116, 121, 122
Stuart, Gilbert, 7, 22, 23
Surveyors, *see* Colvin, Verplanck
  Edwards, A.P.
  Harris, J.L
SUTTON POND, 119, 122
Sylvestor, Nathaniel, 51, 89

Tait, Arthur F., 60, 63, 93-95, 116, 119
Target practice, 137
TEN TOWNS OF THE ST. LAWRENCE, 12
Thatcher, John Boyd, 116, 119, 122
Themanen, Charles, 92, 95
THIRD LAKE, 40, 42, 116
Timm, Ruth, 32, 120, 125
Todd, Rev. John, 35
Tomilson, Rev., 116
TOWNSHIP 40, 35
Transactions of the Linnean Society of NY, 128
Trophies (game), 137
Trout, 46, 48, 76, 80, 81, 83, 119, 121
  Brook Trout, 45, 49
  Salmon Trout (Lake Trout), 47, 49, 119, 122
  Speckled Trout, 41, 47, 88
TUG HILL PLATEAU, 26, 29, 139
TUPPER LAKE, 30, 32, 37, 39, 91, 130
TURIN, 21, 23, 26, 40, 49, 50
TWITCHELL CREEK, 60, 89, 116
Tyler, Wm. Richardson, 82

Union College, 18, 21
Up Old Forge Way, 110
UPPER ST. REGIS LAKE, 130
UTOWANA LAKE, 108, 116
Utowana Steamer, 108

Vane, Henry, 79
Verner, William K., 39

Wallace, E.R., 51, 66, 88, 96, 110-112, 116
Waller, ____, 119
Ward, Mr., 121
Washington, George (portrait of), 22, 23
WATERTOWN, 139
WATSON, 39, 50, 51, 58, 88, 90
Webber, Charles W., 51-53
WEST MOUNTAIN, 82, 139
WEST POND, 111, 116
WESTPORT, 35
WEST TURIN, 21, 26
White, Ann, *see* Ann Constable
White, Townsend, 10
White, Mrs. (sister of Dr. John Constable), 7
Williams, 112
WILMINGTON, 35
Winter Trip, 98-101
Wolves, 98-100
Wood, Alonzo, 58, 60, 130
Wood, Jerome, 119
Wood, Josiah, 53, 54, 58, 60, 62, 87, 130
Wood, William F., 42, 44, 49-54, 60, 62, 76, 78, 83, 128
Woodward, ____, 119
Wright, Daniel (NYC), 116

About the Author . . .

Edith Pilcher has been writing about Adirondack history for some fifteen years. Her first book, *Castorland*, published in 1985, concerned a French émigrés settlement on the Black River. Her second book, *Up the Lake Road*, celebrated the centennial of the Adirondack Mountain Reserve and was published by the Reserve at St. Huberts in 1987. It includes some early history about the High Peaks and Keene Valley area. In addition, nearly two dozen articles have appeared in *Adirondack Life*, *Adirondac* and *The Conservationist*.

Because she spends much time at her cabin on Big Moose Lake, Pilcher closely identifies with the Central Adirondack region so well described in this book. She has paddled many of the same waters and hiked many of the same trails as those traversed by the Constables so many years ago.

A careful historian, she has culled information from many unpublished sources (diaries, letters, maps and family papers) as well as from obscure books and articles long out-of-print, parts of which are reprinted here. She sheds light on topics which have puzzled 20th century historians, such as Who was Bob Racket? and Who were the "intrepid females of Blue Mountain"?

A resident of Schenectady, New York, she is an active member of many historical and conservation organizations and has engaged in camping, hiking, canoeing and kayaking throughout the Adirondacks over the past forty years. She and her husband have also traveled extensively and she has written several articles about trip experiences at home and abroad.